WHAT DO PATIENTS WANT?

WHAT DO PATIENTS WANT?

Psychoanalytic Perspectives from the Couch

Christine A. S. Hill

KARNAC

First published in 2010 by
Karnac Books Ltd
118 Finchley Road, London NW3 5HT

British Library Cataloguing in Publication Data

A C.I.P. for this book is available from the British Library

ISBN: 978 1 85575 719 6

Edited, designed and produced by The Studio Publishing Services Ltd
www.publishingservicesuk.co.uk
e-mail: studio@publishingservicesuk.co.uk

Printed in Great Britain

www.karnacbooks.com

CONTENTS

ACKNOWLEDGEMENTS

To the eighteen volunteers who participated in this project, I express my sincere gratitude. They spoke with candour and openness about very personal experiences in psychoanalysis and I feel privileged to have heard their stories. Without your willing participation, this book would not exist.

I am also very grateful to my two supervisors, Eve Steel, a training analyst, and Janet Spink, a researcher, who guided my original Doctoral thesis at Monash University, and Professor Graeme Smith, Head of Department, Psychological Medicine, for his encouragement and support. I also received very helpful comments from my friend and colleague, Fiona McDermott, and fellow Doctoral students.

I owe a very special thanks to the IPA Research Training Programme, London, 1999, where I received valuable assistance in thinking about this challenging study under the guidance of Professor Peter Fonagy, his Faculty, and my fellow researchers; to the IPA Research Advisory Board for their two consecutive funding grants to carry out this work; and to Professor Horst Kächele, Germany, for his ongoing support and guidance in exploring my research question.

I have appreciated the continuing encouragement of my partner, Tim Healey, and thoughtful comments from friends Ron Gilbert, Stuart Twemlow, Janet Curtis, Doug Kirsner, Ora Bernard, Joy Damousi, Janette Simmonds, and Helga Coulter. I also sincerely thank Daryl Boyd for his tremendous job in proof-reading my original Doctoral thesis. Special thanks go to my two cats, Biscuit and Chocky, my constant companions throughout this journey.

I would like to thank three analysts who have been very important to me during the life of this book: the late Dr Harold Bridger, a mentor and good friend for many years, who gave valuable input into the early research; and Dr Peter Smith and the late Dr George Christie, who have had a significant influence upon my personal life and clinical practice.

Finally, I offer a very special thanks to Vivienne Hill, my sister-in-law, who has given so generously of her time to guide me in the challenging task of converting an academic thesis into this more readable book format. I could not have succeeded without her continuing patience and professional expertise.

ABOUT THE AUTHOR

Christine Hill, PhD, is a clinical psychologist and psychoanalytic psychotherapist working with individuals and groups. Both her Masters and PhD were in the field of psychoanalysis. She has a background in primary school teaching, mainly in remote Maori schools in New Zealand; general and emergency nursing, including a period of voluntary work as a Child & Maternal Health Sister in the West Sepik, PNG; clinical tutoring in both Psychological Medicine and the Masters of Counseling Psych, Monash University; and research and clinical work at the Mental Health Research Institute, Melbourne. Christine is a Past President of the Australian Association of Group Psychotherapists, a member of the Psychoanalytic Psychotherapy Association of Australasia and the Psychoanalytic Studies Association of Australasia, and a member of the International Psychoanalytical Association College of Research Fellows. She is currently Regional Editor for the Southern Hemisphere, *International Journal of Applied Psychoanalytic Studies*. Christine has presented at several international conferences, published papers, and received two funding grants from the IPA to assist with her doctoral exploration of patients' perspectives of psychoanalysis, upon which this book is based.

To the memory of my late parents, Mercia and Doug,
and to all my brothers and sisters in New Zealand,
their partners and families—the Hills, Langleys, and Lauagos.

PREFACE

Since the time of Freud, psychoanalysis has developed into a significant form of psychological treatment, focusing attention on unconscious determinants in human attitudes, emotions, and behaviours. The psychoanalytic literature on process and outcome studies, however, has privileged the practitioner or researcher's perspective. This has occurred in spite of very rich published accounts of personal analyses by analysands/patients and trainee analysts, and through autobiographical accounts of one or more journeys (Cardinal, 1996; France, 1988; Herman, 1985; Saks, 2007). (Analysand is the term often used interchangeably with "patient" when describing a person undergoing psychoanalysis, but for the purpose of this narrative, in all future references I will use the term patient.) Research representing the patient's experience has been sadly neglected (Freedman, Hoffenberg, Vorus, & Frosch, 1999; Kächele, 2001, personal communication; Kassan, 1999; Morley, 2007). As every analysis involves a relationship between two people, analyst and patient, there can be very different viewpoints from opposite sides of "the couch". Thus, I wondered why one voice in the dyad should be preferred over the other. Encouraged by such writers as Casement (2002), and Reppen and Schulman (2002), I set out to examine the patient's contribution.

The importance of listening to the patient is supported by one of Freud's most famous cases—Sergei Pankeyev, the "Wolfman" (1918b)—upon which Freud based much of his initial claim for the success of his theoretical model of psychoanalysis. When Pankeyev spoke with Karin Obholzer (1980), the Austrian journalist who interviewed him over a considerable period of time prior to his death, Pankeyev had begun to question Freud's attitude that patients should be uncritical in the analytic work. He reported Freud as saying, "Don't reflect, don't look for contradictions, but accept what I tell you and improvement will come by itself" (Obholzer, 1980, p. 31). Pankeyev told the journalist that Freud's instruction led to his developing a powerful transference towards Freud, but he also felt that to accept uncritically was a dangerous thing. In the course of these interviews with Obholzer (1980), Pankeyev stated that from his point of view not much in psycho-analysis would now stand up to scrutiny, but Freud himself was a genius whom he worshipped. Reflecting about his personal journey at the end of his life, Pankeyev said that he felt himself to be in the same state as when he first went to Freud many decades earlier. Pankeyev's conclusion was a very different assessment of his analy-sis to that offered by Freud in his case study.

The focus of this book, therefore, has been to allow patients to speak for themselves about their psychoanalytic experiences. They have their own stories to tell about significant factors which have facilitated, or impeded, the psychoanalytic process, and which have led to their understanding of the success or failure of their respec-tive outcomes. To carry out this work, I decided to interview a num-ber of men and women who had already completed, or ended, a psychoanalytic journey. (I have made a distinction between "com-pleted" and "ended" as a small number of participants prematurely left the analysis because of their perceptions that the experience was not working for them. This differs from those patients who felt they had remained to a satisfactory completion.) I believed it was important to share these findings, not only with other "lay" persons interested in pursuing psychoanalysis, but also with experienced analysts and, perhaps more significantly, with analytic trainees. These stories could surely add richness to the more formal method of analytic training; they could encourage a greater mindfulness in the clinical work of prospective analysts as they listened to what patients were able to tell them, from their experiences, as to what they found to be helpful, or not. In today's consumer driven world, and with a gradual decline in psychoanalytic patients worldwide, those who undertake an analysis are eager to be more involved in their own treatment. As they travel on this emotionally hungry journey, patients are seeking something that works for them. This book challenges the preconceived perception that the analytic practitioner "knows best" when it comes to treatment, and responds to the growing sophistication of those seeking the treatment.

Robert Morley (2007) takes up a similar theme in his very interesting "analysis" of published accounts, *The Analysand's Tale*, many of who were patients of Freud and Jung. He teased out the "discordant agendas" between analyst and patient, and discussed what factors he thought had contributed to the diverse accounts of their respective psychoanalytic outcomes. My book differs in its methodology from Morley's (2007) accounts, in that it describes aspects of the analytic journeys of eighteen patients through personal interviews. It subscribes to the thinking that listening to the other, and usually "silent", partner in the analytic dyad can have significant implications for the future of clinical practice. Tessman (2003) conducted a study not unlike mine, but through interviews with psychoanalysts, asking them to revisit their own training analyses. Her book, *The Analyst's Analyst Within*, describes poignant tales of the ongoing effects on the lives, relationships, and professional identities of these analysts.

Pathways to exploration

I was originally drawn to exploring this question by two main pathways: the apparent reluctance of researchers to value the personal narratives of analytic patients and report them as a trustworthy source, and my own personal journey in psychoanalysis. The latter was with two different analysts, each of whom provided me with very different experiences. I will introduce these areas as background to my argument that listening to the patient's voice is just as valid, and significant, as listening to the analyst, generally presented as the "one who knows best". In the following chapters, this argument will be supported through patients' stories, providing personal insights and understanding of what they felt led to the success or failure of their respective analytic experiences. I also believe my professional training has enabled me to bring a capacity for thinking about the material with some objectivity.

Relevant literature

Background reading provided me with an immense volume of literature on process and outcome studies; however, I draw attention only to those areas directly related to my own particular interest. The first published account I found using a patient-orientated format was one by Hans Strupp (1969). Strupp and his colleagues pioneered work that examined responses from both therapists and their patients by combining psychotherapy research and clinical work. Their primary aim was to gain a better understanding of relationship factors that might account for therapeutic change, and was considered an important beginning. However, nearly all early attempts to explore patients' thinking were essentially through questionnaires presented in case reports and mediated by the analyst's thinking.

The most comprehensive review of outcome studies was developed through the collaborative effort of the Research Committee of the International Psychoanalytic Association (Fonagy, 2002). This document covered the principal research conducted in Europe and North America over the past decades, providing an updated and detailed classification of this work. Procedural and methodological problems inherent in psychoanalytic research were presented, emphasizing a fragmentation in a knowledge-based psychoanalysis and the absence of shared assumptions among practising psychoanalysts as to what works for whom. This *Open Door Review* (2002) demonstrated how the nature of psychoanalytic work, which is individual and carried out behind closed doors, makes it very difficult to look at, and question, basic assumptions in psychoanalysis and its clinical application.

One of the major studies that interested me in relation to my own exploration was the Psychotherapy Research Project (Wallerstein, 1986) carried out by the Menninger Foundation. It spanned some thirty years, involving twenty-two cases of long-term psychotherapy and twenty cases of psychoanalysis. As part of this Menninger Foundation Project, Harty and Horwitz (1975) compared the views of patients, analysts/therapists, and independent judges, and rated the degree of success or failure with regard to treatment outcomes in all cases. Their research examined the patient's degree of satisfaction with treatment, the therapist's estimate of the degree to which therapeutic goals had been attained, and independent researcher ratings of the same criteria. It attempted to determine not only the extent of agreement among the three different perspectives, but also whether any divergences could be usefully interpreted.

Findings indicated that, across all cases, there was the tendency for therapists to overrate their success as compared to the patients' and independent researchers' ratings, and, moreover, for the therapists to misperceive patients' dissatisfaction with the therapists' treatment. The independent researchers were the most critical of treatment outcomes. These interesting conclusions drew my attention to the potential for perpetuating an ineffective form of treatment when the emphasis on therapeutic effectiveness is judged from the clinician's perspective only, and is not inclusive of the patient's perspective, the one who seeks the treatment.

The research of Harty and Horwitz (1975) also raised questions as to whether specific criteria need to be delineated in order to guide the therapist and patient in achieving good treatment outcomes. For example, were the human characteristics related to the personality of the analyst/therapist more or less important when compared to interpretations, or were the important factors having sound treatment goals, professional style, and technique?

Central to any analyst–patient relationship is the working through of negative feelings or idealization, an argument that can be made for this being essential for a good analytic outcome. The comparative study by Harty and Horwitz (1975) left me wondering whether the perceived failure by therapists to notice patients' feelings of dissatisfaction could actually have contributed to the unsuccessful outcome in a number of the cases. This important finding was directly related to the question I was interested in, articulated by earlier writers who asked, "What do patients want when seeking analytic treatment?" Erikson (1962) asked what Dora wanted from Freud, and suggested that she had desired her experience to be validated. If Freud had done this, Erikson believed, the treatment would have succeeded. Another analytic writer, Satran (1995), argued that disparities always exist between "what the patient thinks is wrong and wants and what the analyst sees as wrong and wants for the patient" (p. 129).

A few writers have noted the importance of analysts being open to learning from their unsuccessful analytic cases, or from mistakes they have made within the analysis, which could assist them to understand how they could function better analytically. Dewald and Neutzel (1993), for example, drew attention to the essential elements that have been generated from discussion with patients of failed or abruptly terminated treatments by experienced analysts. These researchers stated that problems occurred when the analysis became analyst-centred rather than patient-centred. They wrote, "The difference [was] between seeing the analyst as holder of a superior reality view, or seeing the patient as the source of what can be known" (Dewald & Neutzel, 1993, p. 746). They found that the analyst's theoretical and technical stance was determined by the particular personality characteristics of the analyst and could be detrimental to the outcome. Referring to this as a mixture of "dumb, blind and hard spots" (*ibid.*) they described these "spots" as "cognitive and experiential gaps; aspects of knowing, unavailable through defensive avoidance or repression; and cherished theoretical sets which can either expand or limit the analyst's perceptions" (*ibid.*). The authors argued that a reluctance to alter analytic behaviour was determined by the analyst's own unresolved conflict.

The noted psychoanalyst and writer, Casement (2002), from whom I have quoted at the beginning of the Introduction, identified similar problems to Dewald and Neutzel. He stated that anything going wrong in an analysis is too readily attributed to the patient's pathology rather than to analytic error or problematic clinical style. Casement claimed that analysts were experts in using theoretical notions to support their assumptions about patients' defensive thinking, which could be detrimental to the analytic process, particularly when the analyst was unwilling or incapable of acknowledging mistakes. With an honesty not often observed in clinicians, Casement (2002) provided examples from his own practice. He illustrated how an analyst can so readily misconstrue the patient's communications and make interpretations for which there is not the readiness or appropriate timing for them to be taken in, and thought about, in a context that would promote further understanding.

Reppen and Schulman (2002) follow a similar theme in their edited book, *Failures in Psychoanalytic Treatment*. In this book are contributions from many noted writers, who describe failures from a variety of viewpoints within contemporary psychoanalysis.

An important part of my thinking was informed by the published accounts of personal analyses. As mentioned previously, these included a variety of narrated experiences by patients and trainee analysts, as well as autobiographical accounts. Morley's (2007) book, published in the latter stages of this exploration, provides similar material.

One of the few books published on patients' stories is *One to One: The Experience of Psychotherapy*, by Rosemary Dinnage (1988). Dinnage, a writer for the *New York and London Review of Books*, wrote about patients who had experienced individual psychoanalysis and psychotherapy, recruiting her participants by word of mouth. She reported they had volunteered because they said they wanted her to describe and record their experiences. She asked them to speak as freely and as honestly as possible, thus giving voice to any thoughts and feelings that came to mind about their analysis or psychotherapy. In personal communication I had with Dinnage (1999), she confirmed that she did not add anything to the stories other than very minor editing; she said she wanted the stories to speak for themselves. Her aim was to provide personal analytic accounts for the reader to hear, particularly clinicians, and, ideally, learn from what the patients had to say about their emotional experiences of the psychoanalysis. Her stories provide insight into the diverse therapeutic journeys of these patients, and also the marked differences in style and technique of the analysts/therapists that led to the patients' varied outcomes.

The recorded experiences of training analysts who had published accounts of their own analyses were also critiqued, and I have chosen four here for further discussion. The first three, Simon (1993), Hurwitz (1986) and Guntrip (1975), each wrote of two or more personal experiences in which they identified characteristics of their analysts that they perceived influenced their interpretive style and overall analytic functioning. They discussed how these qualities impacted upon the eventual outcome of their analyses.

Masson (1991) wrote about his experience in a book titled *Final Analysis*. All four narratives were helpful to me when thinking about the experiences of the patients I interviewed and who, in a similar way, described the differences they perceived in each of their analyst's style and technique in working.

Simon (1993) described four experiences, two with analytic candidates and two with experienced analysts. As all four were trained in classical Freudian technique, he claimed there were only minor theoretical differences; however, the "human element" was very important. Simon reports that what stood out most clearly for him as important to the analytic experience was the substantial difference in temperament and personal "style" of the analysts, which then had a significant impact on his day-to-day experience of the treatment. He believed it was this factor that affected the therapeutic outcome. Another central issue for Simon was the important difference between candidates and experienced analysts, primarily in the quantity of words used. The training analysts were much more verbose, whereas with the candidates he believed he was left to talk "too hackneyed and repetitious for my own good" (Simon, 1993, p. 1059), while he would have preferred to receive more feedback from the analysts themselves.

I was particularly interested in the narrative of Hurwitz (1986), as he was able to make clear distinctions between the ways in which both of his training analysts worked, linking these variations with very different outcomes. He recounted his first experience with Dr X as broadly very anxiety provoking; the analyst was a very stern man, "cool, aloof, self-consciously standoffish" (p. 445), and with an air of impatience. He reminded Hurwitz of an orthodox rabbi of whom he was terrified in his childhood. The occasional joking was done in a humiliating way, and in similar experiences of sarcasm and condescension Hurwitz stated how it felt as if the analyst always "had to be right".

Hurwitz reported that he seldom felt understood by his analyst, whose interventions engendered surprise and shock in him, but were interpreted as evidence of resistance. When he tried to explain his reactions to the analyst, interpretations were made around "oedipal strivings, jealousy, and competitiveness" (p. 446), explained to Hurwitz as the wish to defeat a powerful father. These interpretations were experienced as "humiliating submission".

Upon reflection, Hurwitz stated that there was something about the person and style of Dr X which played into his own reactions, and that his constant stirrings of frustration and competitive feelings were never acknowledged by the analyst as maybe a contribution, in some part, from the analyst himself. Suppression of feelings by Hurwitz replaced the freedom for exploration and being enabled to master them. Dr X's unexpected death three months prior to the termination date left Hurwitz with unfinished business, and led him to seek further analysis with Dr Y that, he said, was a totally different experience.

Hurwitz described Dr Y as open, understanding, and non-critical. The analyst offered interpretations for consideration rather than definitive answers, and encouraged open dialogue in an accepting environment. Anything not understood was re-stated instead of being met with stony silence, while responses to Hurwitz's rage and competitiveness were quantitatively and qualitatively different. Another important difference reported by Hurwitz was Dr Y's capacity to be attuned to pre-Oedipal and narcissistic issues, which promoted the uncovering and working through of anxiety and primitive phantasies. (Phantasy with a "ph" is used throughout, as defined by Susan Issacs (1948), denoting unconscious mental processes inferred, not actually observed. Issacs' definition has particular relevance to the patient's emotional relationship with the analyst.) Hurwitz believed that the essential difference between his two experiences was related to the very different personalities of the two analysts, which influenced the way they interpreted his communications and helped him in the process of working through his analytic journey. He also believed that he gained radically different perspectives of himself as a person.

Guntrip (1975) wrote about his analyses with Fairbairn and Winnicott, two analysts who were both deeply rooted in classical Freudian theory and therapy, but who had outgrown it in different ways. He described how he experienced Fairbairn as more clinically orthodox with "very intellectually precise interpretations" (p. 148), while Winnicott was more revolutionary in practice rather than theory. Guntrip ascribed the variation in their techniques to the fact that they had totally different personalities. He argued that this difference enabled him to explore very different aspects of his own past traumas. He believed that Fairbairn provided an Oedipal analysis. Guntrip casts Fairburn as analyst "in the role of the dominating mother" (p. 148), while Winnicott led him into the infancy period, helping him to understand the emptiness left by his mother. Guntrip attributes these differences to the human qualities brought to the analyses by both analysts, in an enlightening and constructive way.

In Guntrip's (1975) narrative, both outcomes for him were positive, although he had two quite different experiences. For Hurwitz (1986), his first analyst was unable to use his own personal qualities to enhance the analytic experience, leaving Hurwitz feeling dissatisfied and with unfinished business. One can hypothesize from these three narratives from training analysts that the personal style of their respective analysts was the most important, no matter what the psychoanalytic theory.

Masson (1991), a former analyst at the time of writing, also placed emphasis on the analyst's personal style, and described in great detail what he perceived as abuses in his training. Of his analyst, Masson said, "I was beginning to suspect that he liked thinking about himself and talking about himself more than he liked talking or thinking about me" (1991, p. 61). He also stated how sarcasm was his analyst's favourite form of attack, lacking in analytic finesse, and demonstrated this with what he called a "blatant sexism" that sometimes took his breath away. On one occasion, the intelligence of Masson's wife was brought into the session, to which the analyst's response was,

> Your wife's intelligence is not natural . . . I find it disgusting. Her mind is so developed because she is so filled with penis envy . . . Her huge brain is nothing but a substitute for a huge penis. Your wife has a cock for a brain, Masson, and you're getting fucked. [1991, p. 75]

Masson remarked that this outburst from his training analyst was a "combination of the worst of analytic theory (penis envy) and the worst of his [the analyst's] own personal prejudices against women" (1991, p. 75). He stated how such personal attacks and other exploitation perceived in institutional life led to his giving up his psychoanalytic profession and pursuing other career interests.

The final group of analytic accounts which influenced me was of autobiographical novels by individuals who had sought analyses for more personal therapeutic reasons, in particular accounts by Cardinal (1996), France (1988), and Herman (1985). (Saks [2007] has since published her amazing account of a very painful journey through schizophrenia, assisted by diverse, but helpful, experiences of psychoanalysis.)

The above-named authors identified long therapeutic journeys, describing the process as it unfolded for them. Herman, for example, describes four analytic experiences and illustrated the importance of the transference–countertransference relationship in each. She suggested that what contributed to the failure of her first three analyses was the incapacity of each analyst to both acknowledge and work with her feelings, her primitive destructive phantasies and fears. She believed that lack of proper use of the transference (the basic fundamental task of every analysis) led to no productive work being accomplished. These experiences were in marked contrast to her later experience with a Kleinian analyst, Dr Z. She described how he effectively brought the "here and now" to life with detailed, close precision, retracing step by step to where her basic problems lay. Herman attributed this to his patience, the timeliness of his interpretations, and the skill with which he undercut the intellectualizing she had always resorted to as a first defence. She reported him as a constant figure who demonstrated how he could survive the worst of her attacks, unlike the father of her past. This analysis allowed for the slow building up of an unprecedented trust in another person. Again, one might hypothesize that the personalities of the four analysts seemed to play a major factor in the success or failure of Herman's analysis.

I have provided these examples of published analytic experiences in some detail in order to illustrate the differences in style and technique that each patient has attributed to the particular personality characteristics of their analysts. These stories contributed to my thinking about "What do patients want?" and alerted me to the growing importance of the analyst's personality to the patient's experience. It prompted my decision to interview "ex" analytic patients and learn from them what factors they believed played a significant part in their analyses.

Personal journey

The second major contributing influence to my interest in this challenging venture was my own personal journey in psychoanalysis. I had two very different experiences, which motivated me to try to learn more about the nature of other patients' analyses and the important elements that led to such variations in the process for them.

While both analyses have contributed to my ongoing growth, the second was carried out within an analytic relationship that facilitated a much greater trust and freedom to engage in internal conflicts, and led to outcomes not possible in the first experience. Both analysts demonstrated understanding and expertise based on their years of training, but the individual personality of each analyst was the catalyst that enabled a more freeing experience or impeded the analytic process.

One of the essential differences was the manner in which each analyst engaged with me in the process. On reflection, in the first experience, it seemed that this analyst's style of relating was based on theory informed by a very traditional model of psychoanalysis, in which the analyst strives to be a "blank screen" and responds minimally. I often felt as though I was left in a vacuum, with a prolonged and unhelpful silence. This had more impact upon me than his often brilliant interpretations. The second experience involved a relationship which respectfully acknowledged me, the patient, as a partner in the process and endeavoured to understand my idiosyncratic way of thinking by a much more interactive exploration. At times, when an impasse seemed inevitable, the capacity of this analyst to employ humour, playfulness, and dramatization of language, enabled a shift in thinking, the turning point leading to more productive work.

Professional background and experience

As mentioned briefly above, I have broad professional experience, having worked extensively in nursing, teaching, and mental health research, before qualifying in clinical psychology, the latter influenced by training in psychoanalytic theory and practice. My knowledge and understanding of unconscious processes has, thus, been enhanced, not only from my two personal analyses and specific training, but also from several years experience of working as a psychoanalytic psychotherapist with both individuals and groups. I believe these experiences have provided me with some thoughtful capacity to engage with the many parts of the patients' journeys I am presenting for discussion.

Format of this book

In the Introduction, I discuss the divergent thinking around some of the basic psychoanalytic concepts which emerged as significant to the patients' stories. The chapters which follow relate to my question and contain the patients' stories, which are formed naturally around particular themes. I present these in the format of a journey, paralleling to some extent the psychoanalytic journey itself. For clarity of purpose throughout the book, I refer to all participants as patients, as their narratives are presented as analytic patients.

The first chapter presents the challenges I met with in attempting this exploration, and provides a very brief journey through important stages in psychoanalytic thought. I decided that this was important in setting the context for the patients' stories. I begin Chapter Two by defining the selection process, criteria, and general characteristics of the patients who volunteered to be interviewed. I then introduce each one through describing the factors that they raised as significant to their beginnings in psychoanalysis. This leads into Chapters Three and Four, with reflections on the nature of the transference and its quality. The patients describe personality characteristics of the analyst, which they believed influenced their capacity for engagement. Chapter Five, which is connected to the previous two on transference issues, illustrates a specific relationship with the analyst as "father", a very powerful theme which emerged. This demonstrates the importance of the working-through process, rather than repeating patterns from early "fathering" relationships without resolution.

Endings in analysis, a crucial stage, are presented in Chapter Six, while Chapter Seven continues this theme with emphasis upon post-analytic reflections. It describes the patients' thoughts and feelings about their overall experiences and includes specific comments on the emotional impact of the analyses. In Chapter Eight,

I discuss responses from the patients to three specific questions I asked them at the conclusion of their interviews. Chapter Nine draws together the various threads and leads into Chapter Ten, which reflects on how these analytic experiences have significant implications for the future of psychoanalysis, both clinically and theoretically.

Conclusion

I have provided the background to my focus on exploring the question "What do patients want?" I now allow the patients to speak for themselves as they reflect on all stages of their analytic journeys. I have listened to patients' experiences "from the couch", and now share their stories with the reader.

Introduction: central conceptual issues

Before introducing the patients' narratives, I thought it might be helpful to define the central psychoanalytic concepts that are used frequently throughout this book, and underpin the basic relationship between patient and analyst within which all analytic work is believed to take place. I have chosen only those terms which are either used by the patients themselves to describe their experiences, such as "transference", or which enter the narratives indirectly. The patients, for example, imply "countertransference" when they speak about aspects of the analyst's personality that they perceived influenced the dyadic relationship. The analyst's interpretative method of conveying to the patient different understanding of their verbal and non-verbal communications is also discussed by the patients, indicating how it combines both the transference and countertransference in the analytic relationship. The conceptual issue of neutrality is explored, defined, and discussed, as it, too, is relevant when attempting to understand its analytic function for particular patients when they speak about how it affects them in the interpretative method of the analyst.

These definitions are, of course, only a very limited attempt at defining such important concepts. I have tried, however, to incorporate a range of arguments, for and against each, which are relevant to the main issues raised by the patients. During the later chapters, I draw attention to these definitions when making links with what I believe the patients are describing.

To provide some consistency, I have introduced each concept by the definition provided by Laplanche and Pontalis (1985) in their book entitled *The Language of Psychoanalysis*. These definitions are then explored in the light of other psychoanalytic understandings.

Transference

> Classically, the transference is acknowledged to be the terrain on which all the basic problems of a given analysis play themselves out: the establishment, modalities, interpretation and resolution of the transference are in fact what define the cure. [Laplanche & Pontalis, 1985, p. 455]

The notion of transference was first introduced into psychoanalysis by Freud in his *Studies on Hysteria* (1895d) and more significantly in a postscript to his Dora case (1905e). In very broad terms, transference is understood as the repetition of past object relations transferred from the patient to the person of the analyst. In his analysis with Dora, Freud acknowledged the powerful nature of the transference feelings, but, at that stage, he considered these an obstacle to the analytic work. Within a few years, his thinking had completely changed, and Freud devoted four further papers (1912b; 1915a; 1916x; 1937c) to identifying this central dynamic force within the psychoanalytic process. He wrote,

> In psychoanalysis . . . all the patient's tendencies, including hostile ones, are aroused; they are then turned to account for the purposes of the analysis by being made conscious, and in this way the transference is constantly being destroyed. Transference, which seems ordained to be the greatest obstacle to psychoanalysis, becomes its most powerful ally. [Freud, 1905e, p. 117]

This "creative leap [in Freud's] unbelievable discovery that transference was in fact the key to analysis" (Bird, 1972, p. 269) was suggested, in part, as an outcome of Freud's own personal analysis, which occurred in the time delay between submitting Dora's case for publication, 1901, and its actual publication (1905). In spite of Freud's further references to transference, this postscript to his Dora case (1905e) is regarded as his greatest endorsement of what has became the essence of psychoanalysis.

Although regarded as "a universal mental function" in all human relationships (Bird, 1972, p. 267) the term "transference" has been assigned a particularly unique function in the analytic situation. Some writers (Bird, 1972; Joseph, 1985; Klein, 1943, 1952a) have argued that transference in some form is always present and active in the analytic relationship and, thus, all aspects of the patient's associations, no matter how remote, relate to the analyst. Other writers ascribe multiple functions, with not all relating to the analyst, as, for example, Baranger, Baranger, and Mom (1983), who defined a broad range of categories. These include instances of transference such as: (1) everything in the patient responding to the analyst's position and function "sometimes erroneously construed as a process of idealization" (*ibid.*, p. 3); (2) the repeated and basically unconscious transferences on to the person of the analyst of figures from the patient's primary objects of love, hatred, and identification; and (3) transference by projective identification in the Kleinian sense. The latter is considered by Baranger, Baranger, and Mom (1983) to be distinguishable from the others because of the "well-defined counter-transferential expressions accompanying it" (p. 4), which then demand interpretation.

Since Freud identified how transference could be used in a particular therapeutic way, it has gained wide acceptance and retained a central position in the psychoanalytic process. Notwithstanding this, the definition of transference has been continually debated in analytic circles and is subject to many and diverse conceptual transformations. As each analyst uses his/her own inner experience to inform the interpretative work, their understanding and use of transference, with "its objective, dynamics, tactics and scope" (Laplanche & Pontalis, 1985, p. 456), differ considerably.

The majority of analysts would appear to think about transference somewhere along a continuum. Some writers (Rangell, 1982; Stone, 1981; Wallerstein, 1990) oppose those who are in favour of total acceptance of transference interpretations (Bird, 1972; Joseph, 1985; Klein, 1943, 1952a); they believe that the support of transference as the only instrument for analytic work would result in the overlooking of vital life elements that belong outside the transference. These analysts argue that this would not be considered in the best interest of the patient who comes to the analysis from within a particular context, and, thus, brings an external or material reality. Other analysts (Gill, 1984; Richards, 1984) have likewise drawn attention to the communications they consider as "extra-transference, genetic transference and genetic interpretations" (Gill, 1984, p. 491). While these writers acknowledge the importance of the here-and-now transference interpretations, they have nevertheless upheld the position that the goal of analysis is not the analysis of the transference as such, but the alleviation of the neurosis. Gill (1984) argues that, "The analysis of the transference, crucial instrument though it be, must take its place together with work outside the transference, both present and past" (p. 491).

Abend and Shaw (1991) have described two basic forms of transference. They state that these fluctuate between the patient's intense involvement in a current relationship "which is defensively displaced or projected onto the analyst" (p. 230), and transference predominantly as "a revival, reenactment, or re-dramatization of past experiences in a new and different format, one in which the analyst plays a special part for the patient" (p. 230). The latter is depicted as occurring when the patient has undergone significant changes in the analytic treatment, while the earlier form is considered transference in a much broader sense (Abend & Shaw, 1991). In these terms, transference has different meanings, depending on the particular stage the patient has reached.

Although debates still exist on how transference is conceptualized, there is general consensus that psychoanalytic work is carried out almost entirely in the patient's transference relationship with the analyst, which facilitates the uncovering of unconscious processes and forms the essential component of the interpretative work.

For the purpose of understanding these patients' experiences, I have used the broader understanding of transference as proposed by previously mentioned writers (Rangell, 1982; Stone, 1981; Wallerstein, 1990). They strongly believed that transference can be extended to external realities and is not confined to a concept in which everything transferred by the patient is related to the analyst.

Countertransference

The whole of the analyst's unconscious reactions to the individual analysand—especially to the analysand's own transference. [Laplanche & Pontalis, 1985, p. 92]

A counterpart to the patient's active role in the transference relationship is the analyst's use of his/her countertransference; the analyst makes sense of, and responds to, the patient's communications by putting into words what is happening in the analytic process at that particular moment. The analyst's task is to bring the unconscious into conscious awareness by listening to more than the spoken content conveyed by the patient, drawing also on external manifestations and other non-verbal communications. In making their interpretations, analysts do not merely function at an intellectual level but, in addition, they utilize any feelings they experience towards their patients that have arisen in the here-and-now of the analytic session. This use of their "emotional" state of mind forms a crucial aspect to their understanding of the patient.

In its original formulation by Freud (1912e) countertransference was understood as a hindrance to the interpretative work through a "neurotic transference of the analyst to the patient" (Hinshelwood, 1999, p. 797). A radical re-thinking occurred, with challenges starting in the late 1940s (Gitelson, 1952; Heimann, 1950; Little, 1951; Winnicott, 1949), and has led to the current understanding of countertransference as encompassing all the analyst's affective responses. Abend (1989) suggests that factors over the years that have influenced this change include:

> ... the introduction of the structural hypothesis, the impact of Kleinian and interpersonal schools on the theory of technique, the effect of analysts' experience in working with more severely ill patients, and the diffuse consequences of certain recent cultural and intellectual trends. [p. 374]

According to Hinshelwood (1999), countertransference was primarily changed "from interference into a principal tool" by Heimann (1950), in her formulation that "The analyst's emotional response to his patient within the analytic situation ... is an instrument of research into the patient's unconscious" (Heimann, 1950, p. 81, cited in Hinshelwood, 1999, p. 798). This change was based on an understanding of the psychoanalytic setting as a relationship between two partners, with each contributing from their personal backgrounds and experiences to the intersubjective analytic space. Little (1951) endorsed this thinking when she wrote,

> The whole patient–analyst relationship includes both "normal" and pathological, conscious and unconscious, transference and counter-transference, in varying proportions; it will always include something which is specific to both the individual patient and the individual analyst. [p. 33]

In spite of the Kleinian influence, opposition continued for another quarter of a century, encouraged by a series of papers by Reich (1951, 1960, 1966), which "delineated a variety of counter-transference difficulties" (Jacobs, 2002, p. 20). The emphasis in Reich's papers was that countertransference, though seen as inevitable, was an interference in the analyst's capacity to understand and accurately respond to patients' communications; thus, it required further analysis for the clinicians themselves to resolve this impediment. As this significant conceptual issue was continually debated, considerable disagreement existed between those who accepted that everything in the analyst's personality had the likelihood of affecting the analytic treatment, and the school of thought which restricted countertransference to meaning only the unconscious processes triggered off in the analyst by the patient's transference. Although differences continue to occur in its conceptualization, the centrality of countertransference has remained as an essential component of psychoanalytic technique.

Boesky (1991) has argued that the broad definition of counter-transference is too inclusive, and has stated that, "If counter-transference means all the analyst's feelings about the patient then we are left with no way to distinguish [the analyst's] learned skill from his unconscious impulses" (p. 25, cited in Abel-Horowitz, 1998, p. 676). Eagle (2000) has supported this contention. Influenced largely by Gill's (1982) writings, Eagle stated that countertransference has been redefined by the acceptance of the analyst's participation in "the emission of cues", rather than maintaining the classical notion of a "blank screen" analyst. The relationship between patient and analyst has, thus, become theorized as a more interactional one. Eagle suggests that,

If the altered meaning of transference is a recognition that the analyst cannot help but emit personal cues to which the patient reacts,
then the altered meaning of counter-transference can be seen as a
recognition that the analyst cannot help but react to the patient in
personal ways. [2000, p. 25]

Eagle cited Racker (1968) as exerting considerable influence on current views about countertransference. Racker's writings included
the following statement:

> If the analyst is well identified with the patient and he has fewer
> repressions than the patient, then the thoughts and feelings which
> emerge in him [i.e., the analyst] will be, precisely, those which did
> emerge in the patient, i.e., the repressed and the unconscious. [1968,
> p. 17]

Eagle's concern, like Racker's, was related to the danger that all
responsibility in what happens in the transference–countertransference relationship would be attributed to the patient rather than
there being any acknowledgement of the analyst's own contribution.

I am presenting Eagle's argument in some detail, as I believe it
of significance to some of the discussion points raised by participants in this study. Eagle maintained that there was a perception by
some analysts (Gabbard, 1995; Sandler, 1987, 1993; Spillius, 1992)
that Heimann's conception of countertransference "might allow
analysts to blame their patients for their own counter-transference
difficulties" (Gabbard, 1995, p. 476). Heimann's view was supported by Levine (1997), who asserted that thoughts and emotional
experiences of the analyst which arise during a session and have
seemingly little to do with the patient nevertheless "can be presumed to have a patient-related component that contributes to their
appearance in a particular way" (ibid., p. 48, as cited in Eagle, 2002,
p. 27). Gabbard (1995) counteracted this by an observation that
if one applied projective identification, "the analyst is viewed as
virtually empty and is simply a receptacle for what the patient is
projecting" (ibid., p. 479).

The viewpoint that countertransference is totally related to the
patient's communications in the transference would seem to suggest that the analyst contributes nothing to the thoughts and feelings which enter his/her mind during the interaction with the

patient in the analytic session. Eagle wrote of a commonly held belief that he disagreed with,

> ... all an analyst (at least a well analyzed analyst) needs do to know the patient's unconscious mental contents is identify with the patient and, through an evenly hovering or suspended attention, permit thoughts and feelings to emerge in his or her consciousness. These thoughts and feelings emerging in the analyst will then be precisely the unconscious thoughts and feelings of the patient ... The analyst is, if not a blank screen, at least a mirror that reflects the patient's thoughts and feelings. Furthermore, like all good (i.e., accurate) mirrors, the analyst brings no prior images of his or her own. [2000, p. 27]

According to Eagle (2000), any critical examination of the analyst's reactions as a reliable indication of what is going on in the patient is thus discouraged and, therefore, monitoring of what is likely to be unreliable is not possible. This definition of countertransference does not allow for the analyst's own personal thoughts and feelings to be acknowledged as influencing his/her thinking about the patient's internal objects and unconscious. As stated by Eagle (2000), analysts, as people, experience a wide range of feelings, and these can occur repeatedly within the analytic session. Identifying all feeling responses as projections from the patient can "constitute reactions to attack rather than identifications with the attacker's internal object" (ibid., p. 31). It has been recognized (Racker, 1968; Sandler, 1987, 1993; Strupp & Binder, 1984) that a therapeutic problem arises when the analyst reacts to certain communications from the patient, not acknowledging his/her own personal agendas brought to the analytic situation, which can then contribute to a retraumatization and creation of a vicious circle characterized by the repetition of the very condition that "helped establish the patient's neurosis" (Racker, 1968, p. 138). This would be considered a countertransference reaction, arising from within the analyst, rather than an interpretation.

A third source of countertransference, the analyst's personal theory, has recently been put forward to complement the traditional understanding of the analyst's emotional responses as being constructed from a combination of personal agenda, which is the analyst's unconscious conflicts and pathology, and the patient's effects on him/her in the transference (Purcell, 2004; Stein, 1991). Emphasizing that there is no practice without theory, Stein (1991) has stated,

> This counter-transference may occur independently of the patient's motivation and independently of the internal dynamics of the ana-. lyst . . . what transpires in a session draws the analyst's theory out of the woodwork where it was only temporarily residing. [p. 326]

This suggestion was also borne out by some earlier research I conducted, exploring the relationship between psychoanalytic theory and practice (Hill, 1996, unpublished). Stein has argued that emotions as well as facts are soaked in theory, and stated that "The analyst's emotional reactions in the analysis depend on the analyst's theoretical convictions of what does and does not constitute good analysis" (1991, p. 326). Stein's notion that theory thus plays an important role in countertransference responses to the patient's communications has been endorsed, and extended, by Purcell (2004).

In affirming the complexity of theory in relation to the practice of psychoanalysis, Purcell (2004) observed that an analyst's theory was becoming much more integral to his/her personality, with an influence not only on cognition, but "more indirectly, through its determining implicit qualities of the relationship with the patient" (p. 636). Given the significance of this, Purcell advocated that theory was a significant causal factor in the formation of countertransference, "by establishing in the analyst a set of expectations for analysis" (ibid., p. 639), and drew on his clinical work with narcissistic resistance in patients to demonstrate his beliefs. He discussed the complexity inherent in his perspective because of the theory in analysts being both preconscious and unconscious. Purcell (2004) also stated, "In our current state of theoretical development there is no one psychoanalytic theory that 'fits' comprehensively and sufficiently all forms of pathology" (p. 647). I have considered this third proposed source of countertransference as I think it does resonate with experiences of patients in this study who questioned, at times, the analyst's theory when difficulties in accepting interpretations ended in them stating that they "felt stuck" or unable to understand where the interpretation fitted with their personal communications to the analyst.

Countertransference, in both the traditional and contemporary conceptualizations, is no longer understood merely in terms of responses elicited by the patient's transference. It has now been recognized that the analyst must not only use his/her countertransference as an indicator of what is occurring in the patient's unconscious and, thus, it becomes the basis for formulating interpretations, but also is required to monitor his/her own feelings in order to resolve personal blind spots. These feelings may arise through unresolved conflicts, anxieties, and defences from the analyst's past, and can block any accurate understanding of the patient's unconscious. Aaron (1974) has also drawn attention to the recognition that the analyst's narcissistic needs can contribute to countertransference (p. 167), while Eagle (2000) has iterated that one can no longer assume that "all feelings and thoughts that emerge in [the analyst's] experience necessarily, and in any simple, uncomplicated way, reflect what is going on in the patient's inner world" (p. 36).

Added to the above discussion about the various understandings of how countertransference is used by the analyst, I would like to refer to McLaughlin's (1981) view that the term "countertransference" is in itself a casualty "so variously defined as to be by now almost unmanageable" (p. 639). He states that he would like to see the term abandoned in favour of the "analyst's transferences", which he believes moved it away from being "confined solely to the patient-centred focus of the analytic situation" (ibid.). This move would then acknowledge the part that is also played by the analyst's personality and unresolved issues. In addition, he noted, "The term counter-transference particularly cannot accommodate the intrapsychic range and fullness of the analyst's experiences vis-à-vis his patient" (McLaughlin, 1981, p. 56).

In my review of the literature, which pertains to the various writings about countertransference, I would argue that McLaughlin's redefinition would seem to fit accurately with what has emerged about countertransference from some of the patients in this study. This is further discussed in later chapters.

Interpretation in psychoanalysis

The procedure which, by means of analytic investigation, brings out the latent meaning in what the subject says and does. Interpretation reveals the modes of the defensive conflict and its ultimate aim is to identify the wish that is expressed by every product of the unconscious. [Laplanche & Pontalis, 1985, p. 227]

The interpretative work of analysis is linked with the transference–countertransference relationship. The analysts use their understanding of countertransference as a primary source for making sense of the patient's verbal and non-verbal communications and then draw on this as part of the material for their interpretations. The analyst's interpretation of what is transmitted from the patient in the transference is considered the central mode of communication in the analytic setting. What aspects of the transference and when these are interpreted, however, continue to be debated. Giovacchini (1993) illustrated this when he wrote,

> There are many analysts who retain the "classical" position, and even though they permit themselves some other forms of communication, they believe that only the transference interpretation is analytically relevant. [p. 474]

This would assume that no aspect of the patient's external world is relevant and can be accepted in its own right, but must be interpreted only in relation to the analyst.

The traditional understanding of interpretation evolved from Freud's (1900a) definition in which he stated that to interpret was to assign meaning to the patient's material (p. 96). This suggested that the patient's psychic life was translated into meaning by the analyst, but limited any sense of the patient being an active participant in the task of interpreting. More recently, interpretation has taken on other meanings, such as described by Aaron (1992) as, ". . . a complex inter-subjective process that develops conjointly between patient and analyst . . . in this sense interpretations contain aspects of the analyst's subjectivity that are made available for use by the patient" (p. 475).

Blomfield (1982) also drew attention to factors that facilitate interpretations, as, for example, the patient's compliance with the basic rule of free association, which is explained as,

> The attempt to put thoughts or feelings into words as they occur, regardless of inhibitory influences, such as fear, embarrassment, guilt or judgments of irrelevance, triviality or irrationality, or,

where these inhibitions are an obstacle, to speak of the difficulty first. [Blomfield, 1982, p. 289]

He described other essential factors contributing to interpretations, such as evenly suspended attention on the part of the analyst as a complement to the free association, and aspects of the setting such as the use of the couch to facilitate bringing the patient's phantasies more directly into awareness with the analyst out of sight, frequency of sessions, and the duration of the analysis itself.

While it is understood that analysts receive cues for formulating their interpretations from the patient's verbal and non-verbal communications in the transference, it can be argued that these interpretations cannot always be considered the last word. As will be demonstrated later through the clinical narratives of the patients, many challenged the relevance and authority of the analyst's interpretations that did not seem to resonate with their thinking. The patients believed that the analysts were "pushing their own agenda". In relation to this issue, Cooper (1993) has quoted Edelson (1975) and Bollas (1989) as arguing that,

> There is always a tension between the analyst "making a difference because he listens and in his interpretations bearing witness to the presence of meaning" (Edelson, 1975, p. 19) on the one hand, and on the other, the analyst "creating" meanings (Bollas, 1989) through the trial-and-error process of interpretation. [Cooper, 1993, p. 96]

Langs (1980) endorsed the argument that interpretations, while entailing "important unconscious contents and processes which are made conscious for the patient", still remained "clinical uncertainties in regard to the timing, formulation, and structure of this intervention" (p. 460). Freud (1937c) also emphasized the notion that interpretation is always a conjecture, subject to potential revision. With reference to the patient's reactions to interpretative constructions he stated:

> We do not pretend that an individual construction is anything more than a conjecture which awaits examination, confirmation or rejection. We claim no authority for it, we require no direct agreement from the patient, nor do we argue with him if at first he denies it. In short, we conduct ourselves on the model of a familiar figure in one of Nestroy's farces—the manservant who has a single answer

on his lips to every question or objection: "It will all become clear in the course of future developments". [*ibid.*, p. 265]

Disagreement by patients, nevertheless, has continued to be understood by analysts as largely within the framework of resistance and negative transference. Arguments have been raised supporting the veracity of the analyst's interpretations, as for example, Paniagua (1985) stated that the soundness of established psychoanalytic theories and the reliability of clinical observations could be considered as proof against the contention that interpretations are nothing but conjectures. The literature would seem to indicate that this contention remains questionable.

In referring to the analyst's function in bringing the unconscious meanings of the patient's subjective experience into the "here-and-now" of conscious understanding, Kernberg (1997) has described a gradual process of drawing together the threads of communication. He links the interpretative work with the search for truth, painful as it may be to the patients, but resulting in feelings of liberation.

> The analyst's search for truth unavoidably will be experienced by the patient at times as an aggressive act; if the analyst's search for the truth is honestly rooted in his wish to help his patients to increase their knowledge about themselves, eventually patients will be able to appreciate that and be grateful for the confidence in their own strength reflected in the analyst's unwavering commitment to the truth. [*ibid.*, p. 109]

In thinking about the patients' narratives in this research, and mindful of interpretations which were not considered helpful, or to be "following the analyst's agenda", I have drawn on a combination of Kerberg's (1997) description of the analyst drawing together the threads in an "honest search for truth", and Aaron's (1992) definition which acknowledges the "complexity" of interpretation as well as the analyst's "subjectivity".

Neutrality

One of the defining characteristics of the attitude of the analyst during the treatment. The analyst must be neutral in respect of religious, ethical, and social values—that is to say, he must not direct the treatment according to some ideal . . . he must be neutral too as regards manifestations of transference . . . finally he must be neutral towards the discourse of the patient: in other words, he must not, a priori, lend a special ear to particular parts of his discourse, or read particular meanings into it, according to his theoretical preconceptions. [Laplanche & Pontalis, 1985, p. 271]

In one of Freud's early papers (1912b), he advocated a non-relational approach for the analyst, a "blank screen" on to which patients' thoughts and feelings could be projected and repressed or disavowed aspects of themselves thus gradually revealed. This was set out by Freud when he wrote that the analyst "should be opaque to his patients and, like a mirror, should show them nothing but what is shown to him" (p. 118). Some analysts have endeavoured to adopt this "non-relational" stance with their patients, mistakenly regarding it as neutrality; however, there is clear evidence from Freud's well-documented case studies that he himself never practised in such a way.

So, how do we understand what Freud was proposing and its relationship with neutrality? It would seem there is still considerable confusion among some practising analysts as well as in the minds of patients, as demonstrated in this research. According to Breger (1984), the misuse of neutrality originated in Freud's early focus on sexuality as the central motive behind all human action. Related to this was the idea that the Oedipus complex was the basis of all neuroses. As Breger (1984) succinctly writes, "If you start with these assumptions, then a sexualized oedipal transference becomes the defining model and being 'neutral' consists in 'abstaining' or not 'gratifying' the patient's sexual fantasies or their symbolic derivatives" (p. 584).

Breger further explained that it was possible to give a more encompassing definition to neutrality. He stated how, in the interaction between analyst and patient, there is a demand by the patient that the analyst, "respond in a stereotypical social fashion: to play his side of the game, as it were" (ibid.). According to Breger, neutrality consists of the analyst not actively participating in the patient's "game", but attempting to understand the interaction by inviting the patient to engage in a process of mutual understanding (ibid.). In addition, by this understanding of neutrality (Breger,

1984) there were no fixed rules with all patients, but each analytic relationship required understanding on its own terms, "Sometimes being neutral means being relatively silent and sometimes it means the opposite" (*ibid.*, p. 585).

Lipton (1977) hypothesized something quite specific about Freud's notion of neutrality. His important paper explored the changes in technique between Freud's work, demonstrated in his analysis of the "Rat Man", and that of later analysts, whom Lipton believed redefined the way Freud worked. The assumption, however, was that it was Freud who changed over the years (Beigler, 1977; Grunberger, 1966; Zetzel, 1966). Lipton argued that the essential difference between Freud and his colleagues and the later analysts was an expansion of technique to include aspects of the analyst's personality affecting the relationship with the patient, which Freud had excluded and claimed as not belonging to technique. Relating this to the concept of neutrality, Lipton (1977) has maintained that Freud's recommendations about the analyst being like a mirror, or "blank screen", to his patients can be understood as purely technical. Lipton argued, "They were meant to emphasize the attitude of neutrality with which the analyst was to comprehend the patient's associations, an attitude which the patient understood. They were not meant to encompass the analyst's entire personality" (*ibid.*, p. 272).

It would seem that, since Freud's era, most psychoanalysts have now arrived at a different understanding of neutrality, or what has become commonly known as "technical neutrality". Variation still exists in its definition, with Lipton (1977) asserting that some analysts have taken the definition too rigidly. However, neutrality generally is considered an essential component of the analyst's task in the analytic situation.

I found the description by Adler and Bachant (1996) particularly helpful, as it clearly delineated the role of the analyst as requiring to be an "emotional presence" in the analytic situation. In a similar understanding to Lipton (1977), they described neutrality in the context of the interpersonal relationship and related it as the analyst's complementary role to the patient's task to follow the "rule" of free association and speak his/her thoughts with as little censoring of the material as possible. In response, the analyst has the complex and demanding task of listening to and understanding the patient's communications, and, in order to fulfil this, to "simultaneously absorb and integrate a host of competing pulls, tensions, and purposes" (Adler & Bachant, 1996, pp. 1029–1030). In carrying out this highly sophisticated role, the analyst adopts a particular position of "neutrality", which is regarded, using Adler and Bachant's words, as "the technical name for a very complex attitude toward the patient's inner life and experience that imbues the analyst's listening in the analytic situation with a unique qualitative dimension" (*ibid.*, p. 1032). This is understood as being a "responsive presence" rather than the "blank screen" mistakenly adopted by some analysts in a misrepresentation of Freud's (1912) dictum, and which is also due to the several different dimensions embraced by the concept (Adler & Bachant, 1996).

In discussing the various dimensions of neutrality, as they understood it, Adler and Bachant (*ibid.*) drew attention to three essential elements which relate to the interactive process: neutrality in regard to conflict, the sequence or timing of issues, and, most importantly, to the patient's transference. Elsewhere, Adler and Bachant (1998) have referred to free association and technical neutrality as "the fundamental pillars of the psychoanalytic process itself" (p. 452).

I think it is important to present a different perspective, which includes two opposing views of neutrality by prominent writers: Strachey (1934) and Loewald (1960), which have been discussed by Cooper (1988) and cited in Akhtar (2000). In comparing the seminal contributions on technique by these two thinkers, Cooper noted how Strachey (1934), in his model of therapeutic action, described the analyst as "a neutral, benign interpreter of reality, internalized as a temporary new object, helping to make the unconscious conscious, and modifying the ego" (p. 19). Cooper states that the classical notion of neutrality was thus preserved. In contrast, he defined Loewald's (1960) position of the analyst as a contemporary object as

> ... an emotionally related object ... mindful of the patient's core of potential being ... offering the patient opportunities to create new integrations on the armature of maturity that the analyst provides. His task is empathic communication, uncovering, and guidance towards new synthesis. [Cooper, 1988, p. 26]

These two sets of ideas on thoughts about neutrality Cooper believed to be parallel, rather than integrated models of how psychoanalysis works and needed to be unified (Aktar, 2000, p. 277). Loewald's (1960) position on neutrality, however, closely resembles that of Adler and Bachant (1996, 1998).

It became clear to me in these patient interviews that "technical neutrality" was loosely defined and thought about by patients in relation to their perceptions of the analyst's style of working with them. However, there are also diverse understandings in the psychoanalytic literature about what neutrality means in its technical usage; it would appear that, from the patients' perspective, some analysts working with them in this research might also have confused the current thinking with the classical viewpoint of "neutrality" as a "blank screen". Laplanche and Pontalis (1985) stated that "it [neutrality] is a technical requirement, and in a way it does imply or guarantee a sovereign 'objectivity' in the person who exercises the profession of psychoanalyst" (pp. 271–272). How technical neutrality is defined and used would seem to have consequences for the analyst's capacity to function in such a way that is helpful to the patient and can enable the analytic work to take place.

Conclusion

In this Introduction, I have defined the psychoanalytic concepts of "transference", "countertransference", "interpretation", and "neutrality", all of which are considered central to the work of analysis and, thus, relevant to this exploration of patients' experiences of psychoanalysis. All concepts have arisen through the patients' communications and, therefore, I believed that they required some explanation in order to make sense of how the patients themselves perceived their usage. In the later chapters, I have linked these definitions with the findings and discussion.

CHAPTER ONE

Meeting the challenge

"Psychoanalytic practitioners sometimes slip into a position of arrogance, that of thinking they know best. Thus, when something goes wrong in an analysis, it is often the patient who is held accountable for this, the analyst assuming it to be an expression of the patient's pathology rather than perhaps (at least) due to some fault of the analyst's"

(Casement, 2002, p. xiii)

If you were a patient seeking psychoanalytic treatment, what would you think of Casement's statement? Or, if an analytic trainee, how would you process the notion that even experienced analysts can confuse, or fail to understand, an inadequacy in their style of working which is then falsely attributed to the patient's pathology? How many people have actually listened to patients and really understood what the experience of analysis was like for them? These are some of the questions addressed in this book.

Casement's (2002) statement struck me as both honest and provocative, and encouraged my growing interest in exploring psychoanalysis from the patient's perspective. How could I find

1

ways to understand the psychoanalytic process as it unfolds within the transference–countertransference relationship, and in the privacy of the consulting rooms? In seeking an answer to this question I decided to ask patients, who had been in an analysis, what led them into this journey of discovery and what the experience was like for them. Did the analysis meet their expectations, or not, and how did they understand what it was that made the difference?

One of the central aims of psychoanalysis is to provide a therapeutic treatment that enables patients to come to a deeper awareness of enduring and pathological patterns of behaviour influencing life situations. I believed, therefore, that one of my tasks was to find a common definition of psychoanalysis that related to this work. Issues that were raised in interviews with the patients, and reading material focused on this area, also motivated me.

Another factor was my attendance at the International Psychoanalytical Association (IPA) Congress in Nice, 2001, entitled "Psychoanalysis: Method and Application", where diversity was the prevailing element. The common feature of these three experiences was the increasing awareness that psychoanalysis is extremely difficult, if not impossible, to define because of its multi-faceted nature, which encompasses theory, research, and diverse applications to its clinical practice.

In meeting these challenges, I saw the importance of briefly touching upon some of the trends throughout the history of psychoanalysis that have contributed to difficulties in a working definition. Therefore, I looked at the literature related to the development and growth of psychoanalysis from the time of Freud, examining the nature of the process, its changing aims, and relatedness to effective treatment and outcome.

Psychoanalysis: the "impossible" definition

Bachrach, Galatzer, Skolnikoff, and Waldron (1991) and Waldron (1997) argue convincingly that defining psychoanalysis has always been problematic. One recent study (Vaughan, Spitzer, Davies, and Roose, 1997) involved interviews with senior training analysts from the Columbia Centre for Psychoanalytic Training and Research, who were asked how they would define and assess the analytic process. No meaningful consensus was found within this group. The authors discussed the implication of this finding, suggesting that it might translate across to other core concepts such as transference and countertransference (discussed in the Introduction).

Psychoanalysis has been defined as a dynamic form of treatment, a method for the scientific study of the personality, and a system of scientific psychology to predict human behaviour (Berne, 1957; Chaplin 1975). Psychoanalysis, however, is not merely a therapeutic method, but an enormously complex, dynamic system of psychology, based originally on Freud's tripartite model of the mind. From the early beginnings of Freud's work, the psychoanalytic method has undergone idealization and collapsed into perplexity. Psychoanalysts are no longer in agreement as to the mechanisms of development or the conduct of psychoanalysis as a treatment method.

In his keynote address to the American Psychological Association on 16 April 1999, Peter Fonagy opened with "It would be a brave or foolhardy man (or woman) who would stand in front of an audience of psychoanalysts and psychotherapists and announce that he (or she) had the 'definitive model' of therapeutic action". This viewpoint is also clearly demonstrated in the psychoanalytic literature, which provides no consensus as to the nature of psychoanalysis or its essential components of theory and practice, even among seasoned analysts (Bachrach, Galatzer, Skolnikoff, & Waldron, 1991; Perelberg, 2005; Vaughan, Spitzer, Davies, & Roose, 1997; Waldron, 1997). Tuckett (2001) stated that knowledge about psychoanalysis and its practical application, in spite of 100 years of practice, is still very much in doubt within the discipline. Perhaps this is a result of Freud's thinking when he said, "It [psychoanalysis] gropes its way forward by the help of experience, is always incomplete and always ready to correct or modify its theories" (Freud, 1923b, p. 253).

The IPA Congress (2001) took up the challenge of addressing confusion around psychoanalysis when they chose the theme for their Nice Congress. Representatives from various analytic institutions throughout the world repeatedly debated the question of diversity; they presented this as a dilemma for more than forty-two Congresses since the time of Freud (Guerrero, 2001). Two central points were raised about the current state of psychoanalysis: (1) how it was highly subjective in its specificity of method, and, hence, lacked the capacity for useful dialogue among clinicians; (2) that it had no internal consistency, therefore presented a difficulty to the clinician in recognizing his/her fundamental task (IPA Congress papers, 2001).

The above concerns offered analysts the challenge to find ways of effectively communicating with those not only within their own discipline, but outside of it as well. Jiménez (2001), a speaker at the Congress, emphasized that unless there was coherence and inner consistency, analysts could find merely what they were seeking, hence turning psychoanalysis into a self-fulfilling prophecy rather than exploring differences.

One of the main problems in searching for a consensus on psychoanalysis seemed related to Freud's continual vacillation over what he considered as the important elements and central aims of analysis. Freud lived in an era profoundly different from today's world, with markedly different social and cultural mores, and influenced by the scientific empiricist thinking of that period. Coming from a medical background, the focus for Freud's learning was through the description and explanation of empirical facts, relying on theories of disease, aetiologies, clinical histories, diagnosis and cure. (Freud, however, was quite clear in his writings [1913c, 1937c] that psychoanalysis needed to be kept out of the medical/psychiatry profession.) The evolving medical paradigm, particularly in that historical period and enduring until recent years, has relied upon a power differential between doctor and patient. Freud's powerful, paternalistic position of authority, which was characteristic of his era, is demonstrated in the following quotes from Freud, "When there is a dispute with the patient whether or how he has said some particular thing, the doctor is usually in the right" (1912e, p. 113), and also, "One must be especially unyielding about obedience to that rule . . ." (ibid., p. 119). The awe in which physicians and other experts were held in the time of Freud has gradually diminished over the years, with patients becoming more critical of the doctor's authority because of their increased knowledge and preparedness to make choices. Living in a different culture, with access to better education, knowledge, and the influence of globalization, patients want aspects of their life outside the analysis understood and addressed.

Freud's original aim, symptom removal, changed repeatedly as he revised his theory of the mind and the analytic process to structural change, and as he became interested in analysis as a method of scientific research. During his vacillations, Freud suggested that preoccupation with achieving a cure could be detrimental to the psychoanalytic process and, in fact, hinder the effectiveness of the method. The contradictions inherent in his works would seem to have contributed markedly to the confusion that has followed. Freud did, however, identify an important transferential component by which the analyst becomes the centre of the patient's preoccupations. The recognition and working with the transference has remained an essential technique in psychoanalytic practice, although, as explained in the Introduction, there are variations in its definition.

Why these vacillations from Freud? According to Holt (1987), Freud had an amazing capacity for tolerating inconsistencies. Holt believed this was the result of the enormous amount of writing produced by Freud, and because Freud liked to give himself up freely to his thinking to see where it might lead him. Freud illustrates this in a letter to Andreas-Salomé in 1917, when he wrote, "You have observed how I work, step by step, without the inner need for completion, continually under the pressure of the problems immediately on hand and taking infinite pains not to be diverted from the path" (Freud, 1960, p. 319).

This, however, has created considerable problems for later generations of analysts and academics, and potential patients, especially when the patient's need is understood as more specific and immediate.

Holt (1987) described how Freud tended to add things to previous publications without any fundamental reconsideration and little synthesis. He believed that Freud's superb command of written communication meant that he rarely had to polish even his first drafts, thus, he did not pay thorough attention to the internal consistency or logic of his works as they went through new editions. Holt illustrates this argument when he writes:

> Freud built theory, then, much as Franklin D. Roosevelt constructed the Executive branch of the government: when something wasn't working very well, he seldom reorganized; he just supplied another

> agency—or concept—to do the job. To tolerate this much inconsis-
> tency surely took an unusual capacity to delay the time when grat-
> ification of an orderly, internally consistent, logically coherent
> theory might be attained. [Holt, 1987, p. 37]

Perhaps this explains some of the more specific ambiguity and
theoretical diversity encountered by followers of Freud. For example, a review of empirical studies conducted by Henry, Strupp,
Schact, and Gaston (1994) generated evidence of no universally
agreed upon definitions of "transference" and "interpretation",
concepts which are considered the cornerstone of most analytic
methods. According to Sandler, Holder, Kawenoka, Kennedy, and
Neurath (1969), and verified with later studies (Luborsky, Barber, &
Crits-Christoph, 1990), definitions of "transference" vary as widely
as the relationships included in the concept, and do not merely
include the analyst/therapist. The understanding of the concept
of "interpretation" varies even more widely (Piper, Debbane,
Bienvenu, & Garant, 1987) while the combination of both terms
generates a number of possibilities. These concepts are discussed
further in the Introduction.

Kächele and Thomä (1999) drew attention to another important
aspect of psychoanalysis when they argued that psychoanalysis
had lost its prime therapeutic position over the 100 years from its
inception. They stated that it has had to actively fight for its special
place among a host of other treatments that have evolved, while
systematic studies have inadequately supported the increasing
variety of psychoanalytic truths. These researcher–clinicians highlighted the impact of new developmental studies as a prime example of why therapists and patients may not want to depend on loose
patterns of theorizing to give them credence.

In this section I have addressed the issue "what is psychoanalysis?", arguing that there are a number of understandings. This situation would seem to have been created by the founder of psychoanalysis, who did not develop the theory logically, therefore his
work led to multiple interpretations. I was hoping to have a working definition of psychoanalysis and its main theoretical components to use when interpreting the patients' material, so formed
one from the following components that I found most useful. The
definition incorporates the essential elements of psychoanalysis
as presented by the Australian Psychoanalytical Society (APAS

website, 2005); they also have links with communications from the patients in this research.

Keeping in mind the difficulties presented in formulating a definition of psychoanalysis, I have chosen to limit my working definition for this research to the therapeutic aspect of Freud's tripartite model of the mind (Berne, 1957; Chaplin, 1975). In simple terms, I define psychoanalysis as a process by which patients seek to understand the unconscious determinants of enduring and problematic patterns of behaviour and human emotions. These are explored through an intense therapeutic relationship with a trained psychoanalyst, and conducted under particular conditions that favour the uncovering of the unconscious. For the psychoanalytic process to work, it must acknowledge the following components: human emotions and behaviour are influenced by the unconscious; symptoms are the manifestation of the unconscious; the work of analysis takes place within the transference–countertransference relationship; the "human" characteristics of both analyst and patient have an impact upon the quality of the engagement; and particular conceptual issues such as free association, resistance, technical neutrality, and interpretation have a significant function. These later concepts are defined in detail in the next chapter.

Complexities compounded by the transference relationship

It is important that any exploration of the unique psychoanalytic relationship between the patient and analyst captures the complexities of the clinical situation (Perron, 2001; Roth & Fonagy, 1996). From my psychoanalytic knowledge base, critical reading, and therapeutic experience, I was aware that the reader would raise questions as to whether the patients' accounts could be considered "trustworthy", particularly with complications inherent in the transference relationship. In simple terms, this relationship can be understood as the patient transferring thoughts and feelings from their own significant early relationships to the person of the analyst, who, as a result, then becomes the vehicle for many projections and understandings of meaning.

Because of this theoretical approach, the analyst's interpretation of what happens in the analytic encounter can be very different from that of the patient's perceived experience. This often reinforces the traditional belief that how the analyst describes the particular treatment is the only true version. An example of this privileging of one account over another occurs for women in patriarchal societies who have posed threats to males when trying to claim a voice, as in feminist movements in the 1960s; a second example is the experience of children not being listened to or believed when speaking of abuse carried out in the family. Within such traditions of doubt about the credibility of the "unempowered voice", I was aware of the challenge of presenting patients' narratives that would be considered credible in an environment where analysts' accounts have generally been privileged.

Matthis and Szecsödy (1998) maintained that "truth" should be understood as a social phenomenon to be continuously explored and transformed. They stated that objectivity is provided by the will and ability to unremittingly question beliefs and assumptions, and emphasized how psychoanalytic "knowledge" or theory was so difficult to test empirically—what changes, how it changes, and why, in the clinical setting. Matthis (1998) described Freud's attempts, often unsuccessful, to present his views and theories to a wider public, and stated that the ambiguities pertaining to the opening up of the closed doors were still prevalent today. He wrote, "Behind these closed doors the clinical psychoanalytic work continues . . . The fact that stormy weather may accompany an opening up of these hitherto sheltered chambers should not be accepted as a good reason for keeping the doors closed" (Matthis (1998, p. xiv).

Questions around the complexities of understanding the transference from the perspectives of both patient and clinician have been raised in this section. I have argued that the trustworthiness of patients' accounts, within the context of powerful transferences, is often questioned. In this exploration of their stories, I am, therefore, choosing to give a voice to their accounts, viewing them with a different lens. In the following chapters of this book, I present the analyses from their experiences.

The impact of unconscious factors

Another difficulty in deciding how to approach this work was related to the value given to specific "truths" or authority from within a psychoanalytic perspective. For example, as argued previously, some analysts believe that patients do not or cannot know what they want from analysis because of the unconscious factors involved; they claim that patients may only know that they want something. Based on this premise, it could be stated that it is only through the analytic process that the real reasons that led patients into treatment will emerge. This question was explored by Hinshelwood (1997) who stated,

> If the psychoanalyst's aim is that the patient should know his/her own mind better than before the analysis, can that be achieved by the analyst knowing better what the patient should think and decide? If the psychoanalyst knows for the patient, does this in the long run contribute to the patient knowing better for him/herself? It becomes a paradox. [Hinshelwood, 1997, p. 105]

To consider the above argument in the context of the question "What do patients want?" challenged me to understand the patients' stories almost outside the psychoanalytic relationship, or outside the confines of psychoanalytic concepts that negate the patient's authority to know.

Keeping these challenges in mind, I set out to explore psychoanalysis from the patient's perspective, at the same time "holding" the paradox.

CHAPTER TWO

Beginning the analytic journey*

"I wanted to be a patient partner; I didn't want to be a patient victim"

(Min)

"The person is kept as blank as possible . . . I came to understand the way the treatment went when I read a book by John Cleese and Robin Skynner . . .

(Simon)

Patient selection for interview

T he participants I interviewed were men and women who had completed, or ended, a psychoanalytic treatment with a professionally recognized analyst. It was important to ensure that the analysis was not current, since I believed that influences

---

*Paper presented to the Victorian Association of Psychoanalytic Psychotherapists, Melbourne, April, 2010.

from the powerful transference relationship could influence the participants' responses. I also wanted the participants to talk about their whole experience, not just part of it. The length of time since ending the analysis was considered as an important factor; however, I decided it would be too difficult to define a particular period consistent with everyone. Given the uniqueness of individual responses, it was not possible for me to estimate the most appropriate time for the patients to feel free enough to discuss such a significant and intimate experience. As it happened, the time since ending their analyses comprised a range of fifteen years.

I sought confirmation from each respondent that the analyst was professionally recognized as a member of any of the three psychoanalytic theoretical schools practising in Australia, which include the International Psychoanalytical Association (IPA) with membership in three state-based Institutes, the Australian and New Zealand Society of Jungian Analysts and the Australian Centre for Psychoanalysis. This criterion was important, because there is often confusion among patients as to who is officially analytically trained. As it happened, there were no volunteer participants who had completed an analysis through the Lacanian School, although one patient had commenced further treatment with a Lacanian analyst following the experience she reported here. This being ongoing, it was not considered appropriate to include. One patient had experiences with two separate Jungian analysts, and the others had all been in analysis with members from the state-based IPA Institutes.

The response to my open invitation was good, indicating an eagerness for people to talk about their analytic experiences. Among those who replied were several who believed that they had been in analysis, but on further questioning and to their disappointment, they did not meet the criteria. I found that this "ignorance" or confusion around what analytic treatment really consists of was quite pervasive, and describe it in more detail in a later chapter, highlighting its problems for psychoanalysis.

Eighteen participants were finally chosen: eleven women and seven men, with ages ranging from thirty-one to sixty, and living in four Australian states. Thirteen participants were working as psychotherapists, three were in allied health, and the other two were professional public servants. Six patients had had two experiences of analysis at the time of the interviews; three had experienced

other forms of therapy following their analyses; one had commenced another analysis that was still current. For some patients,
other forms of psychotherapy treatment had preceded the psychoanalysis. Most of the patients interviewed showed considerable
sophistication in their thinking about their analysis and, thus, their
stories cannot be lightly dismissed.

The time interval between finishing the analysis and responding
to my invitation varied from one patient having just completed her
analysis to two patients who had ended fifteen years previously.
The average ranged from three to five years. As mentioned above,
one patient was in a current second analysis and was excluded from
the stories told here.

Pseudonyms are used for confidentiality. Some names are of the
patients' own choosing while the others were assigned by me with
their agreement. Those who did choose themselves informed me
that the names had a special significance for them. One patient
wished to be called Freud, but as I thought this would cause considerable confusion, we compromised and he is identified as Sig.

Choosing an analyst

This chapter now explores the beginnings of analysis by these eighteen patients, focusing on their choice of analyst and preparation
for treatment. Many speak of the first encounter with the analyst as
one of their most powerful memories. Their stories identify several
important issues that are relevant to how the analytic relationship
is established and maintained throughout the whole analytic journey. A number of questions begin to emerge concerning the
analyst's responsibility when a person in a very vulnerable state
seeks analysis.

I noted that there were three main pathways to finding an
analyst. The first was through some familiarity with psychoanalysis; the second was by direct approaches to the local psychoanalytic
institutes for assessment and referral; and the third group, by far
the smallest, randomly selected from the phone book. The factors
that influenced their choice varied in the first two categories; these
related to the patients being personally assertive or primarily
accepting specialist guidance.

Familiarity with psychoanalysis

Five of the eighteen patients chose their analyst through prior personal experience. A major influence was some knowledge and understanding of the process or of familiarity with a particular analyst through work-related experiences as health professionals. They selected specific qualities they liked in an analyst already known to them, or particular characteristics observed during the initial interviews. These included the demonstration of certain skills. One patient described how she was discouraged from continuing with an analyst after noting his technique of "interpreting too quickly" during the assessment. Another said that physical characteristics such as "a dark-haired man" attracted her, while ethnicity and the analyst's gender were also described as important. The patients' informed choices were, thus, based on characteristics of the analyst, both as a person and in his/her demonstrated analytic style.

Four patients showed some initiative from the beginning. Min said that she scrutinized all analysts in her city and eventually decided on someone who had previously been a case supervisor. She stated that her reasons were based primarily on the personality of the analyst. "I decided which one I could bear; I should say sit with, as I wasn't going to go on the couch. I chose Dr A as someone I could really open up to."

Min was intent on gaining the best possible experience by choosing an analytic style that suited her. She wanted someone who did not use "the rigidity of classical psychoanalysis", but, rather, a very flexible approach.

> "I had made decisions about how it was going to be for me and was clear that was what I was going to negotiate with the analyst . . . Right from the word go I wanted it to be as much in my territory as it was in the analyst's. And I wanted to be a patient partner; I didn't want to be a patient victim."

In a similar manner, Paul, who had been in a previous therapeutic relationship, selected an analyst on the basis of knowing something about his style.

> "I had read quite a bit about it [analysis] and consciously chose the kind of analyst that I wanted to see, someone I knew of and knew

roughly of their approach. There was a sort of benign-ness in his approach that I consciously chose."

Carmel also drew upon her clinical knowledge, and, after several abortive attempts to find an analyst, was finally happy to proceed. She explained this extensive search by saying, "I couldn't work with them. One of them was sitting miles away, a blank screen, and quite old fashioned. I didn't feel safe with him." She was not prepared to engage with someone at merely the intellectual level but desired an analyst who could understand her emotional needs: "I did see a psychiatrist who was a Freudian and my experience was that they work with the head. They don't actually allow themselves to experience me and know me fully. It's about their theory."

She was also determined not to accept someone she perceived in the initial sessions as "sexist".

> "The psychiatrist I went to for about six sessions told me he wanted me to join one of his groups to stimulate my interest in men. I thought about that comment—I couldn't believe it. He was seeing me as a female and not married, and therefore needed to get to like men."

Lucy chose a "dark-haired" analyst with whom she had had some previous experience, though not directly. She had seen this particular analyst give a university lecture some fifteen years previously and, at the time, identified his physical features with those characteristics she remembered about her father. Lucy described how she thought that he would fulfil her desire to have a good relationship with a father figure, replacing her earlier experience of a father who abandoned her when she was very young.

> "I wanted a man, and I chose a dark-haired man. This is entirely significant because I had a very dark father and he left, adored me apparently, and then left when I was three years old . . . And so something drew me to this man."

Lucy's choice of analyst appeared to be a conscious one but, as was later revealed, led to an unconscious repetition of the relationship with her father. She did say, however, that she remembered when she first saw him that she had thoughts of being very afraid of men with dark hair. At that time she had told herself that she would never go to such an analyst.

> "But when it came to choosing someone fifteen years later I remembered him and remembered he had dark hair. And somehow I knew that I was going into the lion's den, but I wanted to. So I went to him, and it was kind of love at first sight. I knew I was gone immediately I was inside the door. And I had a dreadful time."

It appears that being assertive enabled these patients to make considered choices for themselves but, in the situation with Lucy, led to the risk of replaying past negative relationships. I will return later to this important issue.

Marg accepted her analyst through a series of referrals from people she believed were qualified to direct her. "I was referred by a psychiatric colleague to another psychiatrist, who then referred me to an analyst." Although she had a little knowledge of psychoanalysis, she entered without further exploration of the personality or working style of the particular analyst suggested. Marg later regretted accepting this referral without questioning.

Direct approaches to psychoanalytic institutes

Ten patients said that they had no idea of how to choose an analyst and, thus, contacted their local psychoanalytic institute. Four patients from this group suggested preferences for the type of analyst they wanted to see. Kerry explained how she "arrived in analysis in a crisis" after seeing two previous therapists whom she described as "incompetent, inexperienced and a nightmare." Determined that she did not want "to muck around any more", she contacted the local psychoanalytic branch.

> "I was on the list, I didn't want to get another dodgy therapist, I wanted to go to somebody really good. . . . I went to see Dr Z, who became my analyst. I went to see him because he was the person doing the allocations basically, but I really liked him. And I think I got there by default because I asked if I could see him again and in the end he made a space for me . . . I had a funny kind of start because it started with me feeling a bit guilty that I had somehow barged my way in there."

In a similar manner to Kerry, Kate had also experienced other forms of "questionable" therapy. She said that she sought someone with very firm boundaries and who would not disclose personal information in "quite the way the average therapist does". Thus, Kate approached her local institute and, although a couple of the analysts she met in interviews had vacancies, she decided that she was not interested. Something about them did not feel right. "It is funny how you go on different feelings." She described how she dismissed one analyst immediately on two grounds, his physical setting and boundary issues. "He had a really dirty waiting room and I saw him talk to his wife at that first meeting. Because of my boundary issues at that point, I thought 'right, he's off the list'."

Kate also expressed some concerns related to what she called "analytic technique". Demonstrating some sophistication in her thinking, she said, "I didn't like him [analyst], the way he interpreted. I was watching for people who interpreted too quickly, as that kind of thing I was very sensitive to." After interviewing four analysts, she finally decided on Dr S, even though she did not know much about him.

"In fact, it was very hard to get information about anyone. I was trying to because I had had such a bad experience. I wanted someone to tell me who was good and who wasn't good, rather than pathologize me for wanting to shop around, which is what happened with some of them."

She made the comment that, from her experience, she did not believe that the analytic organization that provided assessments and referrals was really interested in looking at the "right fit" between patient and analyst.

Kate raised another important issue that complicated her search and was related to her insistence on clear boundaries. A close friend was also seeking an analyst at the same time as she was, and this ended in a competition between them, particularly as both "needed medical people so we wouldn't have to pay so much". Kate discovered that the analyst she finally chose was also interviewing her close friend, and this led to "such a falling-out" with her friend because both saw this as a boundary violation.

Another patient, Rosa, said that financial affordability for the analysis was also a problem for her, and, thus, she insisted on the analyst being a psychiatrist in order to receive the government Medicare rebate. This had important consequences for patients, as is discussed later. Medicare is the national medical insurance system in Australia, similar to one operating in Canada. All citizens are covered for the common fee set by the government for a particular medical service. Up to the time I was interviewing these patients, this fee was applicable only to those practitioners with a medical background. Non-medically trained analysts, who undertake the same rigorous training and supervised clinical work, are not entitled to claim their fees from the government. Although there have now been some very minor changes to this policy, they are still not enough to enable patients of non-medical analysts to access the government rebate for analysis.

Rosa also stated that she asked for a female analyst. In making demands for these specific criteria she admitted with a laugh,

"I think it was arrogant. I usually believe I should take what is offered. So when I received a call from a male psychiatrist/analyst, saying that he had a vacancy, I said, 'Well, I'll come along and see'."

One patient explained how he requested someone from his own ethnic background. Greg had had a very positive analytic treatment overseas, so when he experienced further difficulties in his life he decided to go back into analysis. As he had problems "shopping around this sort of domain", Greg decided to seek direction from the local institute, but admitted how much he later regretted this.

"I went to [analyst] who gave me a few names. Dr Y was one of them, I think maybe because I wanted someone from my [religious] background, which was a big bloody mistake. The referring analyst subsequently was surprised I went to him. I was enraged. I didn't say anything but I thought 'F. . . stupid', because she obviously didn't think he was any good so why the hell did she recommend him? I was ropable about that."

This particular referral highlights the importance of a good fit between the patient and analyst, an issue that I raise here to be discussed later. According to the patients interviewed, this did not seem to be the common practice during their assessment and referral procedures.

Jenny described how her entry into analysis initially had minimal impact, but she was encouraged by the analyst's interest in her. She explained that her current therapist then, whom she liked, was moving to another position, so recommended someone at the local psychoanalytic institute.

> "It was a woman psychiatrist and she was extremely busy. She said she would see me for a session to talk about it; she could only give me a waiting time but couldn't say for how long. She thought maybe it would be better if I saw someone else. Would I want her to find someone? I said yes, because I had no idea how to approach the whole thing. She rang someone who I then ended up with. She spoke to him and asked if I was happy with a man, and I said yes."

Jenny then explained how she met with the analyst for one assessment and was not quite sure whether she wanted to work with him.

> "He seemed rather quaint, like really old-fashioned on first impression. And, even though I got an impression of an honest sincerity, integrity, I wasn't sure whether I could relate to him because he seemed so different from anybody else I had ever known or been able to talk to."

Deciding to "let him go", she did not follow up the session. Then, with a laugh, she added,

> "And he rang me and I was so impressed by that. He rang me and said 'I thought I would have heard from you by now.' I thought 'gosh, shock, horror!' He was taking the initiative! I'm not used to that. I was so impressed. I felt very safe that there was obviously someone who took my concerns to go into analysis very seriously, and wasn't dealing with that in a light-hearted way. I was really impressed by that and I decided to stay with him."

Ruth initially spent two years in once a week therapy with an analyst recommended by her local institute. She was subsequently advised by her analyst to enter a full analysis but was informed that she needed to move to another clinician in order for this to occur. He told her this was the usual practice.

> "So I went back to Dr M and she gave me some names. That was when I contacted Dr B. Dr M had said maybe two or three times a

week, but when I saw Dr B he said it was four or five times a week or nothing—this was what he was offering. It was a big step. So I thought about it a bit and talked to some people, and there was the anxiety about how to balance it. It was quite a big commitment of time but I thought no, I will take this up and I did."

Audrey recounted how she was happy to accept a recommendation from the analyst of one of her friends. "I didn't really question how he was or anything about him. I guess all I was going to go on was how I was treated."

Another patient, Tony, chose the locality of the analyst as an important criterion because of work commitments. He said that he did not know anyone who had ever done analysis and wanted someone within his vicinity; he was happy to go to someone who was not necessarily known or recommended.

"I knew I would probably have to come after work or in my lunch hour. The way I approached it was that I would go and see the person and check them out and see how it goes. He wasn't recommended. The Institute just said there's someone in . . . so I said that was OK, I would go and check the person out."

Sig discussed two different experiences of analysis, each of which will be discussed separately where relevant. He did, at times, combine the two experiences when he felt that the description applied to both, and when this occurs it will be noted. In relation to choosing an analyst, Sig spoke only about the second experience. He terminated the first after two years because of not getting the help he wanted, and then said he contacted the local branch of the International Psychoanalytical Association for another referral.

"I had a couple of sessions with an analyst with the view to him referring me on to someone he felt was going to be more compatible to me. So I went through that and got referred to this other analyst."

Simon attempted a few different therapies with a variety of practitioners, then finally he was told that perhaps he should try "a sort of psychoanalysis guy", described as a classical analyst.

"So I went . . . At the time I thought my life wasn't in too bad a shape, I just needed a few edges to be knocked off it. I was quite wrong in that regard, but that's what I thought. When those edges weren't smoothed off after two to three months, once a week, I started saying that I was concerned where it was heading and he said, 'I think better results can be obtained by coming more often,' So I said, 'OK let's try it, let's go for the four times a week'."

From this journey into analysis, it seemed that Simon was really unsure at the time what kind of treatment he was actually seeking and had not really considered analysis as a choice.

Selection from phone books

Three patients chose analysts from the phone book; with two patients it was, apparently, a random choice; the third was more selective. Of the two "random" selections, one requested specific criteria when meeting the analyst doing the assessments; the other patient accepted the first person offered to him.

Jean described how she searched in the *Yellow Pages Directory* for the local psychoanalytic association and stated, "I went along and met this fellow and then he referred me to Dr W who was my analyst." She did, however, specify that she wanted a male analyst because of long-standing gender conflicts. "I said I wanted a man, because I had had problems with men. I thought you should face it." In spite of accepting the referral, Jean explained that in the first session she did attempt to maintain some form of control by saying to her analyst, "You're on a three month's trial period. If I don't think it's any good after three months I'm out of here."

Rick admitted to not knowing anything about psychoanalysis or how it differed from cognitive behavioural therapy and other forms of psychology. He knew he needed therapy, but not how to choose someone.

"Basically what I did, I just opened the phone book and picked someone who was registered as a psychologist close to where I was living at the time. And I happened to choose a person who was, I guess, a traditional analyst."

The third patient in this group, Steve, was more selective, and sought analysis following several forms of counselling that he said had not helped him. In talking about his efforts to find an appropriate person, he described one counsellor as "not tremendously effective", then another as a "tremendously nice man", but who provided what he termed afterwards as "fireside chats". At one stage, he went to a psychiatrist so that he could afford it through Medicare, saying, however, "I was betraying my own profession but economics won out." The psychiatrist turned out to be what Steve termed "a shocker", and with whom he experienced "enormous disempowerment". After a few sessions, he left the therapy, stating that he did not know what they were doing in the sessions "apart from me paying money to get advice I found to be very damaging."

Steve spent the next few months phoning around until he finally decided on a psychologist. He said that his experience led him to believe that they were more qualified and skilled. "I finally contacted this psychologist/psychoanalyst, was impressed by him, and started seeing him on a regular basis."

Prior knowledge, assessment, and preparation

Psychoanalytic treatment is not often represented in the Australian popularist culture, so many people would have little idea of what psychoanalysis really involves, not only in terms of time and monetary commitment, but also in emotional investment. This is also not surprising when there are so many diverse understandings of psychoanalysis among its own practitioners. The analytic technique would seem to vary considerably from analyst to analyst, in spite of the analyst's professed allegiance to a particular theoretical background and training. With the current confusion around how analysis is conceptualized, "false" notions very easily arise, and some patients believe that any form of therapy is actually psychoanalysis. Expectations of how the particular roles within the relationship will work also vary considerably.

First impressions of the analyst and his/her relating style are of prime importance, as this initial engagement sets the framework within which the patient is encouraged to speak as freely as possible, trying not to censure anything. This free-floating expression of what comes to mind, generally known as free association, enables the analyst to pick up links between the various spoken, but seemingly unrelated, thoughts. According to Freud, these can lead to the unconscious, repressed memories. This way of working, encouraged in the patient, requires implicit trust in both the analyst and analytic process. A few of these patients had a basic knowledge of psychoanalysis from an early interest in this field and were informed by relevant reading; others had knowledge through being supervised in their clinical work by analysts, or through attending lectures and clinical meetings. Some patients, however, entered analysis without any prior knowledge of this form of treatment, and after an experience of another, quite different therapeutic modality. This was often through the recommendation of a professional suggesting that they needed to work at what was termed "a deeper level".

In general, the patients with some theoretical knowledge reported that they did not consider asking direct questions in the initial assessment period and were happy with this aspect of their early encounters with their analyst. Rosa, however, stated that she was surprised how collapsed she was and acknowledged that she actually felt "totally naïve". She also thought that, having gained some elementary understanding of psychoanalysis through her weekly analytic supervision, to appear ignorant and ask questions would seem very strange.

> "I think partly I assumed that I was supposed to know because I'd been given that kind of supervision. So I didn't ask about how long, or what track, or his particular sort of analytical proclivities. I didn't ask any of those things . . . I don't know whether it's trusting, or naïve, or my eyes tightly shut and saying 'Well here I am, just leaping in' . . . I'm struck by how passive I was . . . I have a friend who knew nothing about analysis. She was only told that when missing a session she would have to pay."

Patients without any prior understanding or knowledge of psychoanalysis described a variety of different experiences when seeking information about the process. Two were provided with elementary explanations about the structure, holidays, and fee paying, while the majority stated that any questions they raised about analysis were left unanswered by their analyst.

Some patients described finding this initial period of analysis enormously uncomfortable and quite bizarre when their questions about the process were met with a blank silence. Others reported on the lack of information and their inability to ask many questions because of not knowing enough about analysis. The effect this had on patients was to render them powerless and with "no way of making sense of the experience".

Among those knowing very little about analysis were Jenny and Rick, who described how different it was from "cognitive–behavioural therapy or family therapy". Thus, they found it difficult to ask relevant questions, but said that they had expected some explanation would be routinely offered to them during the initial session. Jenny emphasized her ignorance and the subsequent lack of information that was provided to her.

> "I had no idea how it worked. What he did do was go over at great lengths about what was the frame, and the issue of holidays. There were other issues, but in terms of what analysis is about, I didn't know much. You need to be able to put the experience down to something, to make sense of the experience. It is such an open process. It would help to say a little about the basics, like 'say whatever comes to mind'."

Rick described his initial discomfort and bewilderment.

> "I didn't have a clue . . . I began to explain why I was there, expecting him to ask me some questions, talk to me or do something . . . What would have helped was some dialogue, like 'Look, this is the way I work' . . . If there had been some conversation about that it might have helped; instead he told me very little about what was going on."

Simon said he was hoping for some overview of how the analyst actually worked and what would be expected of him as the patient. He stated that all the information he ever learnt about the analytic process was from reading a book by John Cleese and Robyn Skinner. In relation to the beginning of his experience in psychoanalysis, Simon said of the analyst's position,

> "The person is kept as blank as possible. They give no oversight, summary, statement, or plan of what they are doing, and why they are doing it and what the basis is for why they are doing what they are doing. If you ask them questions about procedure or

anything like that, you just get a blank silence. I picked it up as I went along . . ."

Another patient, Kate, remarked on how she wanted to learn more about the analytic process than the theoretical knowledge she had gained through a course she had attended. She thought that one was never prepared for the actual experience and described analysis as "like attending a church service".

> "You want an understanding of what the hell this is all about, like 'what are we doing?' I used to complain that there is this incredible faith required and you're not allowed to ask any more questions . . . Going into analysis is like having a faith in something that you don't really have any great evidence for."

Steve and Greg also believed that the process and analyst's orientation needed some clarification.

> "If I was to level criticism at the process I went through, it's the lack of information that the client gets, the lack of the client's right to the bigger picture, about where it's going, what you may experience during this process, what you can look forward to, the pros, the cons, the negatives—all that sort of stuff." [Steve]

> "I said, 'What is your orientation?' and it was not answered. But at the time I didn't follow that through. Retrospectively, I shouldn't have gone back, because it said a lot about him. He did not answer, or would not answer that. I can't understand what lies behind that, where he was coming from." [Greg]

Sig expressed dissatisfaction with his first analyst, who did not prepare him for the analytic journey. He drew attention to a fundamental problem, which emerged several times during the interviews, about the layperson's general lack of understanding of psychoanalysis.

> "Not many people really know the differences between psychoanalysis, psychotherapy, counselling . . . It's not till you have gone through an analysis that you have full appreciation of the differences. And that's a shame, because I think there would be quite a

few people, like my friends, who go into it expecting to get one thing and come out of it having received something completely different."

The above experiences of patients demonstrate their considerable frustration at the lack of preparation for the particular process and structures required when commencing an analysis. Greg said that he regretted returning for what he later described as more of the same "silent" treatment, while others conveyed the impression of being caught in something quite strange to them, uncomfortable, misleading, and perhaps even threatening. Their descriptions of this important phase of analysis did seem to indicate, in a number of cases, a lack of preparation in understanding what the process was about and what was required of both partners.

Expectations of the analysis

During the interviews, patients offered little spontaneous information about any expectations they had when commencing the analysis. Jean was the only one who expressed clarity about what she wanted, saying that her hopes were related to her earlier relationship with an "emotionally crushing" father.

"I wanted to turn my life around—to stop being crushed, emotionally crushed. I wanted to move on. Because I would be all right, then my father would say something to me, or treat me badly, and my whole world would just disintegrate. It was so easy to be crushed and I wanted to be more resilient than that."

Kate and Kerry volunteered more nebulous ideas of wanting a "dramatic" personal change, or learning to deal well with a life that seemed a "mess". When I asked one of my few direct questions towards the end of the interview, Kate responded with, "I guess I had expectations that I would change dramatically and not be who I was. So I think expectations were definitely there. Part of it, I think, was clarifying my expectations, making them realistic."

Kerry said that she did not think she actually had any expectations at the beginning, but "got what I wanted. I knew I was a mess; there was stuff that needed to be dealt with and it got dealt with." She then added, "I think I had this archetypal view of the person sitting behind me and making these very stern interpretations and imposing things on me, and I was constantly surprised by the level of kindness."

Although the central question I held in mind during this work was "What do patients want?", their understanding of expectations generally emerged only after the analytic experience had ended. These expectations also became clearer to me when I reflected on the meanings they attributed to changes that had actually occurred.

This links with the general notion put forward by analysts, that patients' desires are initially unconscious and can only become known through the treatment process. It could also be that the patients needed to go through their story, freely associating to my open question, before being able to express what their expectations had been. Marg, for example, stated with emphasis, "I found it a really important foundation for understanding what I didn't want in an analysis."

When thinking about their experiences after finishing analysis, two patients talked about their unrealized expectations. Steve stated,

> "I'm not sure if I gained anything personally. I didn't come away with any astonishing insights. Maybe that's an unfair thing to expect. I guess I wanted to come away with greater insight into myself, a greater sense of control over myself and my behaviours in my life. Did I achieve that? I don't think I did."

Rick appeared more certain when he said,

> "The reason that I attended there was not really discussed at all—what drove me there in the first place wasn't dealt with much at all. There tended to be a lot of other things and I just felt I was being swamped by it. It felt like I was drowning."

Chapter Eight addresses further thoughts from the patients when I asked them directly about what they believed would constitute a "good" analysis. These thoughts are additional to what came up spontaneously through their free associations.

Discussing the complex issues in beginning an analysis

The beginning of analysis, as reported by these eighteen patients, highlights the complex factors involved in the choice of an analyst and the powerful effect first impressions have on the patient for their future relationship. Maintaining some agency over choice of an analyst appeared to have a considerable influence on how patients experienced the ongoing treatment. Several important findings emerged, which also relate to further themes in following chapters.

Positive encounters

Six of the patients chose their analyst either from previous good encounters with the person prior to entering analysis, or having an experience of the beginnings of a good relationship during the initial assessment. They were attracted by personal characteristics and the demonstration of an analytic style with which they believed they could productively work.

Min was very specific in what she expected from her analyst and said it was going to be for her a "partner" relationship, which implied a degree of equality in the process but, at the same time, acknowledging different roles. She chose an analyst known for her flexibility of approach. This was further demonstrated when Min's request to sit rather than use the couch was accepted by her analyst. The couch is a practical procedure usually employed by analysts; it is based on the belief that with the patient out of sight of the direct gaze of the analyst, this facilitates a better condition for the patient's regression and the work of analysis.

What may have influenced Min's capacity to be so assertive as a patient was her status as a senior medical practitioner, the only one from this professional group who volunteered to be interviewed. This raises the question about whether one's professional identity might enhance or strengthen one's personal authority in life, and, therefore, in this situation, the ability to more readily negotiate a therapeutic relationship. Min was in a position of authority in her own work and, therefore, may have been able to use the system to her own advantage in a way that other patients were incapable of, or reluctant to do. Another factor may have been Min's earlier good supervisory relationship with her analyst that then gave her the confidence she needed to ask for what she wanted.

Kerry's admission of feeling that she had "barged her way in" demonstrated her anxiety and a belief that she did not have the right to choose something good for herself. As she stated, her assertiveness later aroused feelings of guilt. However, Kerry's immediate positive attachment to the assessing analyst provided the stimulus for persisting with seeking the one she wanted. She described how impressed she was by the capacity of this analyst to engage with her in the initial session. He demonstrated personal qualities which Kerry felt comfortable with and led to her saying that she "really liked" him. This indicated the prospect of a good therapeutic relationship. The analyst responded to her wishes and offered to work with her in the ongoing analysis. Her initial feelings of a positive engagement were later borne out by comments that her analyst had qualities of playfulness, integrity, and kindness, all of which helped her eventually to feel freed from the oppressive issues that took her into analysis.

Jenny, unsure about her first encounter in the assessment with her analyst because of his "quaintness", described how her initial impression of "honest sincerity and integrity" later paid off. The analyst, by taking the initiative in following up his offer when she did not respond, demonstrated a real interest in her and that he was taking her concerns for analysis seriously. Her decision to immediately accept the analyst's offer illustrated that her response was intuitively accurate and led to a very positive analytic experience.

Alienating techniques

Kate showed considerable resilience in searching for an analyst with specific qualities to facilitate her personal growth. The setting was also very important, as stated in her comment about the "dirty waiting room". As a consequence of previous unsatisfactory experiences and, thus, her determination to get someone good, she was relying on a referral from the local psychoanalytic institute to provide "the right fit". However, to her amazement, she said that through her discussion with the institute she felt pathologized for wanting to shop around "as if [she was] procrastinating" and would not know what was good for her.

The concerns that Kate identified as significant to her choice demonstrate a capacity on her part to think about how the analytic experience could fruitfully address her issues. Her determination not to accept just any referral, but to assess the prospective treating analyst, shows a certain degree of sophistication and knowledge about the intense nature of the analytic process and, thus, the importance of a "good fit". The needs and uncertainties as expressed by the patients in choosing an analyst highlight the importance of being taken seriously by the referring analyst. Patients wished to be respected in their right to choose which analyst they considered would be the most appropriate for their individual needs. Akhtar (2009) has also drawn attention to this important aspect at the beginning of analysis. He says, "Such assessment, I believe, consists of the patient's looking for the qualities of affinity, empathy, kindness, patience, knowledge and competence. The patient wishes to be understood and feel that the therapist can help him" (Akhtar, 2009a, p. 44).

In Carmel's initial interview with a prospective analyst, she described how indignant she felt at the "gender-laden" suggestion of being placed in a group to "stimulate an interest in men". This comment astounded her, and led her to believe that the analyst did not really wish to understand her as a person, but was focusing on her particular status of being "unmarried", thus making assumptions about the role of women. "I experience them as working through a theory, not working through experience and not working in the unconscious in a way that I anticipated."

Patients who specifically requested information about the process or the theoretical orientation of their analyst described how they received minimal useful information. Ten said they had little or no knowledge specifically about psychoanalysis. Seven acknowledged that they had some basic understanding: for example, one patient said he had had communication with a friend in treatment, but this was primarily theoretical. One patient stated that he thought he knew what psychoanalysis was, but realized later that the actual practical experience was very different from what he had imagined.

These patients gave voice to varying states of anxiety when entering the analytic treatment. For the majority, this was a journey into the unknown, and even those who had some basic knowledge of analysis through their own reading or exposure to professional supervision were critical of the lack of preparation provided by their analysts in this initial stage. All expected to be given some basic information, such as an indication of the analyst's theoretical background and practical procedures. I would think it a reasonable expectation for this information to be given when patients embark on such an unfamiliar experience. Jenny summed it up concisely with her statement that "It would help to say a little about the basics, like 'say whatever comes to mind'", and also Rick's declaration, "What would have helped was some dialogue like 'This is the way I work'."

Rosa made the following suggestion for a more informed beginning to psychoanalysis.

> "Why isn't it in the analytic training that patients are prepared to know what to expect? Why say the minimal? What does this mean? The analytic work depends on the frame, but if you haven't set the frame properly, how do you work in it? It helps you understand from the beginning."

The above statements, which give expression to frustration by some of the patients in this study, are supported by research findings on the same issue some sixty years ago (Balint, 1942; Ferenczi, 1949), which spoke of a resistance in analysts to educating patients in the analytic process. Balint (1942) emphasized the importance of preparation for analysis in both children and adults, arguing that egos of patients were not usually strong enough initially to withstand the demands imposed by analytic treatment. Thus, he suggested, "The first task of analysis is to educate and strengthen the ego" (p. 90). It is of some concern to discover that patients today still continue to report difficulties in being orientated into the analytic process so they can make the best use of it. The preparation of patients for this crucial stage of psychoanalytic treatment would seem paramount to a useful therapeutic experience.

Unhelpful institute practices

Greg's referral raises questions about what could be considered collegial loyalty. It is difficult to understand how a patient can report that the person doing assessments recommended him to an analyst, and then later the referring analyst registers surprise that he has accepted the recommendation. Was this an admission from the analyst that the referral was not suitable from the beginning? If the patient's report was, indeed, accurate, this would appear to set up an unhelpful enactment within the assessment phase, where the patient's needs are not being taken seriously as part of the psychoanalytic process. It would also seem to imply that psychoanalytic institutes maintain a system where referrals are made on the basis of expediency or current vacancies within a practice, rather than the referring analyst being able to think about a "good fit" between patient and treating analyst. In Greg's case, it might have been more helpful for the referring analyst to be more tentative in offering a suggestion or judgement as to who might be the more appropriate. When the match between analyst and patient is not suitable, something can then get repeated in an unhelpful, if not destructive, way in the analytic process.

As in other professional bodies, analysts perhaps are bound by a sense of loyalty to their colleagues, and this possibly restricts them from saying anything that might be perceived as criticism. Such professional loyalty makes it difficult then for the patient or referring analyst to differentiate between who is the most appropriate for a particular person. There is also the assumption that once one has trained and is qualified as an analyst, everyone is the same, not taking into account that each practitioner in the field is an individual with both a unique personality and analytic style of working.

Another question, related to this issue, concerns the authority responsible for referrals being placed in the hands of psychoanalytic institutes as though they would always know better than the patient. One could argue that a professional group would be more informed than members of the public; however, if one considers collegial loyalty as a possibility, this might place considerable pressure on referring analysts when striving to accurately represent their institutes while at the same time attempting to find the best match between patient and analyst. It would seem good policy for institutes to be more open in acknowledging patients' needs, and informing them when their referral is based more on the availability of particular analysts and not necessarily the best fit, as expected by the patients seeking this.

Kate identified what she called a boundary issue, which led to her "falling-out" with a friend. Both were assessed in the same time period for analysis with the same analyst, who was aware of their close bond. This situation could be considered similar to that of an analyst not taking into treatment members of the same family, in order to provide for maximum openness and confidentiality within the analytic process. When representatives of institutes assume the assessment and referral role, I think it imperative to be hyper-vigilant to the crucial importance of boundary procedures which are significant to patients and, therefore, conducive of best analytic practice.

Ruth was referred to another analyst when her treatment changed from analytic psychotherapy to the more formal analysis. This arrangement was decided unilaterally, and it is unclear where this decision originated from and its professional or theoretical basis. This patient, who had already developed a relationship with her current analyst over two years, said she was given no choice in either being able to remain with this person or in negotiating the times with her new analyst. It is difficult to know whether these procedures belong to a personal belief system, or are more perva-sive as part of a perceived "correct" analytic policy to which some analysts rigidly adhere.

Simon's story addresses another question to do with why analy-sis is chosen as the treatment of choice. It was unclear as to why he was actually referred for analysis when he himself claimed that he did not think his life was "in too bad a shape". After months of concern at not getting anywhere, Simon's therapy was converted to analysis of four times per week. Unlike Ruth's experience, however, he was able to remain with the same analyst. But one could ques-tion whose needs were being met. Was it a theoretical belief that Simon would make more progress, or were there other reasons? Again, this seemed a unilateral decision. These are all important issues to consider around the criteria for recommending analysis and referring to the most appropriate analyst.

The power of phantasy

Because Lucy desired to work with issues relating to her father, she was receptive to finding an analyst who had similar physical features. Therefore, she readily projected on to the analyst she chose an idealized, infantile image of a father she had been told had adored her. A very emotionally-charged relationship developed from the initial meeting, and Lucy stated, "It was kind of love at first sight. I knew I was gone immediately I was inside the door." This powerful transference on to the person of the analyst as a visual representation of an early relationship is discussed by Appelbaum and Diamond (1993).

> The transference template ... is shaped not only by the patient's early objects of hatred and desire, not only by images of healers and confessors and teachers of the past, but also by those sexual stereotypes ingrained in all of us from our earliest years and activated by the visible reality of the therapist. [p. 147]

By consciously targeting someone physically resembling her father, Lucy was transferring her intrapsychic conflicts, in all their complexities, to the new father object, and, in phantasy, was requiring the analyst to play out a particular role. The ongoing analytic experience between Lucy and her analyst will be discussed in following chapters. However, it is important to note here that as the treatment progressed, Lucy reported that her analyst did not seem able to use this powerful transference–countertransference relationship and usefully work with her phantasy of him as the accepting "good" father. From Lucy's perspective, the analyst seemed unable to think about her choice of him with all its unconscious determinants, a difficulty raised by Akhtar (1995) when he stated that "The analyst should be unobtrusively curious about the analysand's choice of analyst" (p. 1075).

The important interplay of the personality characteristics and conflicts of both analyst and patient has recently received much more significance as forming the central therapeutic factor in analysis (Anastasopoulos & Papanicolaou, 2004; Kantrowitz, 1986, 1995). Towards this end, the analytic literature advocates very strongly for the establishment of a good match between analyst and patient (Berman, 1949; Kantrowitz, 1986; Lichtenberg, 1985; Shapiro, 1976). Given the power of unconscious predictors, it is, of course, unrealistic to believe that during the initial assessment one can consider all aspects of the personality, of either patient or analyst, which may affect the relationship. As Wolstein (1997) stated, "Any choice of analyst is laden with unconscious patterning and process that may become clear only much later—perhaps, if then, near the end of the analytic experience" (p. 513). This highlights the great difficulties in choosing an analyst, but, nevertheless, this initial step still requires very careful consideration. If patients seeking analysis need an "incredible faith" to go on this journey, as earlier noted by Kate, it is all the more distressing when the basic relationship issues around transference–countertransference are not deemed possible to resolve and, in Lucy's words, lead to a "just horrible" experience.

Stereotyping

While some patients considered the gender of the analyst as crucial, the literature suggests that analysts generally believe transference bears little relationship to the reality of analyst attributes, including the gender (Person, 1985). There is also the general assumption among analysts that it does not matter whether the analyst is male or female. In this work, despite the various ways patients entered analytic treatment, all but two had male analysts. This included the two females who specifically had requested a same-sexed analyst.

A study relating to gender significance (Mayer & De Marneffe, 1992) was conducted in four main psychoanalytic institutes in America in order to address substantial differences in the referral system. One of the main outcomes was clear evidence for referrals being heavily influenced by gender match, particularly the much stronger preference for same-sex referral for male patients than female patients. This finding contradicted a review of the prevailing literature (Mayer & De Marneffe, 1992), which stated that analysts did not consider gender differences when referring. It demonstrated an unconscious bias or reluctance to refer male patients to female analysts (Mayer & De Marneffe, 1992), with referring analysts believing they "do what they think they do in relation to the issue of gender" (pp. 572–573).

The implications from this study of definite gender preferences in referrals raised questions about the findings in these interviews in relation to the enormous disparity between the number of male and female analysts involved. How we might understand this gender imbalance and what implications it holds for analysis is discussed in Chapter Five. There would also appear to be a link with the theme in the following section, which had a powerful influence on the choice of an analyst. This theme will also be raised in later chapters related to experiences in the ongoing relationship and process.

Inequity in funding between professional groups

Five patients stated how they specifically requested a psychiatrically qualified psychoanalyst because of their own financial constraints and the restricted government rebate system. Other patients indicated (Chapter Five) that financial restrictions also affected the ongoing analytic process in important ways. This brings into question the inequity in the funding process, through the Medicare system in Australia, already discussed, and through which only one particular health profession is subsidized for patients, although other professions have identical psychoanalytical training and clinical practices.

As this experience is brought up in quite a significant way in Chapter Five, further discussion will be left for that chapter. However, it seemed important to raise it here, as it did have an impact on the choice of analyst for some patients at the beginning of their analysis, restricting them to an analyst from a psychiatric background.

How the beginning shapes the journey

This chapter has described the reflections of eighteen patients on how they began their analytic journeys. Some talked about very positive encounters in the initial assessments, which generally led to enriching experiences. Other patients presented a number of problems they encountered, which had specific implications for their ongoing analyses. Their experiences demonstrate how little consideration was given by some of the analysts to the power of the patient–analyst beginnings, the patient's enormous struggles intrapsychically, and the intensity of feelings that impacted upon the initial engagement.

Some of these narratives have also demonstrated that if prospective patients have healthy enough perceptions at the beginning, and appear assertive or empowered, they choose wisely. However, if the analyst is chosen out of primitive and gross projections that are not worked through sufficiently, as was reported by many patients and discussed further throughout the book, this can result in less than ideal or negative analytic experiences. Aktar (2009) has drawn attention to failures in psychoanalytic treatment, which he says can begin with the initial assessment "because agreement upon goal and method of treatment was not arrived at between patient and therapist [analyst]" (p. ix). This statement has reinforced for me the crucial importance of the analyst having the capacity to facilitate a process by which the patient chooses well, and also to being hyper-vigilant as to how the patient's choice is made and might be symbolized in terms of unconscious motivation.

The beginning of analysis in terms of analytic technique and its subsequent impact on the patient and ongoing process has generally received very little attention in the literature, a shortfall that Aktar's (2009) recent book has skilfully set out to remedy. Chapters Three and Four will now explore aspects of the continuing analytic jour-ney, focusing in particular on the transference–countertransference relationship and the quality of engagement within this.

CHAPTER THREE

Working with the transference

"It was the most amazing process and so interesting; it just emerged ... and the intensity between the two of us was kind of horrendous, but so intimately tense and sort of wonderful at the same time"

(Kerry)

"I just got the feeling where we were locked into this unbelievable transference; and he took it so much personally. He came back at me at the logical, concrete level rather than the symbolic"

(Lucy)

I n this chapter and the one following, I bring together the patients' reflections on the relationship aspects of their ongoing analytic journey. As there are multiple ways of looking at this, I begin with discussing their understanding of the transference and its importance to successful analytic work. The patients articulate clearly what they found was significant to them in both the content and style of their analysts' interpretations, and the personal or human qualities of their analysts. These characteristics were perceived as what made the difference to their unique experiences.

Transference

Some patients talked about transference, a concept discussed fully in the Introduction, as though they were very familiar with this term. Others described processes that would seem to fit with the general psychoanalytic concept, but used their own words to explain their interaction with the analyst. Where this has occurred, I will cite what the patients have said when presenting the material and then discuss later how this fits with transference in the psychoanalytic sense.

Kerry, with a clear understanding of transference, remarked on the intensity of her relationship with her analyst with some surprise and pleasure.

> "It was the most amazing process and so interesting. It just emerged, and the way that it came out in the transference and the intensity between the two of us was kind of horrendous, but so intimately tense, and sort of wonderful at the same time."

To illustrate her experience, she provided two very vivid examples, one that will be detailed in Chapter Five under "The paternal transference"; the other example is presented here.

Kerry described some ill-defined sexual abuse with an uncle when she was very young. She had also experienced some really bad behaviour with men, and subsequently had bad dreams. While in a relationship during part of her analysis, she suffered from chronic cystitis and occasionally had to make toilet stops en route to see her analyst. She talked about how she would lie on the couch and writhe around in pain, experiencing a great deal of discomfort. Kerry explained how she was also completely paranoid about using the analyst's toilet and used to think "I hope he doesn't come in", even resorting to telling him not to do that. At the same time, she described many florid projections.

> "I was quite mad, like there would be a cardigan or something draped over the back of a chair and I'd think, 'Are they his trousers,

are his trousers off?' It was mad. I was quite fearful even of him sitting behind me and feeling like he was going to reach over and touch me, or something like that. That was a particularly difficult time just because of the intensity of the two of us being in the room. All this stuff was coming out that I couldn't control . . . I don't know how it got broken—maybe it just got worked through over and over again. I remember him baiting me, sort of fishing; and playing with him like he was perfectly trustworthy and friendly. And all the stuff had broken. It went from this incredible fear to playing with him; it was amazing."

When relating this experience, Kerry emphasized the sense of "madness" within her and her amazement at the analyst's capacity for holding this and "playing" with her.

Jean and Audrey talked about the ease with which their male analysts were able to provide them with special "mothering" experiences that had been lacking in their own childhoods. These two patients used words such as "magical" and "special" to describe how they learnt the capacity to mother their own children from this modelling by their respective analysts.

Jean referred to her experience as "repairing lots of damage".

"I would lie on the couch and I would stick my daughter on the breast and she would suck away and fall asleep. And I would talk to him [the analyst]. You couldn't separate me from my child. I thought it was an absolutely magical time. I had my baby on my nipple and I was dealing with things about my mother and my family and I felt I was repairing lots of damage by being mother to my kids. It was great."

Audrey also commented on that the fact of the analyst being male and how this did not preclude the experience from being a good one. She demonstrated how her analyst was able to provide a significant maternal function and emphasized the importance of the experience to her.

"And the mothering of me . . . T [her son] would have come along when I was in my second year of analysis, so I think about six months into it. I used to take him along every day, drag him out and take him along, but essentially that was the only thing that saved me. I wouldn't have been able to do it without that. I think it helped me because *he* [the analyst] *looked after me* and that *enabled me to look after my son.* And that's how I learnt. How he looked after me, I kind of learnt how to do that, which is strange considering he's a male. I have *very positive feelings* about the whole thing; yes, I feel like it was actually quite special."

Another patient, Steve, related how impressed he was with the way in which his analyst sensitively made a "transference" interpretation about a homosexual phantasy he had spoken about in his session.

"And what this analyst did, with great courage and sensitivity, he translated the phantasy into the immediacy of our therapeutic relationship. Something like 'So, I'm maybe the person behind you rubbing up against you or . . .' It was quite a shock to have what was presumably a straight man make a comment like that to me in that context. And I remember thinking this is a very courageous thing for him to have done. I think it was a sensitive thing for him to have done too."

In the four experiences described above, the analysts have shown a particular sensitivity to their patients' issues. There is also the sense of a parallel situation where what is brought to the sessions by the patients is modelled, or discussed in the sessions, in such a way that further exploration is facilitated and the issues satisfactorily worked through. The patients, therefore, were enabled to participate in the process as "patient partners", the term raised by Min in the previous chapter as so important to the ongoing relationship.

Marg introduced a different perspective in relation to her analyst's use of transference. At first describing the interaction as "everything leading back to him", she explained how over time his interpretations became boring and she developed a "perverse reaction".

"I started a game of imagining what he would say next. It wasn't actually part of my treatment; it was 'what does he want me to say, and what would he say in regard to what I was saying'. I found a lot of the time was taken up with that kind of behaviour. Everything was leading back to him, even anything behaviourally—everything."

She then identified the concept of transference. Discussing how her biggest problem was feeling "bludgeoned" by her analyst, she added some thoughts about the silence that she linked to the analyst's interpretive style.

> "There was also quite an element of being persecutory with the silence. I think the patient needs to learn how to speak, be encouraged to speak, the aim of the word is speech, and actually to be left in silence. And the kind of interpretations that are lacerations, interpretations that are lacerations! I don't think interpretations should be lacerations. So, bludgeoning of the transference and lacerations; interpretations that are lacerations."

Sig also reported an unhelpful use of the transference by his analysts. He said that what he brought into the relationship with his analyst from external unsatisfactory relationships never seemed to be interpreted at an analytical level.

> "There were never any connections made between my dissatisfaction with my analysis and the way that I was conducting my other relationships. I would have expected him to have said, 'I can identify that you feel slighted or injured or hurt in this situation with your girlfriend, or your mother, or your father. Perhaps that could be happening here'. It would have brought an understanding of what I was experiencing in my relationship with him. That was never done. I was just always left feeling that it was an issue that could not be explored."

He added that when his "negative transference" began to emerge, he felt it could not be worked with. He believed that what he was presenting was too difficult for the analysts in both his experiences to deal with.

> "I was very surprised they weren't able to work it through with me. I feel like they really let me down. I went wanting analysis and when it got a bit too hard for them, there comes the crunch—I felt they couldn't carry me through it, couldn't see me through it . . . With analysis, their main instrument is, I think, the fact that they are very withholding."

Lucy described something different, at the same time acknowledging her understanding of transference. She talked about a relationship in which both she and the analyst would get "locked in" at a personal level, and, thus, her communications were unable to be sufficiently explored symbolically.

"There were a few occasions where I just got the feeling we were locked into this unbelievable transference; and he took it so much personally. He came back at me at the logical, concrete level rather than the symbolic. He hardly dealt with anything. Most of the things I believe that happen in the transference, or in the frame, are symbolic. But he would never deal with it at the symbolic level."

She added, with great emphasis,

"One graphic example—I went to Italy in the middle of it [the analysis] and I sent him a postcard. It just took me *hours* to write it, and thinking about it. And he told me how wonderful it was and how thrilled he was to get it, instead of dealing with what that was like for me to send it. The focus was never *on me*, it was *on him*."

Rick presented another variation on the patient's perceptions of how the analyst worked within the transference. He reported puzzlement and frustration when he tried to engage with the analyst and was met with long periods of silence, and then a communication that did not seem relevant or helpful to him.

"I would go through weeks when he said virtually nothing. And then, every now and then, he would make a comment and I had no idea what he meant or where that comment came from or what I was supposed to do with it. Was I supposed to do anything at all? What relevance it had was all a bit obscure to me. So, yes, there were periods of weeks when he would say virtually nothing, apart from at the end of the session when he would say 'time'. There were weeks and weeks and weeks of silence."

Kate reported that she saw her analyst's interpretations as an "incredible gift", but also raised issues of her analyst's "imperfection".

"The mistakes that he made! Like sometimes he made mistakes consistently on my invoice with the dates. I imagine that most of his patients went five times per week, and I don't think he had many going four times a week. So often the mistakes on the invoice were him forgetting that I was going four times a week. And I would just get really irritated, because I felt he wasn't paying attention and making mistakes . . . I guess I might have felt like an aberration in his practice or something—that I was the odd one."

She said that what disturbed her was how it seemed pretty clear during those times that "he just didn't know what the hell was going on". I have included this example here as I think Kate's description about the analyst "forgetting" how often he saw her corresponds with one of the definitions of the psychoanalytic concept of working in the countertransference.

Interpretative style

The interpretative style of the analyst covers a very broad area, encompassing the many levels at which the patients perceived their analyst to deliver the interpretations. Examples are provided which illustrate the analyst's flexibility or rigidity; appropriate timing with the patient's capacity to be receptive; the quality of the interpretation and its "fit" with the actual communications; and the analyst's use of language.

While interpretations by the analyst were significant to many patients, particularly in the working through of difficult issues in the transference, what became evident from the patients' experiences was the importance of how the interpretations were constructed and delivered. The patients related this to the analysts' human qualities, as manifested through their style and technique. This was demonstrated by Audrey when she said, "I certainly valued his interpretations but in the early stages it was his personality, the innate qualities that he had. It would have taken me a couple of years to actually really start to value the interpretations."

Some patients expressed frustration about the way their analysts seemed to ignore the material they brought to the sessions. To illustrate, Steve said,

"When I sought interpretative information it was really disregarded. I found that a point of ongoing frustration. Like what do you make of this, what do you make of these phantasies, this behaviour, the way that my father fires me up? That's what I wanted."

Rick stated that so much of the time he could not understand what his analyst was doing. He had no idea where the interpretations came from, leaving him thinking "what am I supposed to do with this?"

> "He [the analyst] would make a comment—it might be just a sentence, or something of an interpretation—but I couldn't understand at that time what it was about. I would be just left with 'What are you talking about? I haven't a clue what you are talking about.' It made no sense to me whatsoever; he left me nothing to work with. It didn't feel like it was linked to what I was saying."

Confusion around the language used by his analyst was also a problem for Rick. "It was obviously couched in terminology alien to me. It wasn't in language that I obviously understood. It was very much in psychoanalytic language, which I had no knowledge of. It doesn't help the uninitiated".

Lucy also described her analyst as not helpful in terms of the interpretations he made. She told me, "I would say 'You don't know what you're doing. You don't give me any interpretation.' I would tell him the most intimate things and he would do nothing with it."

When her analyst did interpret, Lucy perceived him as very inflexible: ""He wouldn't offer, or say 'Could it be this, could it be that?' He would say, 'It's this, or that.' I would say, 'That's just over-simplifying. No, that's not it; it doesn't connect with me at all'."

In a similar manner, Jenny talked about an inflexibility and insensitivity in her analyst at times. She commented on the importance to her as to whether the interpretations were done "sensitively" or "shoved down my throat".

> "This seemed more important than the content of the interpretations . . . Sometimes I think the analyst was gentle, but it was the way he made his interpretations which was frustrating me. He was sometimes quite hard and very strict, and he frustrated the hell out of me. And I always felt there was not enough sensitivity; he didn't understand the intensity of my feelings."

Paul reported that there were times that he was quite defensive or could not hear the analyst's interpretation. However, he said that this was not a problem to either of them, paying tribute to the analyst's flexible way of working with him. "I didn't think like he was pushing anything down my throat that didn't fit. And he would quite easily let go of an interpretation that he had and just allow another one to come up."

Another patient who spoke positively about her analyst's intuitive way of responding was Kate. She remarked on the timing of her analyst's interpretations and the way in which she felt they connected with her material. This will be discussed in more detail in the following chapter, under "Containment".

Marg, as alluded to earlier, spoke of how she felt that her analyst interpreted all the time in a "predictable" way, instead of actually listening to what she was saying, and that this had the effect of immobilizing her. She ended up devising a mental game whenever he made interpretations.

> "It caused inhibitions because I knew what he would do with it; he was so predictable 'That's what happened . . .' And that became a game and no new material was being produced. It was very hard to produce material when you are interpreted in this way."

Two patients linked together several interpretative techniques that they felt were not useful to them. Greg talked about feeling trapped by his analyst's prolonged silence, followed by the use of "authoritative" interpretations that felt disempowering.

> "Was it like he was an authority or powerful figure? Absolutely. I think that's part of what I would call the autism. Like if the analyst says virtually nothing, and once or twice a session he will come out with an interpretation, it sort of appears authoritative—partly because of the infrequency of the responses."

Sig reported that the way in which his second analyst delivered interpretations was both disconnecting and disruptive:

> "I said to him [the analyst] a few times 'Look, I don't feel I'm able to fully participate because when I do start talking I find your interpretations disruptive. I don't feel I really connect with what you are saying, I don't feel understood by them. I feel they impinge on my stream of thought, and it takes me a couple of minutes to get

my head around what on earth your statement might mean before
I feel I can get back into a rhythm or on track'."

In reflecting on both his analytic experiences, Sig said,

"It got to a position where I could no longer use them [the analysts]
to help me, and I couldn't rely on my own resources either. I
was stuck. They couldn't manoeuvre around me so that I could
start using them again or their interpretations. And I was trying
to manoeuvre around them to try to find a way and I found I
couldn't do that either. So I had to leave."

The variation in these perceived styles of interpretation, and the
patients' earlier descriptions of the transference, would seem to
indicate factors other than theoretical training and technique which
had an impact on the patients' experience of their analyses. To
further explore these dynamics, the next section examines the
human qualities of some of the analysts as observed by the patients,
and how these were influential upon their analytic experiences.

Personality characteristics of the analysts

The analytic relationship, with its frequency of sessions over a
considerable length of time, is, by its very nature, of such intensity
that patients cannot avoid being interested in, or getting to know,
aspects of the analyst's personality or personal style of working.
When they reflected on the interpretative styles of their analysts,
the patients not only described how they themselves felt, but also
provided insight into the human qualities of their analysts, which
they believed influenced their capacity for analytic functioning.

Over the years, personality has been defined in a number of
different ways by theorists; however, there is a general consensus
that personality consists of all the particular characteristics that
define the unique quality or identity of the individual (Allport, 1961;
Chaplin, 1975; Samuel, 1981). Here, I have drawn upon aspects of
the term "personality" as understood by Baudrey (1991), who
described the analyst's personality as "the complex organization
of stable recurrent traits, behaviors and attitudes which define him"
(p. 918). I am adding to this definition the way in which these

analysts interpreted the analytic framework and applied rules around the setting, time, and payment, that is, how they functioned as analysts in all parameters. This is closely aligned to the way these patients have reflected upon the characteristics of their analysts.

The use of the word "personal" by two patients indicated their understandable receptivity to their analysts. Min used the term "personal being", and followed this with descriptive words conveying what she saw as very helpful.

> "I think her personal being and her personal way of being with me was the reason why I hung in there. She's very good at what she does. She's very flexible, she's also very patient, and she's very non-invasive. Those things are important to me. I wanted it to be at my pace, not hers . . . She was also, I'd have to say, very persistent. But it probably kept me in there too—probably a challenge . . . And I knew she wouldn't let things go. I knew that she wouldn't forget, I mean, she's like a terrier. At the time I didn't like it, but I mean, when I look back on it, I'd never have done that work, if she had given into it. If she'd just let me run the show, I'd never have done the work."

Min's analyst is depicted as having the capacity for actively pursuing the patient, in a holding, containing manner, which seems very different from those analysts perceived as using a more passive, "neutral" approach.

Rosa portrayed her analyst as "extraordinarily receptive", and wondered if this could be called the "maternal transference". She described, in an emphatic way, how he was "incredibly attuned" to her "infantile states of mind", and then demonstrated how she herself developed a similar sensitivity to his every movement.

> "You'd sort of sniff the air to get a sense of him. Of course, you don't know him in any other way. But I think it's a very personal sense I got over time. The way he moved, the way he would speak, his tone of voice, the rhythm of his voice, the rhythm of his walk, the way he would sit in his chair, the way he breathed. In everything from the tiny nuances to what he wore and how he decorated his room, how he responded to things that cropped up in the external world—all of these had an impact . . . Of course, it's about the journey inward, but it's in relation to another particular person. So

I think his personality had a major impact . . . I feel it was him being him that made the enormous difference."

Steve discussed a different understanding of his analyst, and labelled his personal qualities at various times as "skilful, immensely sensitive and astute", and "ethical and professional"; however, he perceived the analyst as "a victim of his own craft". This, he said, contributed to a state of destabilization in him and the feeling of "a sense that this was some kind of black hole that I would never emerge from".

"I believe that this man was a very skilled therapist, immensely sensitive, astute, as I have said. But I think something of, if I can use this terminology, he was a victim of his own craft, of his own therapeutic approach."

Steve was making a clear distinction between the personality of his analyst and his technique of working, suggesting that the theory exerted such an effect that it negated what could have been a good experience. I think the experiences of Sig and Rick could also fit into this way of understanding their analysts, believed to be following their "own agenda" and working from a theoretical stance. This could be considered as part of a countertransference response that is described in an unhelpful sense in the Introduction.

It was noticeable that, in these examples, and all other experiences related by these patients, no one actually used the word "countertransference" or referred to the analyst's countertransference. However, it became clear to me that their descriptions of the analyst's "personality" or "human characteristics" were their ways of talking about this concept, the counterpart to the patient's transference and in common usage in psychoanalytic language.

Making sense of the patients' communications

This chapter has focused primarily on the interpersonal relationship between the patients and their analysts, particularly centred on the transference as understood by the patients and their perceptions of the analysts' method of interpretation. Patients have demonstrated a vast difference in their experiences, which is based on how they discerned whether their analyst was able to work effectively or not with "transference" issues. They have raised awareness of important issues that may have influenced the analytic work and led to what they considered were inappropriate "countertransference" responses. These include the "real or human" qualities of the analyst in question, and adherence to a rigid theoretical model regardless of its applicability to specific situations in the relationship. It is well noted in the literature that the analyst, as well as the patient, brings personal or human qualities to the analytic relationship that can detract from his/her analytic function (Anastasopoulos & Papanicolaou, 2004). This would seem an important area to address when the analysis itself is floundering.

The therapeutic relationship

Research exploring factors leading to therapeutic change in psychoanalysis has, in recent years, turned specifically upon the importance of the therapeutic relationship. This contrasts with earlier thinking on the significance of increased insight from particular analytic interpretations (Anastasopoulos & Papanicolaou, 2004). In the Freudian tradition, Segal (1962) regarded insight as the precondition of any lasting personality change; however, Symington (1988) asserted that while insight was an integral part of psychoanalysis, this placed too much reliance on the analyst as the centre of truth. It "weighted change in favour of an intellectual cause" (p. 27) and was potentially in danger of a uni-dimensional analytic situation. Symington (1988) emphasized the importance of a two-sided relationship, describing the inevitable creation of an emotional storm when two personalities meet together.

Freud (1912e) proposed a framework in which psychoanalysis could take place with the analyst observing a neutral stance, believing this provided the optimum setting for patients to give free voice to whatever came to mind. In one of his early papers he wrote, "The analyst should be opaque to his patients and, like a mirror, should show them nothing but what is shown to him" (p. 118). As discussed in the Introduction, Freud's dictum about being a "blank

screen" has been misrepresented by some analysts as the requirement to adopt a distant, non-relational approach under the guise of
"neutrality".

Basing their work on clinical examples some early writers
(Ferenczi & Rank, 1924; Jung, quoted in McGuire, 1974) argued that
the patient's experience in relation to the analyst is as important as
Freud's original aim of retrieving repressed information. Other
influential thinkers also challenged the central tenet of neutrality,
emphasizing the effect of the analyst's presence (Adler & Bachant,
1996; 1998; Loewald, 1960), the character of the analyst as an integral factor of the analysis (Chused, 1991; Schafer, 1992), and, more
recently, the unavoidable role of the analyst's personal influence
and subjectivity in the process (Anastasopoulos & Papanicolaou,
2004; Meissner, 1998).

In spite of these arguments, and the now "shaky" belief in
neutrality, adherence to this traditional analytic stance has continued to be an important technique for some analysts (Greenberg,
2001). It is interesting to note, however, that Freud himself seldom
practised in the detached or aloof way that he laid down for his
followers. As attested by a former patient of Freud's, Albert Hirst,
the relationship "not the rationalistic substance of Freud's interpretations" (Roazen, 1995, p. 28), was the key curative factor in his
analysis.

Before moving on to more of the patients' narratives, I would
like to draw attention to countertransference as understood in relation to interpretative work and discussed in detail in the Introduction. Interpretations take shape as the analyst listens with
"evenly suspended attention" (Freud, 1912b) to the patient's
communications, spoken within a particular context, and "do not
arise by chance or in isolation" (Baranger, 1993, p. 15). As the
patient attempts to follow Freud's fundamental rule of saying
everything that comes to mind, the function of the analyst's unconscious is defined by Baranger (ibid.) as a "resonance box" for the
patient's unconscious. This interaction between the two partners in
the analytic dyad is both interpersonal and dynamic. The analyst
monitors the patient's communications in the transference through
being acutely tuned into the feelings generated in him/her in
response, and from his/her countertransference frames the interpretation accordingly.

The use of countertransference

While countertransference is now understood as an important analytic function in interpretation, it is crucial to keep in mind that the analyst can also be subject to feelings that contain repressed elements in him/herself and which are not just generated by the patient's material (Eagle, 2000; Gabbard, 1995; Sandler, 1987, 1993; Spillius, 1992). If countertransference is not processed, these feelings can have a detrimental impact on the timing, content, and delivery of interpretations, which then leaves the patient in a state of bewilderment or believing he/she has not been understood. As in the transference from patients of significant "other" relationships to the person of the analyst, countertransference feelings from the analyst can also contain the mechanisms of projection and introjection. This occurs if the analyst is not accurately tuned in to the patient's unconscious communications, but instead is caught up in personal agendas.

Several themes have emerged from these experiences that relate to this transference–countertransference relationship. I begin with some examples in which the analysts appeared to step outside a theoretically driven, "neutral" style of working, as articulated by Freud (1912b), and where they were perceived by their patients as utilizing personal qualities in quite distinctive and positive ways.

Kerry provided a graphic illustration of an analyst closely attuned to her experience and able to adapt his style in the constructive working through of difficult past issues. Although she recognized in the experience described earlier in the chapter that the relationship was not real, she demonstrated how she became so caught up in the intensity of the recalled memory that she acted as if the analyst was the significant other from her past; this inferred a transferential relationship as understood in psychoanalytic terms. Her analyst was able to make useful interpretations and help her work through this experience in the immediacy of the transference, using humour and playfulness very effectively. Kerry went from an "incredible fear" to feeling that the analyst was totally "friendly and trustworthy". In the end, she found herself able to "play with him" in the analytic space. The unique "playful" style of this analyst seemed to demonstrate innate, personal qualities that led to what Kerry called an "amazing" outcome.

Jean and Audrey described almost identical experiences with male analysts, who not only permitted them to bring their infants to the sessions, but also were able to model for them the maternal qualities traditionally ascribed to females. They talked about deprivations in their own childhood, including the lack of a good "mothering" experience, which had detrimentally influenced their own sense of motherhood. Jean expressed amazement at the analyst's capacity to deal with these feelings of loss and deprivation. It enabled her to "repair the damage" from her early relationship with mother and at the same time enabled her to learn from her analyst how to mother her own child. She referred to this experience as "magical".

Audrey likewise regarded the work with her analyst around mothering issues as "quite special". She described how he had the capacity to "look after" her and demonstrate a holding maternal function that she declared as "strange considering he's a male". For both these patients, the analysts' functioning in this way modelled a role previously unknown to them but from which they were able to take something positive away through this work in the transference relationship. Winnicott's (1988) reference to parents being able to draw on memories of their own experience of parenting to help them, in turn, care for their infants links here with the analysts' capacity, in both cases, to provide what was lacking in the family of origin.

Another rewarding analytic experience was described by Steve, who was impressed with how his analyst could make a transference interpretation about a homosexual phantasy with "courage" and such "sensitivity". It even came as "quite a shock" from someone whom Steve perceived as a "straight man" and yet who was able to understand and translate his communications into the immediacy of their therapeutic relationship. This example and the others mentioned above demonstrate human qualities in these analysts which enhanced their capacity for carrying out fruitful work, contrasting quite markedly to those whose style of working was described by patients as "inhibiting" or even "disruptive". It is useful to note that Steve drew attention to the distinction he perceived between his analyst's very positive qualities, such as surprising sensitivity, and the analyst's theoretical background, which he saw as detrimental to continuing good work. This distinction raises the question of how the rigid application of theory might impact on the analyst's innate personal qualities, and is supported by the proposition that theory can become a third source of unhelpful countertransference (Purcell, 2004; Stein, 1991) as discussed in the next chapter.

Five other patients perceived their analysts as unable to use the transference constructively, and have provided vivid illustrations of where interpretations were found not helpful, or even relevant, to their verbal communications. This is supported by some of the literature and exampled by Abend (1993) when he argues that "the role of the relationship in analysis and technique has become increasingly complex and sophisticated" (p. 639), with a much greater emphasis in recent years on the prominence of the analyst's subjectivity. Abend continues that, rather than blindly accepting that the analyst "can, for purposes of interpretation, reliably distinguish the patient's distortions from reality" (*ibid.*), it is now generally accepted that transference is an interpersonal relationship, with both patient and analyst contributing not only to the relationship, but also to the transference. Gill (1984) also argues that "each participant also has a valid, albeit different, perspective on it" (cited in Abend, 1993, p. 640). The reliability of the once advocated analyst's objectivity has been called into question by these researchers, with a greater appreciation of the emotional reactions of analysts (Abend, 2002).

Marg talked about the excessive use of the transference, which she elaborated as being every utterance of hers reinterpreted back as though having to do with the analyst. She found this so predictable and so "boring" that the interpretations lost meaning for her, and instead were experienced as an abuse and what she described as a "bludgeoning" of the transference. Marg's reported experience as unhelpful mirrors Baranger's (1993) argument in which he stated that confusion can occur between: "the repetition with the person of the analyst of past links and situations (mésalliances), and the patient–analyst link as structurally defined by the contract" (p. 21). Baranger added that in such a situation the transference is lost sight of, and "this forcing of the transference leads ultimately to interpretations that are off-centre with respect to the point of urgency, and may tend to indoctrinate the patient". Balint (1968) has commented on the problems inherent in every transference interpretation being related back to the analyst. He stated that one of the unspoken implications might be that the analytic relationship is "between a highly important, omnipresent object, the analyst, and an unequal subject who at present apparently cannot feel, think or experience anything unrelated to the analyst" (p. 169). Berman (2001) also entered the argument, saying how there was danger of "a new reductionism" (p. 46) when the analyst interpreted everything from the patient's outside life as indirect transferences to him/her.

Marg demonstrated her reaction to what she called a "forcing" of the transference by devising games to counteract the predictability, and spoke of a "persecutory" silence which was then punctuated by "lacerations" of transference interpretations. She has used very explicit and graphic terms for the work of analysis as she experienced it. Because of this, she believed she was not encouraged to speak or explore her issues further. Rick, who likewise said he was left unable to make connections with the material he brought to the analysis, raised similar concerns around silence and irrelevant interpretations.

These experiences are so different from those of patients who reported significant changes in their external relationships and perceptions of the world. It would seem to indicate that this difference was not based on the theoretical learning which takes place in training institutes, but is rather more to do with the personality characteristics of the particular analysts at work. It could also be suggested that the lack of connectedness be thought about as part of a rigid system of thinking which follows an outdated form of psychoanalysis. In this system, it is still presumed that the analyst can remain a "blank screen" in the relationship and make interpretations from a position of holding absolute knowledge and possession of "the truth".

Other experiences demonstrated further examples of minimal or no connection to the patients' verbalizations. In both of Sig's analyses, each lasting about two years, he expressed frustration at their lack of acknowledgement of the material he brought to the sessions. He was particularly concerned at not receiving any constructive interpretations around his pattern of unsatisfactory external relationships, which he believed could have been worked through in the transference. A sophisticated thinker and avid reader of Freud himself, Sig was able to clearly articulate his feelings about the difference between his knowledge of psychoanalysis and the manner in which he experienced the work of analysis by these two analysts. His comments about the analysts not being able to work through his negative transferences, and being very "withholding", demonstrate that the particular approaches of these two analysts were not at all helpful to him. His experiences, related to "fathering" issues, are presented in more detail in Chapter Five.

Lucy was another patient who described experiences in which she felt that her analyst became caught up in the transference rather than being able to interpret what was actually occurring in the analytic relationship (see Chapters Two and Five). In the material here, Lucy discussed how she perceived her analyst as acting out something with her in a personal way instead of exploring the motives behind her wish to send him a postcard, and the hours of seemingly agonized thinking that was behind this. Using psychoanalytic language in a way that demonstrated a familiarity with it, Lucy talked about seeing him working at the "logical, concrete level rather than the 'symbolic'". She described the analyst's responses as self-focused rather than exploratory, and, hence, not helpful to her understanding of her own internal, psychic world. It would appear that he was caught up in a very powerful countertransference reaction, from her projections on to him of an abandoning father, as detailed elsewhere, and, as a result, he lost the capacity to function analytically.

Another patient, Kate, raised issues that could be thought about as the analyst's countertransference, although she referred to them as his "imperfections". She has talked about constant mistakes made on her invoice when he charged her for five sessions weekly rather than for her regular four times per week. Kate said she was not only irritated by this, but made to feel as though she was different or an "aberration"—the odd one out. Far from feeling special, she was not only being charged more, but was also receiving less than those other patients who saw the analyst for an extra weekly session. These feelings of irritation and being an "aberration", in relation to other patients, could be thought of in terms of sibling rivalry.

I believe that the examples demonstrated here by the patients, and articulated with some sophistication about the psychoanalytic process, are worthy of attention. They are supported by such writers as Abend (1993) who said, "The analyst has neither absolute authority nor perfect objectivity" (p. 645), and Bachant and Adler (1997), with their statement that the use and meaning of transference "have been subject to considerable variability even within groups of analysts who share common premises and technical commitments" (p. 1099).

It is important, in reviewing these findings, to acknowledge the variation in the analysts' approaches to working in the transference and to be open to thinking about factors that led to their differences in functioning. Patients' descriptions do demonstrate quite distinct patterns of relating and interpreting, and provide support for suggesting that the personality or human qualities of the analyst are prime factors in the way he/she functions analytically. The patients have provided many examples of the human qualities they perceived in the interpretative function of their analysts that made a difference to them. I suggest that where this has led to an unsatisfactory experience, or even premature termination, it links directly to the particular psychoanalytic understanding of countertransference. This would indicate that the analyst's own agenda can disrupt his/her analytic capacity for thinking in the "here-and-now" of the actual communications from patients. At these moments, the analyst's own personal issues influence the interpretative work to the extent that they are unable to use their intuitive thinking and emotional responses in ways which facilitate the work of analysis; rather, it serves to alienate the patients. Personality characteristics of the analyst, as reported by these patients, would, thus, seem to have had a significant impact upon their analyst's capacity for constructive work.

In the following chapter, I describe more specific aspects of the relationship, highlighting the provision of containment or analytic space, the quality of engagement, and the use, or abuse, of silence and authority.

CHAPTER FOUR

The quality of engagement*

"It was her being with me in this incredible terror and despair, and I felt held . . . I just had this incredible sense of her presence with me"

(Carmel)

"If he had only been willing to give me a little bit of a kick start, that's all I would have needed, a little bit of picking up on what I had said"

(Marg)

I n the previous chapter, the patients' rich narratives revealed a number of key issues that I will now present in terms of central themes. These themes are not discrete, but, rather, interrelated, and include areas of engagement plus issues to do with power and the use of silence. The patients discussed, in quite diverse ways,

---

*Paper presented to the APPWA Conference, Perth, November, 2009, and accepted for publication in *Australasian Journal of Psychotherapy*, 29(1/2), 2010, in press.

their degree of satisfaction with the overall analyses and their understanding of the process. Some reported that they had gone through a profound change, such as feeling "very liberated" or having "a very rich and meaningful experience that I can draw upon and feed off". In contrast, other patients testified to finishing the analysis prematurely because the experience had caused more resentment by staying than what they were gaining from it. One stated that he found the analysis "a fairly intimidating and unhelpful experience", while another patient described his analysis as "a kind of mediocre stew; any good ingredients put in became lost in the process". I will describe these experiences under the following themes that reflect the particular key issues referred to above.

- containment (referring to Bion's [1959] concept of a transformative function, similar to that of the mother in reverie) and reflective space;
  - psychological space;
  - "physical" holding;
- engagement/non-engagement;
- the meaning and use of silence;
- power differentials between analyst and patient; negotiation and expectations of this within the analytic relationship.

As already stated, these themes were difficult to conceptualize in isolation from each other, but will be drawn together in discussion throughout the chapter.

Containment and the use of reflective space

Patients reported that one of the analyst's major functions in facilitating a very good experience of analysis was his/her capacity to provide a reflective space. When this occurred, they felt that it enabled them to free associate, in a spontaneous and liberating way, while at the same time feeling they were being listened to and understood in their pain. To describe these experiences, patients commonly used words such as "contained", "held", "being there with you", and other terms that bring to mind the therapeutic action of psychoanalysis as derived from object-relations theorists (Balint, 1968; Bion, 1959; Gitelson, 1962; Loewald, 1960; Spitz, 1956;

Winnicott, 1965). These analysts viewed the analytic setting itself as containing elements reminiscent of the mother–child relationship, with particular importance placed on the analytic concepts of Bion's "containment" and Winnicott's "holding environment" (Modell, 1976).

In relation to the patients' descriptions of a "containing" function, I identified two specific areas which I refer to as: (1) psychological space; and (2) a "physical" holding. I am using the term "psychological" space in the way defined by Casement (2002). He described it as an emotional space between analyst and patient which can be bridged by either reaching out to the other, and "it may be filled, in one way or another, or be left empty; a space for thinking, a space for relating, a space for experiencing and for being" (p. 100). Casement's (2002) definition resonates with the meanings as articulated by patients. These include the various interventions by the analyst in which he/she was able to convey to the patient a real presence and understanding of the patient's inner world, whether communicated by verbal or non-verbal means. By the phrase "physical" holding, I am referring to those aspects of the setting such as structure, setting, and continuity of time and sessions, which the patients said provided the kind of safe environment where the internal work could be facilitated.

Psychological space

Kerry and Carmel described how they experienced powerful feelings of pain and terror at stages during their analytic sessions, and then enormous relief when they felt that their analysts were present with them in a very liberating way. Kerry, in explaining her appreciation of the space created for her by the analyst, said that it enabled "all the madness to start tumbling out", adding,

> "That pain—I don't know how he could bear it. I would be like this puddle of pain on his couch. He was so kind. Just the fact he was with me and stayed with me . . . I do have this extraordinary experience of having been liberated."

Carmel spoke of a similar freeing experience with her analyst when she felt psychologically held, and illustrated it as follows.

"It was her being with me in this incredible terror and despair, and I felt held . . . I was suicidal and she held me through that; she was able to sit through it. I just had this incredible sense of her presence with me, and her support. I had to go through it but she was there. She was prepared to risk that I might actually do it, and hold me and trust me that I wouldn't do it. It was a very powerful experience."

Another important aspect of the psychological space that patients described was the ability of the analyst to hold them in mind while showing recognition and understanding of their world. Ruth talked about her powerful experience of being known.

"It makes me teary to think that somebody could be there with you, somebody could actually kind of know you at a deep level and recognize what you were going through. To sort of hold something in you is very powerful. It enabled me to kind of enter the stuff, the difficult painful stuff, the difficult feelings, and feel quite held and heard."

Audrey reported that she felt as if the analyst was able to be in her world by the quality of his "mindfulness" about her. "I'm not sure that he was actually in my world, but he certainly gave me the impression that he was. And that was very important." She also described how, at the beginning of her analysis, she felt she needed to be "welded to him, virtually" in order to "exist" and not be "totally forgotten". She described how this feeling changed over time as she worked through the analysis.

"I got to the stage where I realized that you don't actually have to be permanently attached; someone can actually keep you in mind and you can actually be OK. Like just keep a thought about you, that you are OK; that 'I'll see you next week' and it's still OK. It's not like they've totally forgotten you. My fear was that I didn't exist basically, that I didn't exist if someone wasn't thinking about me. I had the feeling I had to be a kind of suction to him."

Kate spoke of another form of containment when she described the analyst's interpretative stance as "an incredible gift".

"Like 'Oh God! Thank you. That was just what I needed to hear'; that feeling when you are talking about your dreams and this and that, and then someone has that wonderful ability of putting them all together in a very succinct kind of way that just feels calming, or containing, or rounding."

In contrast to the above experiences, a few patients described what it was like not to have the experience of reflective space. Sig reported how he felt that his analyst was "unwilling to receive what I wanted to give", and that this limited his ability to develop that part of himself which needed development.

> "He would make these interpretations to me how I was resisting, I was withholding, I was not willing to give in . . . I was giving, I wanted to give, but he was unwilling to receive what I wanted to give. And I felt every time I opened my mouth that there wasn't the reflective space there for me to develop those ideas."

Sig experienced this as "an abuse of power", and that the analyst was not "being mindful enough of the importance of being held, contained".

Jenny commented on her analyst's creative capacity, which she described as contributing to the provision of containment. She talked about him as "a very creative thinker, intuitive and know-ledgeable", adding, "and certainly he had those qualities of containment . . ." However, she said that she occasionally found her analyst unable to meet her needs in such a way that she was reassured that he understood her psychic pain.

> "At times, when in depths of despair, I wasn't sure whether he was able to relate to me on that deep level of feeling—when I was finding it almost unbearable to be with the intensity of the pain. He wanted to go into thinking about it rather than staying with the intensity of the feeling. Maybe a little remark that he understood would have helped."

Tony observed that his analyst displayed a certain rigidity in the way he functioned, saying that it was similar to his own way of working. This was experienced as a lack of containment, and, in a sense, a lack of the reflective space, as raised by other patients. He stated, "The thing that struck me was that he was fairly traditional . . . I'm quite obsessional and rigid and that's the way he struck me. It was all strict and controlled and structured."

The experiences described above demonstrate quite different ways the analysts worked in "reaching out to the other" (Casement, 2002, p. 100), or, in contrast, were unable to provide that important reflective space where the patient could feel psychologically held and contained. It is clear that the narratives of these patients do illustrate an understanding of the importance of a "containing" reflective space.

"Physical" holding

The other form of containment, or holding, which emerged was related to the actual physical setting. This included the regularity and continuity of sessions; the use of the couch; the analyst's waiting area and room; and the way in which payment of the fee was structured. These are all important aspects of psychoanalytic practice that provide the boundaries within which the analysis takes place. Time also featured prominently in many of the patients' stories.

Paul used the word "unchangeability" to describe the regularity of time commitment and the reliable presence of his analyst as important to his therapeutic work.

> "It's the actual frame, the structure, the going four times per week, which is very important . . . I think his unchangeability. That was the really stabilizing strong force in him for me; somebody staying in the same place in the same time creating an incredibly stable holding environment."

For Audrey, structured time provided the "key" to being held and enabled her to bring up issues without fear of rejection or dismissal.

> "There was a lot of structure—for me that was the key. That was the thing that saved me, because in the end it was like 'This is your time—you've got your fifty minutes; he is going to be there tomorrow'. I felt that I could actually bring things up . . . I could get shitty with him, and I felt I could walk out and yet he would always remain the same. He would be there the next day."

Ruth discussed how helpful she also found the regularity of time, plus lying on the couch.

"Going into the space, lying on the couch—it actually felt freeing because you could just let yourself be; it actually facilitated a bit of regression. That was good; it wasn't a frightening experience. So I think it was the setting; that was something powerful, and the rigidity around time."

Jenny and Rosa both described the importance of being able to explore painful issues through the continuity provided by regular sessions and the luxury of time that felt empowering. Jenny said,

"That I was able to go so often, four or five times a week, so that you knew if you were dealing with something difficult you could actually go back the next day . . . It was important also to know that this wouldn't be finished prematurely, that it took time."

Rosa stated,

"I would set my own timing for the emergence of whatever it was. It was really not dictated or pressured in any way. This, in the end, felt like this extraordinary patience on his part, or on the part of the process, and then it empowered me."

The physical setting was quite meaningful in other ways. For example, as described in Chapter Two, a dirty waiting room was one of the reasons that Kate decided not to have analytic treatment from one of the analysts who initially interviewed her.

Sig also drew attention to the physical surroundings when he met one of his analysts for the first time. He described how he was immediately impressed by "A poshy multi-storied mansion . . . a huge consultation room downstairs with a very low heat environment . . ." This led to an initial positive engagement with the analyst.

In thinking about what he found helpful, Rick paused for a few moments, and then replied, "Helpful aspects? I guess, somewhere, there must have been. I went there for two years so there must have been something happening that was helpful." He then added,

"Well I guess one thing that may have been helpful would have been the opportunity just to sit down and try and make sense of my life—what I was doing. And I guess that was the first time I have ever really done that . . . But I guess I could have done that with someone who wasn't an analyst, when I think about it. I could have sat in a corner and done my own thing."

Rick's statement suggests that while "physical" holding such as time and space to reflect is helpful, it is not enough without an "emotionally present" analyst who is available to foster the work expected in an analytic experience.

Engagement with the analyst

The patients described different experiences of engagement with their analysts. They used words like "fit", "connection", "receptive", a "very powerful experience", or "fantastic" and "nurturing". Audrey explained that one of the most important things for her was the analyst's capacity to be internally "in sync" with her.

"I actually needed someone to almost be inside my head, walking along with me, thinking the same thoughts. It took him quite some time to actually be with me, but I can remember it just getting better and better—like he would get with me and we would be in sync. It was just fantastic; you just knew that somebody was actually with you."

Ruth talked about the importance of having her reality accepted. With some deliberation she informed me that what she required of the analyst in order to feel engaged was,

"For somebody to kind of make sense of what was going on so it was a very, very powerful experience, and in some ways very nurturing. It's like you could speak about what was really there and this person is somebody who would accept that this was a reality for you. So you could say anything and know that this person was trying to make sense of it, trying to understand it."

Kerry described a particularly good connection she felt with her analyst.

"I didn't feel him to be removed, I didn't feel like he was just sitting back and thinking, I just feel like I landed in a really good place. There was a good fit between us. I did pull against him, don't get me wrong, I did have fights with him and gave him the shits terribly. But there was a sense of that mutual working together that always was there. I felt connected to him."

Trust in the analyst and feeling respected in return was also of particular importance to the patients' experiences of engagement. Several patients mentioned this. Jean declared, "The most important factor was the trust . . . He never let me down", while Jenny said, "What I did think was helpful was that I could have some trust in him because of knowing he was trained and had been through the process as well himself."

Ruth also spoke about the experience of trustworthiness, and linked it to containment and the analyst's ability to "bear" what the patient had brought to the session.

"You just felt at a deep level that they were trustworthy and that they could manage, contain and bear the shit, the painful stuff— they weren't going to run from it, they weren't going to cover it up, they weren't going to dismiss it, they weren't going to judge it, and they could actually bear what felt unbearable. That was very important."

Rosa described her analyst as "receptive", linking this to what she called "maternal transference", as it was as though the analyst could connect to her infant state:

"I found him extraordinarily receptive, whether you want to call that the maternal transference, I don't know. I just felt as though there was this capacity to understand very infantile states of my mind . . . he was incredibly attuned to the other person."

Jenny, with a background of long-term depression and loneliness, said that the analyst made her feel more human and helped her to engage with him.

"He made me feel I was a human being. And he took seriously my unmet needs; he took the lack in me seriously, and didn't skim over and collude with me. He was able to go beyond that. I felt respected by him. By and large he was non-reactive. That was extremely helpful."

Min described her analyst as having the capacity to engage with her feminine side, which was very important to her as she came from a dysfunctional family with a "phallic grandmother and a phallic mother". She also commented on feeling good about being provided with some space.

> "I think her femaleness, her feminineness, and her understanding of my need to be alone. I have to be alone on a very regular basis, and the only way I can sort myself out is by being alone . . . Some people think it's pathological. I don't, and she didn't. I think that was an important part of our working relationship."

I think that Min's example here illustrates that engagement is a complex concept. Many patients have described engagement as being connected, but for others it can relate to being able to be alone in a containing kind of way, as, for example, the infant alone in the presence of mother and feeling satisfied.

Humour was a quality mentioned by several patients when they highlighted aspects of the analyst's personality that they appreciated. This is discussed more fully in a later chapter. However, I introduce two examples here to illustrate the function it held as a form of engagement with the analyst, in otherwise unsatisfactory analytic experiences.

Marg introduced her analyst's capacity for humour as something quite personal and meaningful for her, and an important part of her understanding of engagement.

> "The only thing I thought I could do was make him smile. It's important, not vital, but important that there is something of humour, because it shows somebody is human if they respond in that way. It's very personal, I think, because that's what I use for engagement."

Lucy also used humour to engage her analyst, but described it in a particularly flirtatious way. Within what she presented as an overall "horrible" experience was an example of some very special moments of engagement:

> "I would flirt with him and that was lovely. A bit like you would with a father, I suppose. We would have lovely moments. Once, the

only time that he laughed, I said, 'It's our anniversary next week and I suppose you've been trailing the shops looking for a present for me.' And he laughed. Things like that. I would flirt with him like a lover."

A few patients described experiences of limited engagement, or even non-engagement. Rick recounted how he had brought to the analysis his problem of feeling disconnected, hoping to explore it, but this was unable to be resolved.

> "One of my issues, I suppose, was feeling connected to others. That's part of my background stuff, feeling disconnected from people. There is a strong need of mine to feel somewhat connected. And I didn't have any sense of connection with him at all."

Greg expressed similar sentiments about how he perceived his analyst's technique of engagement. "He was totally non-relational, and I found it disconfirming. I found it very anxiety making, and I think that played into maybe some masochistic streak in him."

The notion of "technical neutrality" was raised by Sig as an aspect of his analysts' lack of engagement.

> "I think the problem was that the analysts I have seen seem to be very orthodox in their approach and not very modern. They adhere very much to the Freudian notion, it's not even Freudian; they adhere to this notion of technical neutrality."

Simon also reported that his experience of trying to engage with his analyst did not get him anywhere. He talked about his analyst as not being responsive, similar, perhaps, to Sig's experience of "technical neutrality". Simon provided an example. "He would just not respond when I asked him for his views or opinions. He would just not respond. If I was angry with him about the process then I just wouldn't get anywhere."

Marg experienced her analyst as "not very forthcoming", and as "punitive as a school teacher", intent on following a set of "rules". Her description seems to imply incapacity in her analyst to be attuned to her communications:

> "'These are the rules, you break the rules . . .' It was a formula, always the same; I wrote it in my diary. He missed a huge lot of

opportunities. If he had only been willing to give me a little bit of a kick start, that's all I would have needed, a little bit of picking up on what I had said. I remember once, instead of saying 'Did you hear what you just said?', he said, 'Don't you listen to what you say?' See the two different ways of saying something?"

These patients have demonstrated clearly that being able to engage at some level with their analysts was very important to them. Perceptions of not feeling connected, as reported by at least four patients, were linked with the personal qualities brought to the relationship by the analyst.

The use of silence

Several patients raised the analysts' use of silence, and what this conveyed. In most cases, the silence was not reported as a reflective space, but, rather, as unhelpful, or even counterproductive to the therapeutic process.

Kate said that her analyst did not speak often, which she generally experienced as "incredibly powerful and helped me go deeper". There were other times, however, when she felt really stuck, and then the analyst's silences were not useful in encouraging further associations from her. She provided an example of such times.

"I reckon I could have held it the whole session except there is a point where I would think, 'God this is a waste of time and money' . . . I think if he had said something sooner I would have just started speaking sooner. The silence was not helping me go into anything more because I was stuck in 'I'm not going to talk. I've got nothing to say', or 'I'm so depressed I can't speak'."

Simon, likewise, spoke of the problem of silence for him in terms of it immobilizing or distressing him.

"The main thing I encountered was that if I didn't comment, if I didn't speak, then nothing happened. Or I'd say, 'I think I can understand what I'm angry or upset about, but what can I do about them?' There would be silence, and that would usually get me more and more upset. I can't recall a time where, as the result of a silence, I thought more deeply and suddenly thought, 'Aha, wow!'"

Rick also found prolonged periods of silence in his analysis unhelpful. "I would go through weeks when he said virtually nothing, apart from at the end of the session when he would say 'time' . . . There were weeks and weeks and weeks of silence." And Jenny reported, "We discussed it a lot . . . I couldn't bear the silence; I felt I was left hanging."

Marg was more critical of the periods of silence with her analyst. "There was quite an element of being persecutory with the silence. I think the patient needs to learn how to speak, be encouraged to speak, the aim of the word is speech, and actually to be left in silence . . ."

I return to the psychoanalytic meaning of silence and its importance to patients a little later in the discussion.

Power differentials between analyst and patient

Another significant theme that emerged concerned power differentials between the patients and their analysts. By this, I refer to the disparities felt by patients between the analyst's authority, as perceived both verbally and non-verbally in the relationship, and their own ability to question or negotiate issues. Some reported that they were given the freedom to discuss openly anything important to them, and particularly if there was conflict, or they described negotiating successfully with the analyst at the beginning of their analysis about terms and conditions. Other patients expressed disillusionment when they were prevented from negotiating anxieties about terms and conditions in either the analytic relationship or the initial contract. Examples of both experiences are provided below.

During her original assessment, Min described how she successfully negotiated with her analyst to sit up during sessions rather than lie on the couch, the usual procedure in analysis. In stating how she was determined to be a "patient partner", not a "patient victim", Min later talked about other qualities in her analyst that assisted the ongoing relationship to be a negotiable partnership: "She [the analyst] is very good at what she does. She's very flexible, she's also

very patient, and she's very non-invasive. Those things are important to me. I wanted it to be at my pace, not hers."

The two patients, Jean and Audrey, who were able to successfully negotiate with their analysts to bring their newborn infants to
the sessions provided illustrations of very significant mothering
experiences from their analysts. This resulted in not having to break
the continuity of their analyses, and, at the same time, being able to
attend to their infants' needs. Both interpreted this as learning how
to be good mothers through the important modelling they received
from their analysts.

Tony was not so successful in his attempts to negotiate the parameters of his analysis. He described how he felt that one of the
problems he encountered, and which he was still trying to understand, was that he did not actually feel he "had the strength to
negotiate anything". Given his financial restrictions, arrangements
around how he paid for his sessions became a very important issue.

> "A lot of the time I spent trying to get him to understand my world,
> and in a way I think he spent a lot of the time trying to get me to
> understand his point of view. A lot of that was around money . . . I
> didn't have the funds to pay up front, and we had huge arguments.
> He wouldn't let me send it off to Medicare [the Australian National
> Health Insurance System] first—no way. So these were really big
> issues."

Tony summed up his experience with a general comment on his
thoughts about analysis. "I think, personally, this is the way it is
with most analysts. Part of the structure thing is 'The way I do business is this'. And you fit in with that and it's not negotiable."

Kerry described two quite different experiences with her analyst
around money, which demonstrated some individual flexibility. On
one occasion when late, through no fault of her own, she was asked
to pay the difference because of the change in Medicare code, and,
as a consequence, was very angry with the analyst. Another time,
later, however, when expecting similar treatment, she was pleas-
antly surprised at being able to negotiate with him.

> "He was lovely. I was late, something happened, something hap-
> pened with the fees, and I said to him, 'That's really unfair. That's
> grossly unfair to be penalized.' And he said 'How about we split

the difference then?' I said, 'That's really decent. That's good. OK, we'll split the difference.' Pretty good! Pretty good!"

Steve recounted that he asked his analyst how long the analysis might continue, but received no definite answer. This was a boundary issue that Steve said he wanted clarified in order to complete constructive analytic work, even if this time/boundary was later changed through mutual negotiation. He experienced this lack of information around an important issue for him as a loss of agency, which eventually led to "emotional destabilization". In describing this problem, Steve said,

> "I began asking questions like 'How long do you think we might continue working together? What might we explore, what might we not explore?', trying not exactly to set boundaries, but getting some sense of this as a life-long event. I didn't really want to continue an indefinite period in a destabilized sense of state. His response was vaguely along the lines of 'Well how long is a piece of string?' I think the third or fourth time I asked him I felt increasingly dissatisfied, with a sense that this was some kind of black hole that I would never emerge from. I certainly became emotionally quite destabilized. I withdrew significantly from everyone."

Sig explained how he found his analytic treatment confusing after reading Freud's case studies, and other thinkers such as Winnicott, Balint, and Kohut. He said they seemed a lot more supportive and "very able to take on their clients' internal world". He stated that where these noted analysts, cited, saw a therapeutic element in the process, he identified his two experiences as "straight down the line".

> "I guess I was expecting the same amount of willingness to assist me, but there was no willingness. It was like 'You do it my way or no way'. I was forced into the position where I had to say, 'It's causing me more resentment to stay than I feel I am getting out of the process.'"

He added,

> "If you've had a proper analysis yourself, you're supposed to be able to use your own feelings in a way that will help you understand

your client. And there was none of that coming from these guys. It got into a real power play."

Another two patients described how they were rendered powerless by the lack of any real negotiating space. Marg said she was finally driven to find a way to leave her analysis.

"There wasn't any negotiation. It was his way, or no way. He was right. He was always right. That's what led to the stalemate. In the end there just wasn't any space for me. And then I became preoccupied with how am I going to leave? How am I going to get away from this guy?"

Greg described a powerful somatic response to feeling blocked from constructive work because there was no ability to negotiate.

"For long, long stretches it became really, really hard for me to do anything much, and I felt I had physical symptoms. My body was leaden, heavy, and very difficult to think. 'Was I able to talk about that? Was that possible?' Yes. But I never got anything out of it. I didn't have any space for negotiation. No space at all . . ."

He later came to the belief that "I suspect he [the analyst] is cruel", which relates to an earlier remark by Greg about wondering whether his analyst had a "masochistic" streak in him.

As illustrated above, these patients used powerfully descriptive terms such as "cruel", "abusive", and "pathologizing" when describing very different experiences with their analysts around flexibility and negotiation. An example of what Tony perceived as "abusive" was related to the time he confronted his analyst over falling asleep, "even snoring", during one of their sessions:

"I came to the next session pretty angry and said 'What was going on there?' He put it back on me which I thought was abusive. He said 'Maybe you need to ask yourself what it is about you that puts people to sleep', and I said, 'I'm not having anything of that . . .'"

He said that with analysts pathologizing people, they can always turn it around and put it back on the patient because of their position of power, adding, "But that doesn't mean it's the reality."

Giving meaning to these experiences

Patients' perceptions of their analytic experiences ranged from very enriching and liberating to highly unsatisfactory; in the latter two cases, leading to the premature termination of the analysis, including one patient who had two separate experiences, each lasting two years. Thirteen of those interviewed were working in a psychotherapeutic field, but all eighteen patients indicated some sophistication in their thinking about psychoanalysis and its theoretical implications. In this discussion, I decided to combine the different themes presented here into two broad areas related to the quality of engagement between analyst and patient, and the analyst's use of silence and position of authority as experienced by the patients. These two broader areas seemed to encompass the other themes.

The quality of engagement

The patients have produced some very interesting thoughts about what they considered essential to facilitate a good analysis, and convey that evidence of listening is imparted through feedback. They spoke of how they would have liked their analysts to indicate, by accurate responses, that they were really attuned to both their verbal communications and emotional states, and able to work with whatever arose in the sessions. This attunement by the analyst is supported by Chused (1992) who states that to convey an emotional presence, "the major connection to the patient is through the medium of understanding" (p. 294). The patients also expressed the need to be "contained", "held", "supported", "understood", and "cared for", all those important qualities which are defined by the Kleinian concepts of Bion's (1959) "containment" and Winnicott's (1960) "holding environment". By their usage of these terms, the patients demonstrated that they understood something of their expected function in the analytic process. Sig expressed this succinctly when he said that he thought neither of his two analysts understood the "importance of being held or contained".

These theoretical concepts of Bion (1959) and Winnicott (1960) seemed to be used interchangeably by the patients, but, while they do overlap, they have slightly different meanings. The essence of Bion's concept of containment, growing from Melanie Klein's theory of projective identification, is that of a transformative function. Bion described how a mother in a state of reverie (Winnicott's concept, 1956) is able to receive the infant's projections and hold them in an accepting and non-persecuting way. In so doing, she enables the infant to experience an external object, mother, who is not feeling as he/she does: for example, terrified. The mother's response to the infant from an empathic position, not terrified or pushing the feelings back into him/her, but understanding them, changes the infant's own experience.

Bion (1959) compared this to an important function of the analyst, in which he/she would have a similar capacity for reverie, with the presumption of being able to tune in to the patients' needs and, thus, find a way to transform their traumatic experiences. The quality of the reverie is crucial for patients to feel listened to and understood.

Expressed in a different way, but with similar connotations, is Winnicott's (1960) concept of a "holding environment". Winnicott writes of a need for a facilitating environment, of holding the infant, not just physically, but in the mind, by a mother who is not perfect, but "good enough". This holding enables development and growth emotionally as well as physically. Modell (1976) described this as "an evocative metaphor for the human environment" (p. 289), which can be adapted to certain aspects of the analytic situation and the analytic process.

In relation to the analytic function Winnicott (1963) stated,

> The analyst is holding the patient, and this often takes the form of conveying in words at the appropriate moment something that shows that the analyst knows and understands the deepest anxiety that is being experienced, or that is waiting to be experienced. [p. 240]

Modell (1976) elaborated further when he said, "The holding environment provides an illusion of safety and protection, an illusion that depends upon the bond of affective communication between the caretaker and the child" (p. 290).

These concepts of holding/containing functions would seem to be integral to every analysis, so that the patient, within the creation of a thinking space, has the freedom to introduce and explore any issues and expect the undivided attention of their analyst, in a similar manner to the mother "in reverie". By offering meaningful interpretations that address the painful experiences brought by patients, the unknowable and unthinkable thoughts can be transformed into something bearable and creative. While some patients described this sort of containment, others were aware that a containing environment could not be taken for granted.

All patients valued the physical setting and regularity around time and sessions, presided over by the analyst, but, while helpful to a certain degree, this was not considered enough in itself. Rick, for example, remarked how his analyst provided the opportunity for him to make sense of his life, but "nothing more helpful" than what he could possibly have done "with someone who wasn't an analyst", or if he merely "sat in a corner and did my own thing". He conveys little evidence of having experienced his analyst's holding or understanding of his inner world in the sense of the mother/analyst who holds the infant/patient in mind and makes meaningful links to the communications, both verbal and non-verbal, as expressed by the needy infant/patient self.

Rick's comments about feeling "unconnected" to people for most of his life, and finding the same experience with his analyst, highlight an important issue around the patient's hope for a re-creation in the transference of a new relationship, one in which he could make a "connection". As described in his analysis, it seemed, however, that Rick experienced his feelings of no connection to people in the real world to be repeated in the transference–countertransference, rather than being able to be thought about and worked through to a satisfactory resolution.

Other patients talked about the freedom they gained from their analytic experiences and the analyst's capacity for allowing "all the madness to start tumbling out", as expressed by Kerry. They identified as highly significant the provision of a reflective space, which enabled the exploration of personally difficult and intimate problems affecting their lives. The continuity of sessions, with the knowledge that the analyst would still be there the next day, and the possibility of continuing the working through at one's own pace, was also experienced as empowering (Rosa), and facilitative of constructive regression and working through (Jenny). Unlike Rick, who seemed to describe essentially a "presiding" function by the analyst, the two patients mentioned above were able to present their analyst as providing a healing function, the transformative containment espoused by Bion (1959), which offered much more than merely the provision of the time and space of the fifty-minute "hour". They described the intense experiences of being held and understood through the "incredible terror and despair" (Carmel), as though he was "actually in my world" (Audrey), and feeling "teary that someone could be there and recognize what you were going through" (Ruth).

A common thread throughout these experiences was the patients' own endeavours to engage with their analyst. Their narratives demonstrated the numerous ways in which they attempted to reach out and make a meaningful contact. Some patients expressed how they were responded to in very positive and enriching ways, but others were left with feelings of "mediocre" non-engagement, or what appeared to them as a "critical" or "punitive" silence.

Tony stated how he spent a lot of time "trying to get him [the analyst] to understand my world", finally deciding that this must be the way of all analyses, that the patient fits in with the analyst's agenda and "it's not negotiable". Sig described his frustration at the interpretations being disruptive, rather than connecting and making sense with his expressed thoughts and emotions. Feeling misunderstood, he described how he found that, as both his analysts could not "manoeuvre" around him so he could use them constructively, he tried "to manoeuvre around them" in order to initiate the engagement, but felt he could not do that either. Casement (2002) writes that it is necessary for the analyst to know how to engage. "Even such a small difference in how the analyst puts an interpretation can make a big difference to a patient, and can go quite a long way towards either fostering the analytic alliance or undermining it" (p. 20). This observation of Casement's is also reminiscent of infant observation studies, where the infant often tries so hard to attract the attention of the mother and engage with her in multiple ways.

Other experiences of engagement were described by Kerry and Lucy, both using metaphorical language. Kerry spoke of her relationship with the analyst as "kind of like fighting, then musing together". She related the "extraordinary" experience she felt it to be when they were "working really hard, journeying into the madness together". Lucy attempted engagement with her analyst by "flirting" with him "like a lover". His response on these occasions provided for her "a special moment of engagement in an otherwise horrible experience". Marg also talked about her attempts to engage by using humour. "The only thing I thought I could do was make him smile."

While the above-mentioned patients described their often desperate efforts to engage with their analysts, Jean described something different. She talked about the way she did her best to avoid connection, and metaphorically said that they would "dance around each other". From Jean's description, it seemed that her analyst was aware of this attempt to skip away from painful issues, and did try to get her to engage with him in spite of her avoidance. As she explained, "He would say that and I'd dance over here and I'd dance over there." In spite of Jean's attempts to disconnect, her metaphor of dance does conjure up a sense of working together in an almost playful way.

Steve initially sought therapy, and then analysis, to deal with issues around anger, sexuality, and his relationship with his father. He was quite sophisticated in his thinking, and wanted to work with powerful emotional feelings. He said that he wanted to pick the brains of someone who could come up with insights that he was unable to make about himself. Instead, he reported that he was faced with a relating style where the analyst said "very, very little", engaging with him directly in a very "minimal" way.

> "What he was trying to do, I presume, was to free me up from the professional, intellectual side of myself and have me there as a psychological, emotional being, free from the need to engage in discussion about the interpretation. But, nevertheless, I went in as a person carrying all those things with me . . ."

In reflecting on his overall experience, Steve has described how he felt his personal needs were unmet, although he believed that the analyst was a skilled clinician and one whom he liked personally. However, it seems that Steve believed that the analyst's focus was on building the therapeutic relationship rather than working through the particular issues he brought to the analysis.

The analyst's use of silence and position of authority

Interpretations made by the analysts were assessed by the patients as to their fit, their flexibility, their use of language in "lay" terms that could be understood by them, and also how the interpretations were delivered, as, for example, Jenny's statement about an interpretation which was given "with sensitivity or shoved down my throat". Patients believed that interpretations were applied dogmatically and without sensitivity to how they were feeling at the time. They described how these interpretations could block the constructive working through of difficult issues, or even "foster disintegration", as stated by Jenny, and, in Steve's experience, led him to becoming "quite emotionally destabilized".

Working with the patient's transference is the major part of all analytic work and, by its very nature, produces periods of varying states of distress and regression. However, there was such diversity in these experiences that I argue that the analyst's particular personality was what generally influenced his/her analytic function and made the difference.

Patients spoke of some of their experiences in terms of the analyst as a human person with personal characteristics in evidence, and which could not be explained merely as applying theoretical technique. This notion is supported by Abend (1989), who stated that it made little sense "To suggest that analysts' emotional reactions to patients are ever simply realistic, or for that matter, merely accurate responses to the patient's material, wholly unaffected by the analysts' own past and particular psychic makeup" (p. 387).

A large proportion of the patients, for example, discussed reports of the analyst's use of silence. While Kate was able to say that, at times, it could be "incredibly powerful and help me go deeper", generally patients experienced silence by the analyst as prolonged, problematic, and causing an impasse in the analytic work.

Silence is an integral part of analytic treatment and performs specific purposes for both analyst and patient. According to Hadda (1991) there has been a real paucity of literature devoted to the meaning of silence in psychoanalysis. Most of the attention recorded, however, has been to its usage by the patient. Given that this is an exploration of the patient's experience, I have focused on the analyst's use of silence as described here by the patients. However, it is important to look also at some of the analytic thinking about the patient's use of silence.

Considered as a communication from the patient, which needs to be interpreted like all other communications, silence has generally been assigned the two major functions of reflection or resistance. It is also depicted as active and capable of changing aspects of the analytic process (Hadda, 1991). Over the years, many other interpretations have been made about the patient's silence, for example, as "self-punitive" (Loomie, 1961), or "the most effective tool at the disposal of the patient to stimulate transference" (Arlow, 1961, p. 51).

Greenson (1961) describes how powerful emotions can be expressed in the silence "wordless but not soundless . . . In such extreme emotional situations the complicated ego function of verbalization is lost and only the more primitive function of noise production is retained" (p. 81). Greenson added that the analyst could miss the importance of a silent communication by expressing frustration or disappointment, which he believed is picked up by the intuitive patient. Winnicott (1958) discussed silence in the context of the mother–infant relationship, and stated that any disturbance in the early developmental stage would have important implications later for the patient's capacity to be silent in the presence of the analyst.

To return to the patients' assessments of the analysts' use of silence, the majority of patients implied it was over-utilized, and some found it "persecutory", "unproductive", leaving them in states of "anger" or "depression", and feeling that they were "wasting time and money". These statements would seem to depict a very clear message from the patients about silence, in general, being used by the analysts as withholding; and, for the patients, its purpose was very difficult to understand.

Loewenstein (1951), in writing about the important role of speech, stated,

> The analyst's silence has not only the effect of encouraging the flow of associations but, at certain moments, has an important dynamic effect on the patient . . . The gain of insight, however, is

limited if the patient is merely left to associate and is not given any interpretations. [p. 3]

This seemed to be the experience as described by most of these patients. Simon, Jenny, and Rick spoke of very long periods of silence which were experienced as disabling rather than facilitating any effective communications from them; the silence left them "hanging". Marg used very powerful words to describe the analyst's interpretative style and use of silence as "lacerations", while Kate talked about feeling "stuck" and then becoming too depressed to speak to break the silence.

Linked with the patients' descriptions of silence as not always being used in a helpful way were issues related to their understanding of a power differential between themselves and their analysts. Some patients discussed how they experienced their analyst as adopting an "authoritative" style, which they believed left them "no room for negotiation". Min's story of the capacity in her analyst to listen and be willing to respond to her request was markedly different from Tony's story of his futile attempts to negotiate issues related to payment. Tony spoke of an inflexibility in his analyst about payment that he experienced as frustrating and causing further anxiety. These are practical issues that usually can be negotiated between patient and analyst, as they are not specifically related to psychoanalytic technique, or based on a particular theory. So, how can we think about the difference between such experiences as Min's and Tony's?

It could be conceived that the approach of Tony's analyst was based on his own particular personal agenda, a countertransference that was unrelated to the patient's actual financial situation and request. Min's analyst was able to forgo the common practice of using a couch, which allowed her patient to experience working in a flexible relationship where she could feel it was at her pace. Min subsequently felt recognized as a "patient partner", rather than a "patient victim", whereas Tony was left with a sense of not being understood in "his world" but, rather, having to fit in with what he perceived as an inflexible structure which did not allow for any negotiation. Kerry presented a very different picture when she attempted a similar negotiating power with her analyst around financial issues, and, thus, was able to exclaim, "Pretty good!"

Kerry's statement indicated surprise and pleasure at a noticeable difference in the way her analyst, facing a particular financial difficulty for the second time, was able to really hear her concern and negotiate a more equitable outcome.

Greg volunteered information about a non-negotiable analytic setting, and described how he developed unpleasant bodily symptoms of feeling "leaden, heavy, and very difficult to think". His experience of long stretches of time like this left him powerless to negotiate anything, and with subsequent thoughts that his analyst was possibly "cruel". Steve described how he tried to access information about the expected length of time in analysis, anxious about getting caught up in a "life-long event". Receiving no satisfactory answers, he painted a graphic picture of despair, describing a "kind of black hole" from which he felt he would "never emerge", and became "quite destabilized". Sig's experience was not dissimilar when he stated that he felt forced into situations where there appeared to be "no willingness" to assist him.

In thinking about Steve's dilemma of feeling he was being trapped into some "life-long event", it would not seem inappropriate for the analyst to give some response, even if to state the unpredictable nature of psychoanalysis in relation to time commitment. Strupp (1978) noted how remarkably honest Freud was with patients and how he advocated the same honesty in analysts preparing patients for psychoanalytic treatment. In relation to the question asked "how long?" Freud (1913c) stated,

> Psychoanalysis is always a matter of long periods of time . . . longer periods than the patient expects. It is therefore our duty to tell the patient this before he finally decides upon the treatment. I consider it altogether more honourable, and also more expedient, to draw his attention—without trying to frighten him off, but at the very beginning—to the difficulties and sacrifices which analytic treatment involves, and in this way to deprive him of any right to say later on that he has been inveigled into a treatment whose extent and implications he did not realize. [p. 129]

The experiences presented here are, of course, narrated by one partner in the analytic dyad, and we have no access to the analyst's point of view. They could also be influenced by the patient's transference of powerful earlier relationship patterns to the treating analyst. However, these experiences were not individual episodes, but reported by several of the patients and also described as enduring over long stretches of time. As raised in the previous chapter, it does seem that the analysts' personality has a profound impact upon their particular style and technique of working, and, in some cases, as presented here, has precluded an adequate engagement in the two-person relationship. This has led to such diversity in the analyses to the extent that some patients are left at the end with an "extraordinary experience of having been liberated", while other patients talk about a "mediocre stew experience", or prematurely walk out after two years.

The following statement by Abend (1989) supports this argument about personality or human qualities influencing analytic technique. He writes,

> There is no analysis in which issues concerning patients' attitudes and fantasies about authority, expertise, and equality, or assertions of and denials of real and imaginary differences do not play an important role ... If [the analyst's] theoretical preference or predominant character structure bias him or her in one direction or another his or her analytic capability will be compromised accordingly. [p. 389]

Other analytic writers have also written about the impact of what the analyst brings personally to the analytic process. Adler and Bachant (1996) claim that it is "a given" that the analyst's personality contributes to his/her construction of the analytic situation, and again, in 1998, they discussed how patients can be perceived by their analysts through "tinted lenses" coloured by their own personal conflicts, childhood upbringing, and phantasies. Similar issues are raised by other analytic thinkers (Gray, 1982; Greenberg, 1991; Greenson, 1967; Renik, 1995). Adler and Bachant (1998) stated that the analysts' views are "communicated in every decision the analyst makes, from how to intervene and when to be silent, as well as in the tone, tension, and timbre of every utterance" (p. 473).

In relation to the ongoing struggle for engagement by the patient with the analyst, and supporting the patients' experiences as narrated here, I quote from Adler and Bachant (1998),

The analyst's availability as a sustaining source of emotional connectedness, containment, and support to patients during their efforts to change is often crucial. This availability, ultimately an expression of the analyst's own capacity for love and commitment over time, is communicated in countless ways: It is palpable in the analyst's attention to developing a partnership with the patient, a joint process that is continually informed by the goal of fostering the patient's autonomy. [p. 458]

The following chapter will present further examples around the theme of powerful transferences to the analyst as "father".

CHAPTER FIVE

The paternal transference*

"I was able to go away and be angry with him or sort of put him down in a way that I didn't feel like my father would be able to survive ... He just managed it and handled it and kept bouncing up"

(Paul)

"I said, 'I don't think you are fostering the kind of relationship that leads me on to be more open, more willing to use your interpretations. I feel like in a way you are repeating the relationship I had with my father'"

(Sig)

I n the previous chapter, I introduced the emergence of a central theme involving the patients' relationship with their fathers, which was then re-enacted in the transference to their analysts.

*Paper presented at the IPA Congress, Berlin, July 2007, as part of a panel discussion on "Father Hunger", and submitted for publication to the *International Journal of Applied Psychoanalytic Studies*, August, 2010.

While some patients presented significant issues to do with their fathers as part of their reasons for seeking analysis, with others this relationship only became apparent throughout the analytic process. Thus, I became interested in exploring this as a particular theme. The most useful way for me of thinking about this was in metaphorical terms as the analyst as father, or the "paternal transference".

Two broad themes emerged: the "emotionally present" and "emotionally absent" analyst. In an analysis, the analyst is, of course, unmistakably present physically; some patients, however, described experiences in which they felt their analyst to be absent or unavailable to them. They provided illustrations that they identified with early "fathering" experiences, and said could not be worked through in the analysis. Other experiences were very different, with the patients describing their analysts to be emotionally present and highly attuned to early relating patterns with absent, weak, or punitive fathers. This analytic work was productive and liberating.

In seven of the eighteen narratives, the analytic experiences were lived out almost totally in the transference to a father figure; thus, I describe these in some detail. I also include two other experiences of patients who, elsewhere, have expressed feelings of overall good analyses, but nevertheless provided illustrations of dissatisfaction in working with anger issues to do with their fathers, and which they felt they could not deal with satisfactorily in their analyses. I have called this the "not good enough" analyst.

The "emotionally present" analyst

Kerry described how she entered analysis in crisis following two unhelpful and "nightmarish" therapeutic experiences. Through her analysis, she discovered she was carrying a lot of guilt from memories to do with her father's death, from cancer, when she was five years old. He had been nursed at home and, during his last six months, Kerry was sent to live with grandparents. She described how she then experienced powerful feelings of "survivor guilt", accepting the loss of her father and abandonment of her family as being her fault; she believed that she should have taken responsibility for caring for the family. This guilt was compounded by other feelings of wanting to hang on to her father, but at the same time feeling that she should not do so. This experience and her previous one, related to sexual abuse by an uncle (Chapter Three), were part of the unfinished business she brought to her analysis; they became central issues.

Kerry described her father's death as a "gross kind of land-mark". When Kerry was aged two, her mother was hospitalized and absent for six months; then, after her father's death, she experienced a mother who became emotionally absent. Kerry talked about this as a generational problem. "A lot of loss and separation and uncontrollable absences of parent, something I'm sure that I generationally carried."

Stability in the analysis thus became extremely important. Kerry wanted her male analyst to fulfil both parental roles and have the capacity to work constructively with powerful issues of attachment.

> "I constantly had this little phantasy that I wanted to be put in his pocket. I wanted to live in his pocket, and would love nothing more than to curl up and stay in his pocket. So I'm sure there was stuff about being close and being held."

Memories of father emerged through Kerry's powerful projections on to her analyst within the transference.

> "For several months I had this idea that he was getting thinner and I was very worried about him. I kept looking at him suspiciously when I arrived, to check for signs of colour and stuff. I had images of him in flannelette pyjamas, very weak. What came out was this incredible contempt I got for him for being so weak and useless, that he couldn't pick anything up and that he had just become really hopeless."

Other phenomena arose at the same time, which Kerry described as an incredible sense of mania, where she would be lying on the couch and would suddenly have the following thoughts,

> "I wanted to go running over the top of the furniture, run over the desk, jump on the chair, run around the room. I didn't feel destructive or anything, it was completely manic. And the aliveness of the child stuff was extraordinary."

She understood this mania to be a defensive manoeuvre away from her perception of a weak and useless father/analyst, who was phantasized as wasting away with cancer. "I think it was a state of not being able to cope with the trauma of it all, feeling like a kid twirling, making noises all the time."

In her penultimate analytic session, Kerry explained to her analyst, with feelings of sadness and regret, that she used to have a few broken belongings of her father's, which were rosary beads and a pipe. In an earlier therapeutic relationship, Kerry had given this little package to her therapist with the words, "I shouldn't be holding on to my father, I should be getting rid of him. You can take care of these things." In this current experience, her analyst interpreted that she had given away the father's belongings, not to be disposed of, but for safe-keeping. He told her they represented the brokenness of her relationship with her Dad, which she really wanted preserved. In spite of protestation by Kerry that he had it wrong, the analyst reinforced his comment with the words, "No, he's yours; you're keeping him alive inside you." Kerry found his words so liberating, as though he was saying to her, "Have yourself, have your Dad, have your own thoughts, have all the madness. Have it, it's yours. Keep it. Don't feel like you have to fix it, get rid of it, whatever".

Looking back at her analysis, Kerry remarked that she now felt so emotionally alive. She attributed the success of this experience to her analyst's sense of "being real, his kindness and integrity", and also to the creation of a playful space where she could work through the powerful projections on to him of a weak father and learn to survive the guilt. She explained how, in his transferential role as a parent and a caregiver, the analyst was also the first person who had ever played with her. "The playing mattered, which is funny really, because you are only playing with the words. But that was there, that was part of it."

When Paul entered analysis, he sought someone he knew, a male analyst, but said that at the time he did not consider the gender was an issue. However, on thinking back on his experience, he believed that he worked through far more father issues than he would otherwise have done. He considered that this was due to the particular transference relationship with the analyst, and because he was male. He described his father as a weak and passive man for whom he had always needed to take full responsibility, and initially he perceived his analyst in a similar way. The analyst's response to his anger, however, was very different. He demonstrated the capacity to deal with Paul's expression of strong emotions without repeating the experience of a passive, weak father; he was able to withstand the attacks and survive.

> "Because he was the way he was, it really fitted the image of my father perfectly—the nice, gentle, weak man. I went through a stage when I thought he was really useless, and he was able to hold that and manage very well. He really tuned into my father issues and that was good. I think it was my transference on to him that he was not good enough and he was able to survive that. He just managed it and handled it and kept bouncing up."

Paul also talked about how he felt he had incorporated the analysis rather than being left feeling that he was dominated by it. His analyst would often make an interpretation around this theme, asking whether he was doing it for himself or for the analysis. Paul linked this to the experience with his father. "That was part of my father; the sense of duty and sacrifice, or guilt for going off in my own direction."

In her analysis, Audrey, too, spoke of the capacity of her analyst to help her think differently about the relationship with her father. Prior to commencing her own treatment, she spent several years devouring books on psychoanalysis, with a particular focus on the relationship between mother and child. She felt the relationship with her own mother had been problematic all her life. Depression finally led Audrey to seek analysis for herself, saying that she now believed she had a real reason to pursue it. What then emerged for her as a central issue was the working through of her relationship with her father. For this to occur, she gave considerable importance to the gender of her analyst.

> "I wouldn't have needed another woman to join me in matching my father. I needed to say to a male, 'typical bloody male', but have that sort of somehow heard and respected. If I had someone saying 'Oh yes bloody me', I would have just wound myself up into another frenzy. Instead, I had a male who heard what I said, and could actually inject another perspective in, a bit more reality, a different reality."

This experience was very helpful, and enabled Audrey to challenge her earlier thinking about men. She stated that her analyst's way of working through the "father" transference, and not colluding with her, provided a very important boundary.

Jean entered analysis with several personal issues precipitated by the death of her mother. She particularly chose a male analyst, as she wished to explore problems she was experiencing with men. She also talked of a father who treated her very badly. When she completed her analysis six years later, she felt that the freedom to be honest and talk about anything was one of the most important aspects of her experience.

> "I've always been burdened—felt this heavy burden of my parents and their personalities and their parenting. Even when ten or twelve years old I used to think I would only be free when they were dead."

Jean reflected on how, through the analysis, she came to the realization that her parents could die and she still would not be free. This was an important issue she had to work hard on for herself. With regard to problems with her father, she said,

> "I wanted to stop being crushed, emotionally crushed. I wanted to move on. I would be all right, then my father would say something to me, or treat me badly. My whole world would just disintegrate. It was so easy to be crushed and I wanted to be more resilient than that. I wanted to actually build up my life."

Jean then described a really positive and different experience with her analyst, emphasizing his unbelievable stability, reliability, and consistency. The acceptance of her when she would say the vilest things to him was so unlike her father. Proclaiming that it was difficult to articulate, she added that she was able to say the vilest things and her analyst "wouldn't bat an eyelid"; when she discussed the preposterous things that had happened in her life, her analyst would say something like, "yes, that was preposterous", or "that was outrageous, that was way out of bounds". This was so good to have her reality acknowledged and hear him say "that's not on". By the end of her analysis, Jean felt that it had totally turned her life around.

Early assumptions among writers were that the gender of the analyst did not matter. This notion was based on Freud's "impossible" dictum that analysts be trained to work as a neutral "blank screen" in order to facilitate the re-enactment of past relationships within the present context. There was a belief generated that the actuality of the analyst was irrelevant to the analytic process (Appelbaum & Diamond, 1993), and, thus, until the 1970s, the importance of gender was never really confronted. One of the primary reasons given in the literature was that most papers depicted narratives of female patients with male analysts, while women analysts treating men were severely under-represented (Gornick, 1994). A reluctance to grapple with the question of gender-related significance was reported to be based on fears that the analyst's gender might provide some advantage and that the transference could be threatened by acknowledgement of the impact of reality factors (Gornick, 1994; Karme, 1979). Interest in gender-related issues, however, gradually began to emerge with prominent analytic writers (Chasseguet-Smirgel, 1984; Goldberger & Evans, 1985; Lester, 1985; Mitchell, 1974, Person, 1985; Samuels, 1985). Added to these is the interesting American study by Mayer and De Marneffe (1992) (reported in Chapter Two)

This change in thinking led to a new focus on the interaction between patient and analyst in the curative process (Gill, 1982; Anastasopoulos & Papanicolaou, 2004) and, with this, an increasing acceptance of the real characteristics of the analyst, such as gender and personality, in the therapeutic interaction (Appelbaum & Diamond, 1993; Kulish, 1984) and rejection of the analyst as a blank screen (Kulosh & Mayman, 1993). Some writers have even argued for gender playing an essential role in the transference–countertransference relationship (Chodorow, 1989; Gornick, 1986; Kalb, 2002; Kulish, 1984, 1989; Lachmann, 1992; Person, 1985). These articles address substantial differences in the female analyst–male patient relationship, such as the pre-Oedipal maternal transference, the possible defensive uses of the erotic transference, and the merging of aggressive and sexual impulses (Gornick, 1986). Other writers, however, have continued to reject the relevance of gender, as, for example, Brenner (1992), who claimed that the most important factor was the therapist's personal maturity, which enabled a patient, male or female, to feel comfortable with an analyst of either gender.

With many of these patients, the gender of the analyst was, in fact, identified as what generally made the difference. Each one who spoke about working through "father" issues to a positive outcome attributed much of this to the analyst being male. For example, Audrey declared the male gender to be crucial, while Kerry and Paul signified the importance of being able to work through past relationships with a "weak and useless", or "gentle, weak" father in their transference to male analysts. When listening to Kerry's story, I think her analyst also had the maturity (Brenner, 1992) to hold the dual transference of a very primitive quality, which enabled his patient to remember, repeat, and work through to a very different outcome from her childhood days. She was able later to exclaim with amazement about the learning that took place, and cited personal qualities in her analyst that she found so liberating, rather than experiencing an analyst who demonstrated adherence to a rigid, theoretical system.

The "emotionally absent" analyst

The relationship has always been fundamental to the ongoing analytic work but is now generally considered as the most important element of any analytic/psychotherapeutic treatment (Anastasopoulos & Papanicolaou, 2004). Psychological understanding leading to development within the patient requires the presence of an analyst in tune with the patient. "When the analyst is not emotionally present and available there is a certain level of connection that simply will never occur, and a certain level of work that may never be possible" (Ehrenberg, 1996, p. 281). Interpretations are not always effective, as was recounted by Audrey. She described how it was the analyst's personality and innate qualities that held her together when she was feeling so unwell during the early stage of her analysis. Her experience demonstrated the importance of an environment where initially she could feel emotionally nurtured. If this does not occur, the patient needs to construct defences to overcome the lack of his/her own internal resources and soothing mechanisms.

Three patients described experiences which, to them, demonstrated an "emotionally absent" analyst, and one with resemblance to their own fathers. Tony cited "personal" reasons for entering analysis, and raised serious issues to do with an uncomfortable relationship with his father, whom he described as "very traditional and non-nurturing". He said that from his father he had inherited an inability to talk about feelings, which had had an impact on most of his life.

> "My father would probably only talk to me when he had me alone, like driving in the car if there was a distraction or something. But if we were sitting alone in a room we would both feel very uncomfortable."

As his story unfolded, Tony explained that he had developed the same transference to the analyst as his relationship with his father, which was "very superficial and quite cold". He referred to his wife's experience of a nurturing analyst, and said that he was never conscious of nurturance in his own analysis. He suggested that his analyst might have tried to be caring, but that his prior experience with a non-nurturing father probably hindered his own capacity to be receptive. His comment resonates with those of patients who tend to see failures in an analysis as their fault (Casement, 2002). Tony explained how the analytic sessions felt like a repetition of his sitting alone with his father. "We [father and he] never really talked that much, so maybe that was part of the problem with the analysis."

One of his big issues, which has been referred to in the previous chapter, was feeling that he did not have the strength to negotiate anything. He provided an example of a time when he felt quite unwell and wanted some acknowledgement of this from his analyst.

> "I was in a lot of pain and I still kept going to my appointments. And I didn't feel I could negotiate anything around that . . . I wanted him to actually say to me 'You are very unwell'. I wanted him to nurture me. I suppose I was trying to turn him into a mother that way and I wasn't that successful."

Tony uses words denoting a maternal function, implying the wish to be held, contained, and/or listened to in a way he had not experienced in his family environment. Perhaps he was also more acutely aware of this lack in his own analysis as compared to that of his wife's nurturing analyst, as noted earlier. Instead, he understood his experience of analysis to have been centred on rules: money, appointments, and missed sessions. Throughout the entire analysis, he said these were the basic issues discussed.

> "It's all quite strict and controlled and structured. Maybe that structure is there for you to have those sorts of battles around it. But it seems like they have all the rules on their side."

Providing a structure is frequently symbolized as a male function. Previously, Tony described how a battle around money figured prominently, for example, the demand by his analyst that he pay the full amount of his fee up front before claiming his refunded portion back from Medicare. These additional charges are imposed at the analyst's discretion and for which the patient must pay.

This battle about payment occurred when Tony was experiencing monetary difficulties, and led him to believe that his analyst was unable or unwilling to listen to his struggle. The payment issue had other consequences for Tony, who experienced enormous anxiety around either being late or missing sessions; he would then be required to pay the full fee, as the Medicare rebate cannot be claimed if you do not attend sessions.

> "Part of it would be that you had a fear that your analyst was some sort of all powerful, paternal figure, who was going to sanction you in a dramatic way because you didn't do what he said."

Tony linked this with his early parenting: "I think I probably had that kind of relationship with my father." However, he also reflected on his anxiety as "totally irrational", and gave an account of a specific occasion which he said had caused him to act in an atypical way:

> "Once I had an accident. I don't think it was caused by me, but I had to stop and I had incredible anxiety about being late for my appointment. The other person wouldn't have understood, they would have thought I was trying to drive off without giving my licence."

Reflecting on his experience, Tony acknowledged that his analyst could have been "quite a soft person" underneath, but there was no way he perceived that through the transference. He questioned his analyst's technique, saying,

> "For me the softness didn't come through, but I don't know whether he was working against that or something. He seemed quite traditional in the sense he didn't really say that much, and he didn't really interpret that much."

This financial arrangement with a third party can be a stumbling block, even counter-productive to treatment, as reported by Tony. It has an impact upon the actual time spent in sessions and, as a result, how much analytic time can be subsidized. The significance of late or missed sessions has received much interest in the literature (Miller & Twomey, 2000). Special attention has been drawn to the rationale for charging (Blackmon, 1993; Tulipan, 1983), its meaning for the patient (Mitchell, 1993), and the need for proper handling (Gans & Counselman, 1996). Whatever the policy decided upon by the individual analyst, there does seem a clear message that the patient can feel "traumatized and inadequately held" (*ibid.*, p. 47) by these policies. Arrangements around payment for missed sessions, therefore, require adequate discussion in the assessment stage of the analysis.

As described in these narratives, this third-party reality seemed rarely taken up and talked about, with implications for the patient's capacity for honesty and openness. The importance of exploring impingements from external parties is supported by the literature (Busch, 1997; Gabbard, 1997; Shapiro, 1997), the latter advocating that any uncertainties and limitations imposed by outside need to be brought into the analysis for meaningful transference–countertransference dynamics to develop and be interpreted

Confidentiality issues are also at risk. The patient's awareness of the probability of some reporting agreement to determine the continued eligibility for benefits has the potential to give rise "to doubts, hesitation, and conflicts, both conscious and unconscious" (Rudominer, 1984, p. 773). Unless these can be openly faced and explored by the analyst, the analytic process itself may be undermined.

I return now to other patients' stories. Sig described how he sought analysis to help understand himself a little better, be more open, and able to express feelings. He had hoped for a relationship that would differ from that which he had experienced with his father, someone with whom he could never get angry, assert himself, or disagree. He ended up having two analyses, both of which he considered failed him. The first was for two years, followed by a four-month break before commencing the second analysis, also for two years. Sig terminated prematurely with each when he felt that they did not have any more to offer him. He stated that whether it was due to their technique or his own particular personality, it was just not working. Again, this is a reminder that when there is a failure, the patient can feel that he/she is probably to blame.

> "I got around to the decision that it wasn't resistance and it wasn't just that I was having a hard time free-associating or getting in touch with my dependency or conflicts. It was more that I could feel the use of the technique wasn't facilitating my exploration of the analysis."

In his first experience, Sig demonstrated an immediate positive transference to his analyst based on external factors (see Chapter Four). His initial impression was that this was the father he had always wanted. However, by the second year, he said he felt stuck in an "impasse" where he was continually told that he was "resisting".

Sig explained how there was a period of some six months in the analysis of nearly total silence, broken only by the analyst at fifty minutes saying the session was over. When Sig did speak, he felt he was "not heard, unable to feel connected, and any interpretations were disruptive, impinging on my stream of thought". He said that it took him a couple of minutes to get his head around "what on earth the statement might mean" before he could get back into a rhythm or on track. His frustration was conveyed quite palpably during the interview.

> "I said to him, 'I'm looking for someone who can help me understand myself a little better. And I don't think you are fostering the kind of relationship that leads me on to be more open, more willing to use your interpretations. I feel like in a way you are repeating the relationship I had with my father."

A similar impasse occurred in the second analysis, which again started with positive feelings towards the analyst. After a honeymoon period of about twelve months, Sig described what he referred to as "a negative transference" again developing. He believed this to be a problem of "orthodoxy" within the analytic community, which he defined as an attempt to adhere to "a notion of technical neutrality". He reported that, in both his experiences, he felt that the analysts followed an agenda of their own at the expense of encouraging the expression of his own thoughts and feelings, again a repetitive experience with his father. He said that any of his own attempts at exploring this were not heeded.

> "Whenever I was expressing hostility towards my analysts they weren't interested in exploring this. They would always say, 'You are using this to disrupt the analysis'. So I would be left then with having to deny the reality of what was happening. And rather than make an interpretation, something like 'You're frustrated because you're not being fed well', I got the impression they would withhold from me almost like it was a power game, which was exactly the same relationship I had with my father. I couldn't express any hostility or disagree with him. He'd just say 'up your face!' This was what I was also experiencing in my analysis."

Sig recounted how, on one occasion, when he felt that his second analyst's comments had nothing to do with what he was bringing to the session, he actually accused him of following his own agenda. To his consternation, the analyst laughed at him and said, "Ha, ha, of course I'm following my own agenda." Sig felt outraged, and said to the analyst, "For one, I can't believe you laughed at me. I feel really angered and humiliated by you. And secondly, if you're following your own agenda, then what the hell am I doing here?"

He recalled clearly his analyst's response. "Look, I'm here to offer you my insights and my comments which come from my training and my experience. And if you don't find that useful, that's up to you." Sig described how these words left him feeling very angry and deflated, and that this response from the analyst was "just like my old man".

Sig was a sophisticated patient, with considerable knowledge of psychoanalytic theory and its clinical application. He had even given some thought to analytic training, but became disenchanted by his two experiences. Shortly after his interview, I learnt from Sig that he had left clinical practice and joined a musical group. This could perhaps be interpreted as a positive outcome from the analyses, or as a rebellion towards a father who could not meet his needs. Nevertheless, it does not explain the continual sense he had that these two analyses were merely repeating the relating pattern he had experienced with his "old man". In both experiences the analysts did not appear to have the capacity, or willingness, to meet the patient on his own ground. And being laughed at was not only humiliating, but led him to consider whether his position in the analytic relationship was futile. Even if Sig had, at times, misinterpreted the analysts' comments, there does seem clear evidence of unproductive work for him to have twice ended the analysis prematurely and each time after two years. The timing in itself could be significant, bearing in mind the theme of repetition, and I wondered what may have happened to Sig when he was two years old and whether this had actually been explored in the analysis.

Lucy's analytic experience revolved around seeking a "good" father. During her interview with me she became terribly distressed, demonstrating that the painfulness was still very much alive in her.

Lucy's father abandoned her family when she was very young. She described how she grew up with her sister and a mother who never recovered from the separation, "metaphorically and literally" taking to her bed with depression. Lucy became the mother/carer and "proxy" father of the family. When she entered analysis, she deliberately chose a male, and one who physically resembled her "abandoning" father: "A dark-haired man, entirely significant, because I had a very dark father and he left, adored me apparently, and then left when I was three years old."

She admitted she was knowingly "entering the lion's den", stating that there was an immediate transference, "a kind of love at first sight", and then reported having had a dreadful time. In the analysis everything from the past came up, reducing her to a constant, deeply regressed state. Lucy described the analysis as "a horrible experience", in which she and her analyst became entangled in continual verbal battles, neither of them able to work these through. "I thought that I had found my father again, that he had come back, and I was completely and utterly overwhelmed, overpowered."

Lucy spoke of an analytic relationship in which they "tortured" each other.

"I said everything to him that I wanted to say to my parents . . . I would like to have been stopped from beating him up as much as I did. Like a good father, I would have liked him to have said, 'You will not speak to me that way; what is this about?' rather than getting into a verbal fisticuff. I would say things like, 'You're an intellectual bully', and he would then say, 'Well, of course you're not'."

In response to a comment by me that she had seemed stuck in a re-enactment of her abandoning father, Lucy agreed, adding, "And I suffered like you would never know the pains I suffered." She believed that her analyst did not seem to understand what she was going through in relation to her search for "a good daddy", one who made her feel special, adding, "a strange thing, given the work he was doing." The child-self was enormously powerful within her, illustrated with the following example:

"One day one of the worst things happened. I said to him, 'I saw a leggy brunette coming into your place when I was leaving the other day', and he said, which I think was a terrible, terrible thing: 'That was my youngest daughter; what did you think of her?' Well, of course, then the whole house blew up. The world just disintegrated. And we never worked through it."

Thinking back on her experience of analysis after two years, Lucy stated,

"Most of the anger has gone, and it has settled down into a feeling of loving him. That's lovely. The pain has gone out of it. Talking to you now it's bringing it all up, but my tears now are not painful. It's more a sort of sadness, a sadness about the whole thing of fatherless-ness, and in a way motherless-ness. A bit orphaned. I feel it so, so deeply. It's like how can you comfort a paraplegic who can't walk?"

She admitted, however, that she did gain something positive from the experience. At first a little emotional, then moving into a very distressed state, she declared in a halting way,

"On the good side I felt like I've had this incredible experience that
I would have missed out on. In some ways, I feel I've had a father
through him. Not a very good father, a terribly disappointing
father. But I don't know that he could have been anything else
because I had such a phantasy built up. And I also believe, in a way,
he had to disappoint me."

Lucy demonstrated that, over time, she had developed the capacity to accept the disappointment of an analyst/father who could
not give her what she wanted; this was something she was unable
to think about when actually working with him. Her experience
seems to demonstrate what Herzog (2001, p. 34) described as a kind
of "father hunger", experienced by children who have early loss of
a father. He referred to this as an effective state of "considerable
tenacity and force" (p. 35), where the child feels a lack of something
essential in life. If the father is kept alive in the child's mind, by a
mother who reveres the memory, Herzog believed the father
hunger is lessened. Lucy, however, was prevented from loving her
father, or any memory of him as good, by a mother who constantly
put him down, telling her that he exhibited typical male behaviour.
Her attempts to benevolently hold in mind a traumatized father,
returning from the war and then unable to cope, was undermined
by this continual berating by her mother, "This is what men do to
you, what your father has done."

The experience of meeting the "leggy brunette" at her analyst's
rooms seems a clear illustration of an Oedipal wish for an exclusive
relationship with father. The analyst, by pursuing the discussion
about his own daughter, appeared to demonstrate little understanding of this desire. To Lucy's way of thinking, he was incapable
of helping her work through the special place father held in her
mind. Among the devastating consequences to a child of the loss of
a parent at the Oedipal phase, through death or abandonment, is
the creation of rivalrous triangles and the inability to tolerate attention to sibling figures during later life stages. It would seem that the
analyst working with Lucy was unable to provide the kind of facilitating environment "that tolerates the emerging wishes" (Abend,
1984, p. 93), in which Lucy's desires could be acknowledged, confronted, and worked through to a satisfactory outcome. I have
referred elsewhere (Chapter Three) to Lucy talking about her

analyst working at the concrete level, rather than the symbolic. This illustration of the Oedipal triangle would appear to fit Lucy's observation of her analyst's inability to symbolically work through her primitive phantasies.

Her strong identification with a paraplegic—one who cannot walk—demonstrates the lack of a nurturing, containing analyst who could help her face and work through the mourning process and the phantasy that if she was special she would not be abandoned. She expressed something of what she wanted from the analytic relationship, but instead was left with the repetition of her early fathering experience.

> "I wanted to love him, not criticize him all the time. I really think to do any re-enactment of this early relationship you have to be very, very skilled. And you have to have an enormously strong sense of yourself and keep it separate."

Lucy's statement about "fatherless-ness", re-experienced by her again in the analysis, and the other experiences reported by Sig and Tony, can be thought about in relation to the meaning of absence as defined by Schafer (2003). He identified four main areas in which the patient experiences the absence, in each of which the expectation is that the analyst note, explore, and interpret, at both emotional and phantasy levels:

- imagined: the analyst never speaks;
- patient addressed at wrong level: interpretations are too abstract, too complex, or not attuned to the patient, or the patient is not psychologically or emotionally ready;
- withdrawn, unresponsive, inattentive and;
- patient's oblique reference: "we are not together". [Schafer, 2003, pp. 70–74]

The psychical, emotional absence is often more keenly experienced than the real absences, such as weekends, holidays, and unscheduled breaks. Memories from these patients' early childhood experiences with fathers generated feelings that were powerfully re-experienced as emotional absences in the analytic relationship. The non-responsive and protracted silences, and the analysts' interpretations which were felt as counter-productive or with little relevance to the patients' material, were all experienced as "emotional" absences by the patients. They conjured up memories of early relating patterns with punitive and abandoning fathers.

The "not present enough" analyst

Two patients from essentially good experiences (discussed in other chapters) described an important aspect of their analyses which they felt was not usefully addressed. This was related to dealing with anger, specifically in the context of earlier relationships with their fathers. I have thus introduced a third theme of an analyst who might be regarded as "not present or good enough", although both patients were satisfied with their overall analyses.

Kate said that one of the big issues she wished to deal with was her relationship with a very aggressive, angry father, of whom her whole family was terrified. She described her father as someone not interested in her, her achievements, or whether she was good at anything.

When reflecting on her analysis, Kate said that she had mixed feelings. On the one hand, she claimed that it was very important to her personally that the analyst was a man and not interested in how she looked, but, rather, able to be in her internal world, her thoughts, and feelings. This was a very different experience from her father. However, she stated that she ended the analysis with "a hell of a lot of anger", which she felt she had never really had the opportunity to express. She wondered if it was to do with the fact that there was nothing her analyst did that made her angry enough. With a laugh, she added,

> "I mean, what can you do? Make a mistake on the invoice, something like that? And I think I needed it because it is such an issue for me that I had a very aggressive, angry father, and we were all terrified, including my mother. It is such a big issue, and I'm not sure that it really got addressed."

Kate commented on a lack of warmth in the analytic relationship, describing her analyst as "A little bit like the stone father, which is exactly what my father was like. What I admired about him [the analyst] was his brain."

The other patient, Ruth, described how her father had walked out of the family when she was a teenager, leaving her with many angry feelings towards him; she had hoped these could be dealt with in the analysis. He had himself been in analysis for several years, so there was some understanding in the family of the importance of working through issues.

Ruth talked about the wonderful experience of being listened to and understood by her analyst, providing an overall very positive experience: "There was a presence that allowed you to be in a sacred space.". However, she described how she was never able to get angry with him. She reflected on what she felt prevented any productive work, and said, "I spent my life trying to be the perfect person, this good girl."

According to Ruth, this did not seem to be noted and addressed by the analyst in a way she had hoped might happen. She explained how she was a very compliant person at heart and, in terms of her temperament, implicitly accepted the structure and framework as set out by the analyst. She argued that it was probably a transferential thing, because of the many years she had difficulty in getting angry with her father. "He left and I thought, well, I don't have much contact with him so even if I did get angry, I needed to hold on to what was good in it."

Ruth likened these experiences to her feelings towards her analyst and, with some emphasis, stated,

"I probably haven't got angry enough, because my analyst actually forgot to tell me that he was moving his practice. This had a profound impact on me. He forgot to tell me. I could have been outraged but I just thought he has probably been so busy and he has to move. I feel angry now."

Beginning to laugh while discussing this, Ruth said she probably should have been angry with the analyst at the time, but instead directed her anger towards other people.

"Because of the closeness with the transference with my Dad, I could start feeling something, but know it was really about my Dad and not about the analyst, so I would interpret it myself. But it was probably bad because I think that to enact more stuff with him might have been helpful."

In response to my comment about her appearing to pre-empt any kind of conflict, she agreed, and iterated how she just accepted the rules and, hence, prevented the emergence of tension.

"I mean, he might make an interpretation which I felt defensive about and he would pick it up and say he was making an observation. Then I would see that it was me projecting on to him my critical Dad. I would see I had taken it as judgement rather than observation."

Ruth considered that the analyst being male and close to her father's age could have aroused all the "fathering" memories, which probably would not have come up with a female analyst. She admitted that he did have qualities of a "good mother", feminine capacities which to her seemed to fit Winnicott's (1963) description of "the maternal object". But this had its own problems for her, as she felt obliged to be forgiving and compliant instead of angry when the appropriate occasion arose, such as being forgotten about in an important practical issue.

It is conceivable, with both Kate and Ruth, that a problem arose with neither wishing to disturb a relationship with an idealized analyst—maybe one whom they observed as too perfect or unable to withstand a "non-compliant" patient. They were not able to bring into the analysis a fear that their anger would destroy what they needed to keep good. This appeared to lead to a collusion in their respective analytic dyads without any challenge, a phantasy which needed to be protected and left both patients regretting a lost opportunity for some resolution to their anger.

Bringing together the main issues

I will now draw together some of the main threads under two central themes: the relevance of gender, including a contribution by psychoanalysis to role stereotypes, and the influence of the analyst's personality or human qualities on the countertransference.

Gender relevance

This emphasis on the father, compared with references to early mothering relationships, was striking. Given that there is argument for the significance of gender, and the ratio in this study was 16:18 patients with male analysts, I began to question the reasons for this "father" imbalance. I believe it could be argued that this phenomenon reflects (at least in part) the peculiarity of the Medicare funding system in Australia, already discussed. The majority of medical psychoanalysts in Australia are male, with only two exceptions at the time of the interviews. As this is the only group that receives government funding, there was, therefore, little real choice for patients who were compelled to seek out analysts with a medical background. This predominance of males could then be responsible for the father's prominence in the transference.

The literature on how fatherhood and its functions have been defined has illustrated the stereotyping of fathering and mothering roles historically, with origins in traditional psychological and sociological theories, such as role theory, social learning theory, cognitive development theory, and labelling theory. People feel and act according to the mental images they have constructed of people and events, rather than to what those people or events are really like. These images are believed to be "the truth" and not a representation of one's inner world, and can be referred to as personal constructs (Berne, 1957, p. 16). Psychoanalysis, since its inception, has contributed largely to such stereotypes, with its institutionalized, patriarchal structure. The literature provides many illustrations of how analysis has been perceived as a male domain, specifically conceptualizing women in terms of "the unconscious fantasies, wishes, fears, and longings that men have about them" (Gonchar, 1995).

From the time of Freud and other early psychoanalysts, such as Ferenczi and Abraham, the father was viewed as the central figure in mental life. With their theoretical framework essentially phallocentric, mothers and their nurturing functions were relatively neglected. After the Second World War, a shift occurred with an emerging group of female thinkers, such as Klein (1952b), Anna Freud (1952), Mahler (1958), and Bick (1968), who drew attention to the study of motherhood and its important functions. Bowlby

(1958, 1960) was also an influential thinker, with his post-war work leading to the development of attachment theory; and Winnicott's (1960) efforts with children at this time led to a body of work relating to the importance of the maternal function and facilitating environment.

In spite of this shift, some of these patients have demonstrated how psychoanalysis has continued to be structured around the stereotypical male functions, and limited the capacity of some of its practitioners to work through important issues. Goldberg (1979) has argued that the non-responsive style of psychoanalysis resonates with traditional male interaction, while Gornick (1986) described how both the method and theoretical metaphors of psychoanalytic treatment are located in the ways in which male authority is assumed (p. 300). He noted the influence of the very different cultural meanings ascribed to power and sexuality for men and women and its subsequent relationship to analytic treatment. "There are male associations to the interpretive method, such as the analogy between interpretation and penetration and the link with the usually masculine trait of intellectuality" (Gornick, 1986, p. 305). Recent psychoanalytic research, however, has challenged the belief that interpretation is the primary mutative factor (Kächele, personal communication, 2001).

The above thinking about role stereotypes, and not only by those working in the field, was substantiated by one of the speakers at the Annual Meeting of the American Psychoanalytic Association, Honolulu, May 1973 (Aaron, 1974). Marian Tolpin discussed the phenomenon she had observed in some of her patients of how she was seen by them as the "admired father imago". Reflecting upon this, she described how she came to realize the significance of "an ubiquitous tendency to idealize the parent imago's work roles", such that her valued analytic function and identity, in spite of being female, was seen as "mental activity belonging to the 'higher, wiser' father, in contrast to the mother who cares for bodily and psychological needs" (Aaron, 1974, p. 160).

In relation to Aaron's comments (1974), questions have been raised frequently in the literature about the differences between parental roles and whether fathers can have nurturing qualities, or are generally attributed other characteristics specific to the male. According to Etchegoyen (2002), the general psychoanalytic view is that of a fundamental template of a couple with differing functions. Within this perspective, the father is perceived as offering emotional support and containment to the nursing mother, responding to anxieties about the infant, and managing the practical external demands, a position which relegates father to the protector, caretaker role. He is also considered a significant figure outside the mother–infant dyad (Etchegoyen, 2002), providing a separate and different mental space for the child and, thus, identified as fostering the child's awareness of its own identity. An alternative view has been offered by Samuels (1985), who believed that while the maternal and paternal functions are different, they are not necessarily gender specific.

Lacan (1953) offered a further perspective of father, linking him with the development of symbolic thought in the child's psychic structure. He expressed the belief that it was not the actual father, but what he represented between the union of mother and child, "breaking open the collusion between the two" (cited in Target & Fonagy, 2002). Developmental psychologists have provided a more traditional view of fathers, defining their role as the "structuring of the child's inborn predispositions to activity and motility" (Marks, 2000, p. 98). Typically, the male is defined in terms of "aggression and activity", while the female is seen as "indulgent and passive" (*ibid.*).

These definitions are related to my argument, evidenced by the case material, that as psychoanalysis historically has been structured around typical male functions, it has possibly had an impact upon the nurturing aspects of the treatment and contributed to the "traditionally" perceived masculine attributes of power, status, and money, as articulated by Tony, and also limited some patients' ability to properly use the analytic experience in order to achieve both their expressed and unconscious reasons for seeking analysis. In spite of this, other patients have described very liberating experiences resulting in "life changes".

The analyst's personality

The transference–countertransference relationship, as perceived and recounted by these patients, has demonstrated either a space for the restoration of a good and liberating father, or the repetition of a punitive, angry, or abandoning father. Patients' experiences in the latter relationship with the analyst led to dissatisfaction and, in three cases, to premature termination of the analysis.

Tony described powerful issues around masculinity and the incapacity to express real feelings because of what he termed his "traditional fathering upbringing". According to him, this lack of emotional responsiveness was replicated in his analysis with an analyst perceived to have a similar temperament to his father. By the end of the analysis, Tony believed his issues had never been addressed. How might this be understood? When one goes into an analysis, a significant aspect of exploration is trying to understand one's identity and how the relationship with parents was experienced and can be worked through and reframed in a more positive way. However, the method espoused by this analyst seemed to have made it difficult for Tony to form a relationship with him that enabled the constructive working through of his important issues.

Tony's experience of his analyst's lack of support when he wanted acknowledgement and validation of his pain could also have been worked through to a more satisfactory outcome by addressing this in the here-and-now of the transference relationship. It would appear that emphasis was placed on structure, money, power, and silence, rather than a more open engagement with the patient. According to Herzog (2001, p. 10) "Being supportive and allowing for exploration are not contradictory; rather both are essential and facilitative". It could be argued that Tony's analyst followed the traditional male analytic model without being able to allow for the type of nurturing as espoused by Herzog (2001). Similar stories were recounted by patients such as Sig and Lucy, who described their analysts as adhering to strict, authoritarian models of working. This had the effect of recreating previous punitive, non-nurturing, or abandoning father experiences.

Sig presented two analyses in which both his analysts appeared not to have the capacity, or willingness, to meet the patient on his own ground; for example, there was the time Sig was laughed at for verbalizing how he perceived one of the analysts as following his own agenda instead of working with the material he, the patient, brought. This was not only humiliating, but also led him to question the futility of his own position in the analytic relationship. He likened the analyst's comments to repeating the relating pattern he had experienced with his "old man".

Sig was also baffled by the refusal of his analysts to accept the venting of his angry feelings without being accused of resistance. Again, this was experienced as a reminder of his relationship with a punitive, authoritarian father. How can this be explained? Even if Sig was, at times, misinterpreting the analysts' comments, there does seem to be some evidence of unproductive work if he consistently came away from the analytic sessions feeling as though he was reliving a power game from his early childhood. The analyst's statement of "following my own agenda" does not seem to recognize the frustration felt by Sig or the desperate attempts by Sig to make a fruitful connection with him in an attempt to understand and work through similar power plays he had encountered with his father.

Other patients' experiences, however, were very liberating and resulted in "life changes". It was these differences in outcomes, particularly with almost all analysts being male (16:18), which led me to try to understand the reasons for this. Those analysts who were described as having the capacity to work with whatever emerged in the patients' transference would seem to have incorporated not only skills and techniques based on theoretical training and clinical experience, but also portrayed specific personality characteristics. The patients depicted them as not bound by the perceived "traditional" male style of working with a focus on such aspects as structure, rules, and silence. Rather, they had the capacity to use their innate nurturing qualities with very good effect, enabling the patients to work through issues to new and positive experiences

Kerry, who felt loss and abandonment by her father, highlighted the importance of her analyst's stability. She described how he created a "play" space within which they could explore together the brokenness of her relationship with father and demonstrated the capacity to survive her transferential attacks on him as the "weak and useless father". These very powerful experiences were enabling for Kerry, who was able later to exclaim with amazement about the learning that took place, the sense of building the capacity to tolerate and contain things and not feel so victimized by them. Audrey, Paul, and Jean cited similar illustrations of human qualities in their analysts, which they believed made the difference.

According to Herzog (2001), the patient brings his/her story to the analyst for "an unravelling and reconstruction of the past as it is encountered in the present" (p. 2). The analytic aim is to help develop a fresh and reparative perspective on problematic issues narrated by the patient. This created space Herzog (2001) termed the Spielraum, or play space (*ibid.*), is conceptualized as a safe and contained place which enables deep personal pain to be expressed, accepted, and worked through in conversational style. The analytic relationship is a crucial part of this constructive work, developed through responses both felt by, and engendered in, each player, and significantly affects what does or does not happen in the analytic work. Its fundamental purpose is to help the patient make psychological changes to enable him/her to live life in a more fully human way. In the process of carrying this out, the personality of the analyst cannot be divorced from his/her style and technique, demonstrated clearly by the different experiences reported by these patients.

Conclusion

The power and predominance of this theme, as it emerged through the interviews, not only highlights the impact of gender, but, to some extent, also demonstrates the significance and reality of "father hunger". However, this is a separate study and goes beyond the limits of what I am presenting here.

These patients have talked about a particular way of relating to their analyst, influenced by their own relationship with fathers, and described very different experiences. The transference relationship is a two-way process, not just projection by the patient on to an analytic "blank screen". An exploration of central issues, which are considered to have contributed to such variation in these analytic experiences, has drawn attention to the significance of the analysts' personal characteristics, which seemed to have played a crucial role, and is supported by recent trends in the psychoanalytic literature. Their narratives have demonstrated the very powerful nature of the transference–countertransference relationship, the significance of early relating patterns which need to be understood and skilfully addressed, and the difficulties encountered when repetition occurs and the analytic task of working through does not take place.

CHAPTER SIX

Ending the analysis

"There was a sense of loss and sadness, but mostly that had been worked out. I was ready to leave . . . I worked right up until the end and that was it. So I think I felt, for the first time in my life, that I'd completed something"

(Rosa)

"I said to him, 'I know this isn't completed. I know I haven't finished, but I can't complete it with you' . . . I stayed too long. I didn't find it very useful, but I was a good little girl and stayed well over eighteen months when I wanted to leave"

(Marg)

E nding an analysis is one of the most important aspects of the whole analytic journey. It is the process by which the patient consolidates the learning that has taken place and is assisted to create the capacity for continued self-analysis. How the ending is experienced by the patient affects the post-termination mourning process and the loss of the analyst. If conducted at a stage where both analyst and patient have come to a shared understanding about the readiness to finish, the patient is enabled to move forward on his/her own by internalizing the analytic relationship. The ending can also have a crucial impact on how patients remember the entire analysis. However, as noted by Craige (2002), little is known about how analytic patients actually experience post-termination mourning. In this chapter, I present reflections on the process of ending analysis and its meaning to these patients, which then lead into the post-termination phase in the following chapter.

The time span from when patients ended their analyses to their interviews with me ranged from one having just completed to two at fifteen years. Most were between three and five years. The termination process was generally carried out by a mutually agreed upon decision between patient and analyst. A few, however, who found the analytic experience not helpful, ended it abruptly themselves, or with minimum preparation and discussion with their analyst.

Premature endings

I begin with the premature endings. Sig and Marg recounted how they left the analysis as a result of feeling "stuck".

> "It got to a position where I could no longer use them to help me, and I couldn't rely on my own resources either. I was stuck . . . And he [analyst] couldn't manoeuvre around me so that I could start using him again or his interpretations. I was trying to manoeuvre around him to try to find a way and I found I couldn't do that either. So I had to leave." [Sig]

> "I could say he wouldn't let me leave, and that was part of it because you want to be a good little patient for the analyst. So I wouldn't leave. I should have left way earlier because it had become stuck and I didn't face that he would not have the flexibility to be different." [Marg]

After finally ending her analysis, Marg felt she had stayed too long.

"I said to him, 'I know this isn't completed. I know I haven't finished, but I can't complete it with you.' I overstayed in that first analysis. I stayed too long. I didn't find it very useful, but I was a good little girl and stayed well over eighteen months when I wanted to leave."

Simon described a similar experience of not finding his analysis helpful, and chose to finish following a holiday break.

"When he [the analyst] finished his holidays I thought about coming back in the following year and then decided not to continue. I didn't think I was benefiting enough from it. So I chose to discontinue. It wasn't an agreement; it certainly wasn't anything at any stage he had talked about. I rang him during the holidays and I remember that being a very nerve-wracking phone call. It was not the done thing to speak to him outside of sessions. He asked if I would like to come in and tidy up some loose ends, which I agreed to do. And I had one regular appointment; that was all."

His reference to a nerve-wracking phone call suggests conflicting thoughts about breaking a taboo with some powerful, authoritative figure.

In an earlier chapter, I have described how Steve began to feel destabilized in his analysis and questioned his analyst as to how long he thought the process would last, feeling concerned at not receiving an answer. In relation to finishing up, he said,

"At the end of it we discontinued—I initiated that. It was quite clear the therapist wasn't happy about it, and there was always the sense that if I continued longer there was so much more to do. It was kind of like a Pandora's box. I had no intention of disclosing everything about my life—I wasn't going in for the 'warts and all' treatment. I was open to any process but I didn't ever achieve closure."

Rick thought that one of the triggers for him leaving analysis prematurely was because of his inability to develop a relationship with his analyst. Connecting with people was a crucial issue he had taken to the analysis to work with, but after two years he decided it was futile.

"It [analysis] had no impact whatsoever on the reason that I presented there in the first place, and I stayed there for some time. So the initial presenting problem had absolutely no impact whatsoever. From that point of view, it was a dismal failure. I think the relationship aspect is so vitally important because it sustains people. It is certainly what sustains me and I don't think I got that from analysis . . . And I think my desperation at the beginning at getting some sort of relief from what I was experiencing was so great that I was prepared to put up with anything. I was desperately hopeful."

Readiness to finish

Those patients with positive analytic experiences describe something very different. Kate ended her analysis feeling that major changes had occurred, facilitated in the process by her analyst.

"The lead-up to leaving was when I started to feel like my plumbing had changed. I don't know; it was just these feelings. I just felt different inside, like something had been arranged differently. And I think that was about a year before I finished."

Jean discussed how she took the initiative and gave a year's notice.

"I was quite determined to leave because I wanted to try on my own. And it was difficult to leave . . . but I just wanted to try on my own. I've achieved what I wanted to set out to do."

Rosa also felt a readiness to leave, and finished in a very positive way.

"There was a sense of loss and sadness, but mostly that had been worked out. I was ready to leave . . . I worked right up until the end and that was it. So I think I felt, for the first time in my life, that I'd completed something."

Carmel described the ending of analysis in relation to her two experiences. She explained how she felt ready to finish her first analysis after two years, but later started having nightmares again and realized she may have left prematurely. After interviewing several therapists, she once more found an analyst and one she was comfortable with. "At first I didn't want to see her [analyst], I did it out of desperation and I really liked her. I was really desperate at that point—I was getting close to not coping." This time Carmel worked through to what seemed a more timely and satisfactory ending, met with her analyst for one more session a year later, and then considered that she no longer needed further work. "While they were both very positive—I don't want to do it again", and, with a laugh, she added, "I mean it has been terrific now but the time—Oh God! . . . the ghastly pain and the obsession about your-self, not to mention the expense!"

Variations in the termination process

One of the commonly raised aspects in terminating the analyses was the amount of time it took to go through the process. Kerry described how she and her analyst set a tentative date for "finish-ing", but ended up prolonging the analysis for a further productive year.

"I was going to finish analysis after five years and then some stuff emerged—a kind of narcissistic thing that was unworked through. We were fighting a bit and I felt like there must be something going on. So I just relinquished basically; I gave up and yielded to him the idea that there was something still unworked through and I changed my mind and decided not to finish. I had the extra year . . . We actually had agreed and it was all sort of settled up then this stuff started coming out. I stayed another twelve months, which I'm really pleased I did."

In spite of some ongoing big stressors in her life, Kerry said that she was now capable of consolidating the work done with her analyst and felt so proud that she could do this without him. She also acknowledged that she herself played a significant part in the ongoing process. "It's not like it all lies in the analyst and pearls of wisdom dropped from the chair behind me. I contributed too, and what he's got is learnable. I learnt it." She described how she was able to internalize the experience.

"It was a very treasured relationship and I feel that he's always with me. All the work is internalized and I guess that it's like he's in me, but I'm him now. It's how I think and how I take care of myself and how I can look after the stuff inside. I just feel such a healthier person . . . It's really wonderful, it's exciting, and there is a whole lot more to the world."

Ruth's ending of analysis followed a similar pattern to that of Kerry's in the sense of discussing a termination date with her analyst and reaching a mutually agreed upon time. However, after the analysis had ended, she realized that she had some unfinished business relating to the separation process with her analyst which was not fully addressed. This paralleled an earlier experience with her father.

"I can see looking back now a few years on, that the year after I finished the analysis, I actually think I went into quite a reaction—something like my dad leaving. And it wasn't worked through really enough at the end and it wasn't really talked about where I kind of closed down like I did after my dad left."

Unlike Kerry, who realized that the ending might be premature and was able to ask for and stay another period of time until "it came to a natural end", Ruth felt that she was unable to discuss this with her analyst. In thinking further about finishing, she added, "We sort of came to it together. I suppose that last year going to two days was like a weaning or something." This specific reference to a reduction in sessions during the "last year", also referred to elsewhere, related to the government policy change in Medicare. (Medicare has been discussed elsewhere. In 1996, this government policy limited full psychiatric rebates to only fifty sessions per year, with 50% of the rebated fee continuing for all other sessions. This changed policy resulted in many practitioners reducing their number of sessions rather than receiving a reduction in the government co-payment.) This affected the number of rebated sessions available, thus the reduction in Ruth's sessions towards the ending appeared to occur for financial reasons rather than a decision mutually arrived at with her analyst.

Audrey described how she was the one who initiated the ending of her analysis and went through a weaning stage.

"It was me who brought it up. I think I was over the commitment, the constancy of it, after nine years. I went down to three days, I think, and I said right-o we'll start to finish, and I kind of went down and down. It was always me instigating it. But by the time I'd got to one day, he was virtually agreeing with me and that was the only time I ever remember him having any say about when I finished or how I did it. The rest, the entire thing was up to me . . . I got to the point where I could just finish. I remember that was it and I haven't been back. And I was OK about that. It was a bit weird and I thought 'Oh God! Christmas is going to be a bit . . .' But it was fine."

Two patients ended their analyses in mutual agreement with their analysts, but returned for brief periods again at a later date. Jenny described how, after about eighteen months, she felt that she had not really finished, so her analyst agreed to take her back for another year of weekly sessions, which she found very helpful.

"I sat in the chair and really used the time to work through something that hadn't been completed. But it only could have emerged after my analysis, through the relationship, and I felt I completed that with him. And we also looked back at my analysis and tied up loose ends. It was really good that year, it was really good. We were so productive, we worked so well together."

Jean's experience was slightly different.

"I left, and about a year later I went and saw him a few times because my brother was dying. And I talked to him but it wasn't analysis, it was just sitting there and talking. And then I had an appointment that I cancelled twenty-four hours beforehand and I haven't seen him since."

She added that she then felt all right, and no longer needed to see him.

The significance of endings

The importance of the termination phase, and any difficulties likely to have an impact upon the treatment outcomes, cannot be overestimated. It is advocated in the literature that this phase should take place over a long period of time, and after the patient and analyst have reached mutual agreement that major therapy goals have been attained. Researchers have considered termination as a "major psychoanalytic intervention" (Novick, 1988, p. 307), and one which arouses the new psychological tasks of having to accept the possible limitations in the treatment outcome, as well as the experiencing and working through of reactions stimulated by the separation and loss of the relationship with the analyst (Dewald, 1982). The termination phase of analysis requires the analyst to be particularly sensitive and skilled in order to allow for this process to be sufficiently worked through and resolved. However, as noted by Peterson (1998), "Because of the uniqueness of the analytic couple and every patient's specific starting point it is impossible to formulate a general theory on the ending of analysis or any all-embracing criteria" (p. 54).

Given the difficulty raised by Peterson, it is not surprising that these patients have presented very different experiences of ending their analyses. Some were able to leave feeling they had achieved very good outcomes, although the actual ending was very painful; others terminated prematurely or with little preparation, later explaining that their overall experience of analysis was unsatisfactory or even disabling, and left them with unfinished business. One patient spoke of the opportunity for a later review period on a weekly basis in which her experience was consolidated and felt completed; another said he was still finding it difficult to process the experience after fifteen years, which was quite uncharacteristic of him.

The ways in which the termination process in analysis are facilitated, with subsequent painful feelings of separation, loss, and abandonment, have become more of a focus in recent analytic literature. A broad distinction has been made by Novick (1982) between terminations that are timely, "a mutually agreed upon decision", or premature, which are "initiated by one person only" (p. 230). Within these diverse processes, he defined two forms of premature terminations: "arrived at and initiated by the analyst ... usually called forced terminations", and "that initiated by the patient, or unilateral termination" (*ibid.*).

A review of studies into attrition in psychoanalysis by Novick (1990) highlighted how premature terminations were as high as

70%, with no difference as to whether the treatment was carried out by qualified analysts or trainees (Hamburg, 1967; Novick, 1982). Novick noted that many years earlier, Glover (1955) had expressed the view that most adult cases of analysis were discontinued rather than actually terminated, leaving a form of stalemate and "creating the illusion that a unilateral decision to terminate was arrived at by mutual agreement" (Novick, 1990, p. 423). Novick drew attention to Glover's observations some fifty years ago on the negative effects of premature termination on both the patient and the analyst, which still remained a concern. It has also been revealed (Limentani, 1982) that abrupt endings occurred more often than was generally recognized, while Schachter (1992) noted that the proportion of analytic trainees who completed their analyses seemed higher than that of patients.

As I reflected upon the endings of the analyses as described here, I noted a link between most of the patients' ongoing analytic journeys and their termination processes. The patients who were most positive and described "internalized", "rich and meaningful" experiences also talked about a more mutually agreed upon termination period, where they were able to consolidate the working through to a satisfactory ending. For example, there was a "readiness to leave" in Rosa, who spoke of her analysis as a "joyous thing" which she was "taking with her" and gave her the basis for a "mind of her own", while Kate left after "her plumbing had changed", but spent a year in preparation before actually finishing with her analyst. Kerry spoke of a "treasured relationship" and feeling "much healthier". She said she and her analyst worked towards a mutually agreed finishing point, even allowing for extra time when some unfinished business unexpectedly arose and needed to be addressed.

These experiences were very different from those of the patients who felt stuck, for example, Marg, who informed her analyst that her analysis was not completed but she could no longer work with him, and Sig, who said he had to leave his second analysis because neither he nor his analyst could manoeuvre around each other. Simon also chose prematurely to finish his analysis when feeling he was no longer benefiting from it. His very abrupt termination after a holiday break, described by Simon as his analyst "asking me to come in and to tidy up loose ends", would seem to negate any understanding of the crucial importance of this phase of analysis.

Ruth described a different experience again. Hers was a mutual agreement with her analyst to finish, but later she found that she had "unfinished business" which had not been dealt with during her analysis. She also talked about a kind of "weaning" process in which the sessions were reduced for the last year, which no other patient in the research seemed to experience, or, at least, did not talk about. I wondered if this particular way of ending the analysis made it difficult for Ruth to ask for more time, as Kerry had done. The "weaning", however, was not directly linked with a negotiated move to less frequent sessions because they were nearing the end of the analysis; instead, it was contingent on a reduction in the full Medicare payments, which led to the analyst unilaterally reducing the number of sessions for financial reasons. This would seem to fit in with the concept of "forced" terminations rather than a "mutually agreed upon decision" (Novick, 1982) that is timely for both partners.

For Ruth, this change was quite abrupt, and elsewhere (Chapter Five) she spoke of how she could never respond to her analyst in anger because of her self-acclaimed "good little girl" demeanour and not wishing to displease him. The perceived "weaning process" seemed to have a negative impact on Ruth's capacity to ask for more time when new difficulties emerged for her during the termination phase; in her mind she was required to remain the "good little girl".

Experiences of premature or abrupt terminations of analysis, initiated by the patients themselves, seem relevant to Simon's views of a "frustrating" ongoing analytic experience, and those of Marg, Sig, and Rick, who also described overall unsatisfactory analyses. However, without further follow up at the time to clarify issues, perhaps the less satisfactory experiences and impressions of the analysts in question could be understood by findings in a recent study (Conway, 1999). This research indicated "that the experience of the pre-termination process may have a particular impact on how the analyst is held in mind after the analysis has been terminated" (ibid., p. 563). Could unsatisfactory and premature endings actually have contributed to some of the patients' very negative views of their ongoing experiences and perceptions of an unhelpful analyst, or was it the reverse as indicated? Whatever the answer, the termination process warrants further exploration, which Conway

(1999) and others before her (Glover, 1955; Limentani, 1982; Novick, 1990) have indicated has received little attention to date.

Where there has been recognition of a failed analysis, or what patients have perceived as unsatisfactory experiences, a recommendation to another analyst for a "review" period could be beneficial and go some way to affording closure. Casement (2002) has also suggested that if analysts themselves can acknowledge that the analysis was not satisfactory, or even a failure, it is hoped that patients could be referred elsewhere for some healing work. Termination procedures are highly significant to experiencing the analysis as a positive (or not) ongoing journey; they require thoughtfulness about, and consideration of, the painful mourning which takes place, and a timing for ending the analysis which is mutually agreed upon by both patient and analyst.

Implications of using the word "termination"

An issue that I believe is relevant to the ending stage of analysis is the actual psychoanalytic use of the word "termination", which analysts have continued to employ since the time of Freud. It is interesting to note, however, that in spite of its common usage by practitioners, the word "termination" has only just appeared in a psychoanalytic dictionary (Akhtar, 2009b).

The patients themselves did not use this terminology when describing their experiences of ending their analysis, and I wondered if this was because of the death symbolism implied by usage of the term. "Termination" has connotations to such common experiences today as the abrupt ending of a significant life event, for example being made redundant at work, or an actual death experience as in abortions. I checked the thesaurus for alternative meanings and came up with the following examples: extinction, annihilation, execution, slaughter, butchery, and massacre. These conjure up very powerful images of an abrupt and frightening death.

The inappropriateness of using "termination" has been commented on by Pedder (1988), who says, "I have felt it is a rather odd, unsatisfactory and inappropriate term for what should be a healthy developmental process" (p. 494). Berenstein (1987) has also drawn attention to the restricted meaning of this term, and says that "in a wider sense, it would include an appreciation of the analysis as a more extensive process" (p. 29). He compares the therapeutic experience of patients with trainee analysts, noting that the former is of a specific duration and with spatial and temporal limits to the mental process, which can be conceived as having no end.

Bergmann (1997) has written about the difficulty that analysts often have in bringing the analysis to a closure, and says that there is a fundamental lack in the literature in offering a paradigm for termination. In an earlier paper, Bergmann (1988) has addressed the question of how patients might perceive termination. He stated, "There is no analogue in real life to the experience of termination. No wonder that analysands so often associate termination with death" (*ibid.*, p. 137). However, he does not take up the issue I am now raising about the continued application of the word "termination" to such a significant phase of psychoanalytic treatment, in spite of the very traumatic images it can create with its reference to a "deathly" experience. The working through of this stage of the analysis and how it is understood by the patient would seem a crucial aspect of the analyst's function. I believe it is made even more difficult by the usage of such a frightening term, implying "death" or "annihilation".

Freud's paper, "Analysis terminable and interminable", was written in 1937, a year before his death. Prior to this, Freud had only alluded to this phase of treatment in 1913 (Novick, 1997). Novick commented on how it took around seventy-five years for analysts themselves to begin to think about the ending phase of analysis. His statement, "As noted by philosophers from the ancient Greek, Epicurus, to the 20th century philosopher, Wittgenstein, death is a subject that does not exist" (Novick, 1997, p. 146) seems related to my suggestion that the analytic terminology implies traumatic death experiences which cannot be thought about. So, why the ambiguity by continuing to use this term and what is its significance for both patients and for analysts? This is something that could usefully be explored further.

Conclusion

These stories have demonstrated important issues to do with termination procedures, which I believe are not always understood from the patients' perspective and adequately addressed. The analysts themselves experience something very different at the end of their training analyses; they are initiated into the psychoanalytic "family" and continue the relationship as a colleague and "perhaps even intimate friends" (Novick, 1997, p. 152) of their training analyst, while the patient must say goodbye. With little or no real acknowledgement of these differences, as "the candidate can avoid the mourning that is seen by many as the central task of the termination phase" (Novick, 1982, p.152), analysts can become unmindful of the huge separation and loss experiences of their patients. This is endorsed by Pedder (1988), who questions, "then are we not asking patients to face something that we as analysts may never, or seldom, have to face?" (p. 500).

Schachter (1992) has also commented on the multiple contacts that analysts have post-termination with their training analysts, many of which go beyond professional situations. He draws attention to Hartlaub, Martin, and Rhine (1986), who state,

> Perhaps we analyst are ill-prepared to help him [the patient] with the impact of this reality [absence of post-termination contact] because we have been silently, as it were, profiting from the effects of continuing contact without conceptualizing its nature or understanding the psychological necessity for certain experiences which go with it. [p. 904, cited in Schachter, 1992, p. 147]

Unlike the authors above, who can openly discuss this very different termination process between the experiences of patients and trainee analysts, it is interesting to note that I have found it quite a difficult area to discuss with analysts within my own community.

In the following chapter, I will focus on reflections from the patient's post-termination phase which extends beyond the immediate ending of their analysis.

CHAPTER SEVEN

Post analytic reflections

"It had the seeds of something very alive and vital. It gave me a foundation, a very good basis to the whole idea of beginning to have a mind, and a mind of my own"

(Rosa)

"Overall, when you put everything in the pot, and mix it up to see what comes out at the end, the whole experience was a kind of mediocre stew. Any good ingredients put in became lost in the process"

(Steve)

The way in which patients ended their analyses seemed generally consistent with how they later recalled their overall experiences. Ten spoke very positively about the benefits they had received; the other eight patients were more or less negative, but were still able to describe some helpful aspects which they took away with them.

Life-giving experiences

Among the many positive outcomes expressed was the capacity of the analyst to impart something to the patients that was "learnable", enabling them to internalize the experience and continue the work on their own.

Ruth, who managed to negotiate a mutually satisfactory ending, spoke of gaining "enough tools" to continue on her own.

> "It's made a profound difference. I don't think I could be doing the work I'm doing therapeutically, or manage all the complex work relationships. I don't think I would have the level of understanding that I do have or manage as easily the difficult things in the world if I hadn't had that experience. I think I would be back in a really distressed state . . . Not that at times you don't now get anxious but it just feels like life would be very hard. I feel that there has been enough resolution—that I've been given enough tools to continue the work in myself . . . It feels like a very rich and meaningful experience in my internal world that I can draw upon and feed off."

Rosa talked of a continuing struggle throughout her analysis, but, nevertheless, described it as providing a good foundation for moving forward.

> "It gave me a very good basis to the whole idea of beginning to have a mind, and a mind of my own . . . I guess it's the feeling that I was taking it with me. I was really taking it with me; it was a very joyous thing."

Kerry also described a painful experience of being brought to a state of "rawness and vulnerability", but then able to emerge from it all with a sense of having her whole self returned.

> "I think there is something about going there, being in it, like really being in it, sitting with it when you think nothing is happening, and feeling totally disintegrated and just demoralized. I don't know whether anyone else has emphasized the utter humiliation of analysis (laugh). That it is one bit of being exposed and humiliated after another, after another, after another. And the rawness and vulnerability are just hanging out there with your entrails all over the floor. And then somehow there's this kind of emerging that

comes out of the process where for me, I felt as though everything that belonged to me was given back to me, so to speak, like I'm left there with the sense of having myself given back to me."

Two remarked on the profound difference the analysis had made in their thinking and perception of the world; one patient said that it had "turned my life around", and another described considerable "psychic change" and "peace". Paul talked about the impact on his life's work, not just as a therapist, but also within the organizational system within which he consulted.

"I think what it does is a way of thinking about things, which is very profound and I very much appreciate that . . . I love the depth of the thinking involved, and the mixing of the emotional and the thinking. It's a very profound experience."

Audrey, referring to the analysis as the "best thing I've ever done", expressed its significance to her as an ongoing experience.

"I think it changed my life forever really. I don't think that I'm a different individual by any stretch of the imagination, but it has certainly changed the way I perceive the world and how I perceive others."

Jean, too, was very positive, saying that she still thought about her analysis and smiled. Although she found it "gruelling", she nevertheless was able to show appreciation. "It was terrific. It was gruelling, sometimes it was tedious, but it was good. I have improved out of sight. It really turned my life around."

Linked with the above theme of analysis helping patients with the way they think, Kate described a downside in the potential for "too much" thinking.

"I think there is a tendency to over-pathologize oneself, to just question a decision, or an interest, or something I might want to do. This constant 'You want to do that because . . .' Sometimes I've regretted completely going into analysis. You can't get rid of it once you've done it. It's almost as if you should sign a pact before you go into analysis: 'be warned, your life will change forever and you will never go back to that naïve state'."

She added that there was, however, a helpful aspect in that she did learn some things from her analyst that she was now able to use. "I can put things into a wider perspective, maybe understand myself a bit more and use that thinking that I internalized from him."

Min described a noticeable change in herself, both psychically and emotionally.

> "I have undergone a considerable psychic change in the three years, which at the beginning I didn't recognize. I think it's something very difficult to talk about and write about it . . . I feel inside now that I have a considerable peace, which I didn't have before . . . It's been a major change for me personally and I'm very happy about that."

The analyst's humanity and creativity were very helpful to Jenny and made her feel that she was a human being. She also said that the analysis had changed her life. She reflected how she had grown more positive about the experience over time, and more appreciative of her analyst's capacity to hold her in mind. She referred back to the beginnings of her analysis and his offering her the space where things could be thought about, which was so special. "It was a privilege having someone taking the time to think about my needs in such a reliable and thoughtful way."

Carmel reported that her experience was also very positive in its outcome, but from a different perspective. She spoke about not feeling so anxious and depressed now, and gaining the will to live and move forward.

> "I'm much more trusting and more able to make and enjoy life. But also I don't get depressed. I used to get terribly depressed. I really fought with depression all my life, and after analysis with my first analyst that stopped. And then with the second analyst it made an enormous difference to my professional life, a huge difference to my work as a therapist. I'm much more able to move on . . . I just feel great. I'm sure if I hadn't worked with them I'd be dead, I would have killed myself. I'm still a little anxious, but I'm more able to hold it and deal with it."

Unsatisfactory or "mediocre" experiences

Less useful experiences were spoken about by other patients. As Steve reflected upon his analysis, he seemed to have difficulty in explaining his thoughts about the process and its "unfinished' business". He described how, in the fifteen years since he had finished the analysis, his thoughts about it had never changed.

> "I was open to any process, but—I didn't ever achieve closure through that therapy. To this day I have quite a degree of ambivalence about it. The whole process has sat with me in a very odd way, in a very unfinished way. I find that disturbing for me, that I haven't really ever achieved closure . . . It's an uncharacteristic thing for me."

He added that it had "quite a negative effect", and defined the experience in paradoxical terms: a therapist "skilful" and "professional", but the process "not working".

> "It's like a lasting impression of a slightly bad taste. If I could gargle and get rid of it I would. I haven't been able to rationalize it. I felt very much at the mercy of the therapist. I was lucky I was working with a therapist who was ethical and professional and all that. But despite all his skill, and despite my own skills, I don't think it really worked for me . . . I would really like to have closure but I don't know how to achieve it."

Rick was more explicit about the "damaging" effect of his experience.

> "Certainly it had no impact whatsoever on the reason that I presented there in the first place, and I stayed there for some time. So, from that point of view, it was a dismal failure . . . In fact, I don't think it had any impact at all. What it seemed to do was open up a Pandora's Box—a whole lot of things . . . When I reflect on it, I think it was a fairly intimidating and unhelpful experience . . . I just thought that at the time I was fairly vulnerable and probably looking for someone to help. I'm not sure if that really came. That was really my experience of psychoanalysis. I think it was more damaging in some ways."

He questioned why he kept continuing the analysis.

> "I guess there must have been something because I kept going back, but there was no therapeutic benefit . . . Sitting back now thinking

about it, I think there was no relationship, there was nothing in it. When I got angry it was all just a waste of time. There were certainly times when I was very angry; there were times when I was very happy with him. But there were many occasions when I remember walking out shrugging my head and saying 'What on earth am I doing? What's this bloke doing?' The more I think about it the more I really think that experience was—unliveable."

Greg expressed similar sentiments about the analysis not being productive, and said it left him with adverse bodily symptoms.

"I think that for long, long stretches it became really, really hard for me to do anything much. And I felt I had physical symptoms. My body was leaden, heavy, and very difficult to think. Was I able to talk about that? Was that possible? Yes. But I never got anything out of it."

Lucy described feelings of being left with "a hell of an experience", similarly linked to Rick's statement about the analysis being "unliveable". She then talked about her various roles in the transference to her analyst, but nothing was worked through. She commented on how he seemed to lack the required skills to work with someone like her.

"I was everything in there, and I would go from one position to another. I would be the terrible mother, the dreadful child, the psychotherapist. I discovered that I knew absolutely nothing about men, or myself in relation to a man. Nothing. It felt like I was about one year old and I was very, very critical of him and I felt he didn't help me. I think that actually I needed someone who was much, much more skilled than he was."

Lucy recalled that at the end of the analysis, her analyst did, however, make a comment to her that she felt was quite meaningful. He said, "We haven't been able to be very good analytic partners." To which Lucy replied, "No. I don't feel like I've had it; I've had something else. I had a very, very significant relationship, that's how I feel. But I don't think I had a lot of analysis."

Here, Lucy was distinguishing between the analytic process and the actual relationship. This relates to an earlier observation by Steve about the apparent paradox of the "skilful" analyst, yet the experience of analysis "not working".

When Sig reflected on his two analyses, although he reported them as generally negative, he said that he thought his own personality may have contributed to the outcome.

"I don't think you could say with either of the analysts I had a full analysis, but that's because I felt that they didn't have any more to offer me. So, whether it was due to their technique or my own particular personality—it wasn't working."

It seems that both Lucy's admission of being "the terrible mother . . . and very, very critical of him" and Sig's statement, above, were acknowledgements that difficulties in the analysis can be attributed to both parties in the relationship through each person's "particular personality". The patients were taking some responsibility here for the problems they encountered.

Two further patients described little personal gain from their analyses. Simon expressed frustration at not really having his issues addressed but being required to adapt to the analyst's agenda.

"I found most of my experience of it was a frustrating one; it was all very much the same. I was just frustrated at the fact that I had lots of issues, and nothing seemed to get anywhere. He offered some insights and I never really felt they were leading anywhere. I often had the sense he was trying to make theories fit into what was going on."

And Tony indicated considerable ambivalence.

"I'm sure it did help me but I'm not sure how. Maybe that's because changes are more subtle than I know or on a level I'm not aware of. And it's over such a long period of time I would have changed as a person anyway, so it's difficult to say."

Diversity in what patients took away from the analysis

When reflecting in general on how their lives had been affected by the analyses, the patients described significant and quite varied experiences. Three related how what they had achieved from their very enriching experiences was "learnable". They were able to internalize aspects of the analyst's work, which Ruth said she could "draw upon and feed off", Kerry was able to take care of herself as "I'm him now", and Rosa claimed, "I was taking him with me." These patients had not only journeyed through "madness" and "pain", but had worked through issues to the extent that they could move on and take their analyst with them as a good internalized object. Jean spoke of "my life turned around", Min described "considerable psychic change", and both Paul and Audrey talked of "profound" differences in the way they now perceived the world and thought about issues.

Carmel added another dimension to her description of very good analytic work. She reported how her two analyses enabled her to survive a lifelong depression, admitting that the work had prevented her from killing herself. She makes a very significant statement in the light of increasing demands by government bodies and insurance companies for short-term psychological and/or medication focused treatments. Severe depression and suicide rates are on the increase, often attributed to the more prevalent relationship break-ups and competing societal and life demands. Patients trapped in self-harming behaviours, and fighting for survival, cannot easily be treated with symptomatic relief and quick fixes. They require the understanding and working through of pervasive and self-destructive forces in a treatment modality such as psychoanalysis, where the clinician is trained in the exploration of unconscious influences on thoughts and behaviour. This type of treatment takes time, and Carmel, who described how much she benefited, was able to express gratitude to the two analysts who kept her alive. She has also acknowledged the particular sensitivities and skills that her two analysts brought to the relationship and how they facilitated her capacity to survive.

The above experiences demonstrated significant life changes and very productive analytic work. They differed markedly, however, from those described by Sig, Rick, Marg, and Greg, who either terminated prematurely, or left their analyses with feelings such as Lucy's "horrible experience" and Steve's "mediocre stew". Two patients mentioned specifically their difficulties in leaving and how they had "overstayed" in what they described as "stuck" experiences. As clinicians, it is not uncommon to be confronted with such problems, and having to strive hard to understand what is most effective for these patients at a time when they do feel caught in unhelpful situations and relationships. Questions can also be raised about whether there is some inevitability in the repetitions that are described so painfully, because of early life experiences. Nevertheless, how these repetitive patterns are worked with does vary with different analysts, as demonstrated in these stories.

Tony's reflections about his overall experience suggest some ambivalence. "I'm sure it [the analysis] did help me but I'm not sure how ... I would have changed as a person anyway so it's difficult to say." However, I wonder if he was indicating more than this—that he needed to say the analysis helped him because to admit it was not helpful was too awful for him to contemplate. Would it actually reflect badly on Tony himself if he were to tell anyone that he spent "such a long period of time" in something that provided no good outcome for him?

I return to my earlier comment about there being three analysts each with two patients in analysis whose outcomes were consistent: two pairs described very positive transformative experiences and the working through of painful issues to a successful outcome. The patients with Analyst X stated that their experiences left them feeling "such a healthier person ..." and realizing there was "a whole lot more to the world" (Kerry), and "it was a very joyous thing ..." providing "the basis of a mind of my own" (Rosa); the two patients with Analyst Y similarly expressed positive sentiments, for example, "It changed my life" (Jenny), and "I could put things into a wider perspective" and "felt my plumbing had changed" (Kate). In contrast, the two patients with Analyst Z spoke very differently, but consistently, of experiences which left them totally dissatisfied; they described non-engagement by their analysts, in spite of genuine attempts themselves to engage. Greg spoke of long stretches of silence and being left with "physical symptoms ... body laden and very heavy, and very difficult to think" and never getting anything out of it, while Sig emphasized his position of being constantly "stuck" in a relationship similar to the one he had with his father, with no room for either to "manoeuvre around each other". This number of patients is small, but I would argue that its consistency over three pairs of patients, with the same analyst per pair, suggests these accounts are worthy of consideration.

What has emerged powerfully as the most important contributing factor to a "rich and meaningful" or "mediocre" experience was the relationship with the analyst. Key words, such as "learnable", gaining "enough tools", and "changing my life forever" demonstrated a lasting impact of the analysis on these patients; they were able to talk about major changes to their "internal" worlds and also about the way in which they could now relate to the "external" world. They reported having internalized a significant other, the analyst, in such a way that they felt now that the analyst was not only always present as a benign and helpful figure, but that they could also continue to "draw upon and feed" from him/her. These patients described analyses which had had significant impacts on their lives and which were continuing after the analysis had finished.

Other experiences, also based primarily around the patients' reflections on their analysts' personal characteristics, were likewise remarkable but for very different reasons. These patients talked about analytic experiences in which they felt "no therapeutic benefit", being "stuck" to the point of needing to terminate, and an "unliveable" or "horrible" experience. Steve described how he felt "very much at the mercy of the therapist" and was left with "unfinished" business—a "lasting impression of a slightly bad taste" which he would have liked to "gargle and get rid of". After fifteen years since completing his analysis, Steve said he still could not process the experience adequately, which was very uncharacteristic of him.

Linked with these experiences were those of patients who expressed, in quite powerful ways, how they felt totally controlled and even frightened in the relationship with their analyst. Simon spoke of a "nerve-wracking phone call", Rick recalled a "fairly intimidating experience", Lucy described being "completely and utterly overpowered". These patients reported how they were unable to find a way to connect and sustain a meaningful relationship within which they could do productive analytic work. In contrast, Jean could describe how "gruelling" her experience was, yet it "turned her life around", while Kerry with her "rawness and vulnerability hanging out there with entrails all over the floor" could exclaim at the end, "It's wonderful, it's exciting, and there's a whole lot more to the world."

Analytic qualities perceived as lacking

The difference in these experiences is profound, with the working style and technique of the analyst presented as a central issue. Some of their comments reflect what they felt was missing in their respective analysts which could have provided a more constructive experience for them. Lucy said she needed someone "much, much more skilled" in order to contain her outbursts as a "terrible mother and dreadful child", which she admitted she transferred to the person of the analyst. Kate would have preferred her analyst not to over-pathologize and question her decisions, to the extent that she sometimes regretted having gone into analysis. Simon considered that he had to "adapt to the analyst's agenda", which appeared to him to be based around theory, rather than having his own personal issues addressed. Rick described feeling "very vulnerable and looking for help", but being left in an experience that felt "more damaging" than the difficulties which had led him into the analysis. Other patients described prolonged silences that did not convey a listening presence, with the addition of interpretations perceived as "lacerations" or with no relevance to the material presented. These were among the general criticisms expressed by concerned patients.

Both Steve and Lucy implied an interesting distinction between their analyst as a person and the actual process of analysis. Steve reported that he would recommend his analyst, who was still on his preferred list of practitioners, but he would not recommend the analysis itself because of it being a "damaging experience". He described how he perceived the person of the analyst to be affected by a theoretical model of working which prohibited the analyst from doing useful work with him, yet the analyst's personality shone through enough for Steve to appreciate and recommend him. Lucy said she had a "very significant relationship", although "not a lot of analysis". I believe that these statements, and examples from other narratives above, demonstrate that the person of the analyst, with specific and unique qualities, plays a more significant and powerful role in the success or failure of outcomes in psychoanalysis than the actual training, or theoretical framework, which guides the analysis. This finding is supported by the recent literature (Anastasopoulos & Papanicolaou, 2004). It raised questions for me about the individual capacity of each analyst to be open and flexible in working with the unique characteristics and problems brought by patients, and again whether any analyst can really analyse any patient. I also thought Steve's comment was worth considering, on how traditional psychoanalytic theory may have an influence on the innate personal qualities in the analyst to such an extent that the analysis is perceived in a detrimental way.

Listening to the patient

Aspects of the analyst's personality have figured prominently around what has been significant for a successful or prematurely terminated analysis. Patients have thoughtfully considered the positive attributes brought to the relationship by their analysts and recommended for the facilitation of satisfactory analyses. Issues have also been raised by patients about the rigidity and adherence to rules rather than the analysts focusing on listening to the patient. Some have talked about instances of perceived harshness and even "cruelty", and how much the humanity of the analyst is important for successful and "liberating" experiences. Hearing what patients have to offer about their analyses challenges the prevailing orthodoxy that anything they say is merely a statement of transference. This, I think, can be argued as a methodological assumption and not a statement about reality as it is. What is being denied is that patients have the capacity for authentic insight and for analysts to hold that position is enormously disempowering of the patients.

In the next chapter, I present responses from the patients to three specific questions I asked them at the conclusion of their interviews.

CHAPTER EIGHT

A difficult question:
to recommend analysis or not?

"It's the best thing I've ever done. I would recommend it;
however, I would actually always say it's not for everyone"

(Audrey)

"Recommend psychoanalysis? No. Would I recommend that
therapist? Yes. Now that was a contradiction"

(Steve)

D uring the interviews, I encouraged spontaneity in patients'
responses to an open question about their analytic experiences, not wishing to lead in any direction. I was interested,
however, in leaning about their personal views on specific issues
that did not arise, in particular whether they would recommend
analysis to others. Associated with this was my interest in seeing
what patients thought constituted a "good" analytic experience. I
was also curious to know why these patients volunteered for this
study, which involved them revealing aspects of a very personal
journey and, at times, getting in touch with powerful feelings.

Thus, towards the end of the interviews, I asked the following three direct questions.

- Would you recommend psychoanalysis to a friend or colleague?
- What do you think constitutes a good analysis?
- Why did you volunteer to be interviewed?

These are their responses.

Recommendation to friend or colleague

I framed this question in such a way that might generate more careful consideration than if only asked about a general recommendation. Fifteen of the eighteen patients replied to this question. I was surprised at the very mixed responses, even from those who had previously reported good experiences.

Two patients, Simon and Marg, both had a very instant "No", with Marg adding that she would not have known about alternatives to analysis at the time she herself was considering it. Lucy, who has described her overall experience as "horrible" was a little more tentative.

> "I have to say no. I have to say I have too many queries. I'm not sure that I would want to take any client of mine to that place, and certainly I think you need to be enormously skilled to be able to do that."

Steve separated out the process of analysis from the practitioner when he responded with a laugh, acknowledging "a contradiction".

> "Recommend psychoanalysis? No. Would I recommend that therapist? Yes. Now that was a contradiction. Would I recommend psychoanalysis with that therapist? No. But he is still on my list of preferred practitioners. About psychoanalysis? When people ask me I have to say I have some ambivalence; it can be a damaging experience."

He added that he certainly told clients of his who asked about therapy to "shop around", and that "You don't have to go with the first person you see. You're a consumer—you choose the right person for you."

Tony declared that he would not "necessarily recommend it as the first experience". He expressed similar sentiments on the necessity for being able to choose one's own analyst and then being able to leave if it was not working.

"But I'm not quite sure how you do that. I would have been too frightened to say to him 'look, I don't think this is working'. Maybe I should have, but I didn't think I could do that. I lay there thinking 'This isn't working, but if it's not, maybe I should stay here and try to work it out'."

Carmel also stated that she was not sure "whether analysis is always the answer", and the matter of choice again came up.

"I think I would tell them to be very careful as to whom they chose. I suppose I would be happy for them just to go and see a good psychotherapist and not necessarily have an analyst."

Other patients responded in a way that indicated that they would not recommend analysis except under special circumstances. After a brief reflection, Greg stated,

"No, I probably wouldn't. I know that probably most people in analysis are doing it because they are professionals, so doing it for professional reasons—that's fine. But if somebody came to me and said they were depressed and should they go into analysis I'd say 'no'. I'd suspect analysis wouldn't help them this way for obvious reasons. On the other hand, if someone seemed to be functioning reasonably well and thought of analysis as a space where they might gain insight, if they were a functioning adult, I would have no problems with that. But for an adolescent or an adult with everyday problems of depression, anxiety, and relationship problems whatever—I think not."

Rosa, who had talked about an overall good experience, was also clear in her thinking about whether or not to recommend analysis.

"If one was in a lot of distress, no. Knowing how harrowing it is, how involved, I wouldn't want to sell it. If asked about it I would

> talk about what I had gained but it is such an individual thing. I probably wouldn't have done it if I hadn't been in this kind of work. You need to be well informed."

Jean thought her experience was "fantastic", but did not believe there were many patients "receptive to it".

> "I'd be very wary to recommend it to somebody unless I knew them so very well, and I knew they were really troubled, or really unable to find a contentment or happiness. It's a delicate matter. I think it's great, but I'm not evangelical about it."

Rick and Jenny stated that they would not recommend it to just anyone. Rick introduced the importance of prior knowledge about the analyst's work.

> "If I did it would be to someone who had had other experiences of therapy and was looking for much longer term, deeper exploration of things. And I would want to make sure if I was going to recommend someone that I was fairly confident that the person doing the analysis had some knowledge of the analyst's work."

Jenny also stipulated that "not everybody is suitable for it". She added, "It's hard, and it's also hard on the analyst. I would recommend it to some people—someone wanting to change something more structural and is psychologically minded."

Three other patients who had previously spoken positively about their analyses were also hesitant. Min advocated strongly for carefully checking out the analyst and was critical of the decreasing affordability of analysis.

> "I would think very, very carefully and talk to them at length about therapists' strengths. It is absolutely essential. But I also think that you have to be able to afford analysis. Unless you've got a psychiatric illness, and you can use one of the Medicare numbers, it costs a lot of money. So I think it needs to be there, but it's rapidly becoming not very affordable. Sadly, it's coming to be seen as a luxury and navel-gazing, and a bit narcissistic."

Paul described analysis as the "Rolls Royce of therapy" and not necessarily helping people to change.

"But I wouldn't call it a therapy necessarily; it's an analysis. It's not about trying to change anything about you. It's really trying to understand you at its depth and you then decide what you do with that. So, if somebody came to me who obviously needed to sort through things quite quickly or wanted something, I would probably recommend them to go somewhere else, at least to start with, and if they needed to go somewhere deeper, then into analysis. Depending on their personality, if they were open and more intuitive in that way, I would certainly then recommend analysis, but if they were more concrete thinkers, no, I would recommend a different kind of therapy."

Kate had similar thoughts. She described the importance of "educating" people about the process.

"And checking where they are at, whether they have done anything else before. I actually have done this as a coach; not that I've ever referred anyone to analysis, but even referring someone into therapy I spend a bit of time preparing them and I think 'God I wish someone had done that for me'. But I certainly wouldn't not recommend it, especially if someone is really struggling with deep-seated issues that don't seem to go away."

The patient who showed the most enthusiastic response to recommending analysis was Audrey.

"It's the best thing I've ever done. I would recommend it; however, I would actually always say it's not for everyone. It requires a big commitment, it's hard work, it's not just a picnic in the park and really it is not for everyone. It's huge. At the time when I started I never realized."

Kerry also agreed she would recommend it, although added, with some emphasis, "But it's absolutely not for the fainthearted. I think you have to really want to do it. And I needed it."

I was taken by surprise at the generally negative responses as reported above. Only one person really showed enthusiasm, and even that was qualified. Perhaps Audrey's statement explains some of the ambivalence when she enthusiastically described her experience but then went on to say how difficult analysis was. "It's hard work, it's not just a picnic in the park." Of the other fourteen patients who offered comments, only five more said they would recommend this form of treatment, but they also had some reservations. This was in spite of most having described generally very good experiences of their own. Kerry, in spite of her positive affirmation of analysis, also graphically described the "downside" with the use of such words as "humiliation", "rawness and vulnerability", and "just hanging out there with your entrails all over the floor". Perhaps recommendations were, therefore, given reluctantly because of the immense mental pain experienced, an unexpected "side effect" for patients, which, for many of them, outweighed the benefits they had received from their analysis.

So, how can we understand this further? A search of the psychoanalytic literature did not reveal any papers addressing this question. This finding raises a significant issue about the absence of any such interest in seeking patients' views on recommendations for analysis. I believe it also relates to an important point raised by one of the patients, Steve, who said, "Recommend psychoanalysis? No. Would I recommend that therapist? Yes." This statement about referring a colleague or friend to a specific analyst rather than to the actual psychoanalytic mode of treatment reinforces the relationship with a real person as the important factor. It would seem that the interpretative work based on theoretical knowledge and understanding is considered by patients as secondary to how the analyst uses his/her own personal characteristics.

What constitutes a good analysis?

I established earlier that my primary aim in interviewing patients was not merely to describe "good" or "bad" analyses. Rather, I wanted to provide a space for patients to speak about their experiences and give voice to what they really found helpful or not. I believed that much could be learnt from what patients can tell us about aspects of an analysis which, from their perspective, facilitates or impedes productive work. Such understanding would be very useful in the clinical work of practitioners and particularly, but not exclusively, to analysts in training.

I soon discovered that these patients had enormously different experiences, ranging from high praise of their analyses to others feeling they had not been understood or helped to any satisfactory outcome. The personality of the analyst came in for considerable scrutiny when patients were asked what they believed to be essential for a "good" analysis. As well as noting significant human qualities perceived in their own analytic experiences, they also brought up those qualities which they believed to be missing, but were considered crucial for a good working relationship. Expressions used to describe what was helpful were: "kindness", "love and being cared for", "humaneness", "warmth", "empathy", "humour and playfulness", "thoughtfulness", and "accurate listening". There were also comments on the importance of a "greater presence", more preparation for "the broader plan" when referring to "boundaries, parameters and practical issues", and the analyst being "skilled enough" to work with any confrontation without becoming embroiled in conflict with the patient.

Kerry presented some thoughts about the significance of the analyst's active presence in the relationship. She believed that the analytic model had a potential flaw in it. "They are so careful about the boundaries, guarding the space, that they are not there enough. And there's not enough kindness; it can be harsh."

Having heard a lecture from a prominent analyst on "what psychoanalysis is", Kerry questioned the relevance of love.

"Can analysis work if love is not felt by either person at any time in the whole relationship? Can this really work and really deeply touch people if there's no sense of love or being loved by the person you are there for? It doesn't have to be expressed in terms of love but the feeling of being loved, of being cared for. Can analysis work without it?"

Kate specified that she would have liked to see "more of the analyst's personality" and more thoughtfulness "on the impact of interpretations on the client".

"Like when I was saying to you before about not being able to be angry. It's hard to be angry at somebody so bloody neutral. Like if he would just—if he had a bit of a personality that was a bit arrogant, that would probably have triggered off my ability to get angry more. When it's so neutral there's nothing to hang the anger on. I think someone who could be warm and self disclosing, a little bit educational sometimes, but always thinking about what impact they have on the client, not just going into that and not thinking. And just being a little bit looser, not completely losing the frame, but a bit looser as a human being."

She also added that she would like the analyst to be "a tad more active". "I don't remember him particularly asking me any open questions to help me explore something. I just think that would be good."

Audrey spoke about her analyst's "innate quality that was quite humane", and advocated for this as a basic requirement in analysts. "Sometimes I think that's possibly the only thing that you actually need. You can do all sorts of behavioural stuff, but I think essentially, if you're not humane and can empathize with someone, then what?"

She added some thoughts on the significance of the analyst's personality. "I actually think that it is the personality of the person doing it. I think there are probably some people out there that probably couldn't or shouldn't be doing it."

Aspects of the analyst's style and technique were also addressed. Carmel presented ideas around the need for some congruence between the patient's verbalizations and the analyst's interpretations. This would indicate that the analyst has listened carefully, and accurately picked up on the verbal communications.

"Some comments have nothing to do with the client and the person has no idea; they [analysts] don't even notice that it has nothing to do with the client and that's what fascinates me. I know when I've said something that's wrong. You see it in the eye or in the movement of the body or a twitch in the nose, and think 'Oh that's wrong'. And I think there are some people who just work from a space where they believe they know what is right and not from the person being right. And that is very dangerous, if you think of transference and the fear and pain. And they are considered the experts. Very dangerous!"

Two other patients, Simon and Sig, drew attention to the same point made by Carmel about the importance of accurate listening and interpreting in a way that is meaningful to the patient.

Three patients raised issues to do with boundaries and analytic technique. Steve was concerned about what he felt was lacking in the preparation for analysis.

"The sense of the broader plan and where we are going with this and boundaries and parameters, like let's give it a go for three or six months then review it. Those sorts of thing for me are really important. The sense of a life sentence to me was a real killer."

Sig acknowledged the importance of "strict adherence" to a particular technique, but stated how there were times that this could be detrimental to the ongoing process.

"I think there are times when it is warranted that the analyst steps out of the technique to be able to give you the space to realign yourself with the method. And then to go back to conducting it again on orthodox lines so that you keep your client in the analysis and they get what they want."

Issues that concerned Sig and Steve were similarly raised by Lucy.

"What I would long for was more egalitarian, more of a collaborative effort together. More positive interpretations of my behaviour . . . there was always the negative view of me, like 'you're very controlling', rather than getting to the pain underneath. I do think you need some confrontation but in a holding way, almost leading the client to it rather than rubbing their nose in it . . . someone with very firm boundaries."

Lucy is speaking here about the desire for a more open and trusting relationship that included some occasional positive reinforcement. This might then have enabled her to tolerate, or even accept, appropriate confrontation from the analyst when she was aware of behaving badly, as detailed below. Instead, she draws attention to her analyst's incapacity to confront in a meaningful way.

"Surprisingly, I would like to have been stopped from beating him up as much as I did. Like a good father I would have liked him to have said, 'You will not speak to me that way. What is this about?', rather than getting into a verbal fisticuff. Because I would say things like 'You're an intellectual bully', and he would then say, 'Well, of course you're not . . .' You have to be very, very skilled, and you have to have an enormously strong sense of yourself and keep it separate."

The "collaborative" aspect was significant for Min as well, together with the prospect of an "open door" if there was more work to be done after termination.

"I think a good analysis is both a shared experience and a personal experience. I think a good analysis leaves one with the feeling one could continue to share it. Also the confidence that one can in fact reflect, and analyse for oneself what's going on, and still continue to make some change . . . I think it's important that a good analysis, when it terminates, it doesn't close the door. It's about having a good beginning, a good middle and a continuing end."

Marg emphasized how actually being listened to was one of the most important attributes she wanted from an analyst.

"No more than this—someone who hears what you are saying and who can work with you on what they hear, and with logic. I think one of the things—and this is not even my own perception but what I hear patients saying as well—if the patient comes to talk to you, and it can be for a whole lot of reasons but they are confused because they can't sort something out for themselves, they say, 'Can you help me sort this out?' So, that's what you do. In a nutshell, that's what you do. You help them sort something out so they can think for themselves about what is going on. And to have assistance with that, with the analyst, that's pretty profound work."

These examples all illustrate how patients were mindful of elements in their analysis that were either provided by their analyst in the facilitation of good work, or they found lacking and contributed to general dissatisfaction.

Reasons for volunteering to be interviewed

Two patients expressed the wish to help out because of their perception that it is difficult for researchers to recruit participants for studies. For example, Min said,

"I just thought I'm doing a PhD myself, and also because I work with a lot of post graduate students who have great difficulty in getting subjects. And I just wondered if you were getting enough people. So, a little bit of altruism."

She also added, "It's not the type of thing you sit down and talk about with a friend."

This was a more common response from patients, saying that there was little opportunity to tell anyone of the experience. Kate iterated what Min has said, adding her interest in understanding whether analysis actually worked, or not.

"I thought it would be a good opportunity to reflect on my analysis because you don't really get a chance to do that about lots of things, unless someone is interested to listen to you for an hour . . . I suppose there is also an interest in research about analysis and whether it works or not—I guess anything that is going to help find out whether that is true or not, because sometimes I don't know myself."

Kate also commented on how a friend had told her about the interview and how helpful it had been. "And I thought, 'Yes, that would be helpful, just to give you a chance to remember it and reflect on it.'"

Rosa had a similar response, in that she had also been told about the interview and decided she wanted psychoanalysis to be more known.

"Someone who heard about it [interview] spoke to me and asked if I was open to it. I think the more this is opened up academically and the process thought about, the more it becomes accessible."

Several patients wanted their stories told because it had been such a positive experience for them. Kerry stated, "It was a really good experience and I wanted it to go on record", while Audrey declared, "I thought, wouldn't it be nice to meet up with someone and talk about it, it being a successful thing, and wasn't it terrific."

Jenny explained that she wanted to change the misperceptions about analysis because of annoyance at "the bad press analysis gets, and usually from people who haven't been there." She added,

"I mean, that is the impression I get . . . I don't know, but yes, it is often people who haven't been there who comment on analysis and they usually refer back to Freud and anal-retentive characters. And I think it's just such a shame that there is such a misconception of this and it's really not what analysis is about."

Simon, however, who was not very encouraging about his experience, said, "I just thought I've got a story to tell—where the analyst has virtually complete power over you, something a lot of people who do it don't talk much about."

When I developed an interest in interviewing patients, it was suggested to me that only people who had had bad experiences would wish to talk, thus my sample would be skewed. It seemed that my exploration of patients' perspectives was perceived as an attack on psychoanalysis. However, as discussed in Chapter Two, the participants came from a very representative group of analytic patients. There was also the surprising, overwhelming response to participate. The answers to my direct question to patients as to why they volunteered demonstrate that there is actually a widespread interest, or need, for people who have been in analysis to tell their stories, regardless of outcome. I think perhaps this does have a link with endings in analysis, which may leave patients in prolonged mourning or with unresolved transference feelings. These patients needed to go public, an interesting area for further exploration.

CHAPTER NINE

Drawing together key findings*

"There's this kind of emerging that comes out of the process ... I felt as though everything that belonged to me was given back to me; like I'm left there with the sense of having myself given back to me"

(Kerry)

"The question always arises—is it due to the nature of the treatment, a reluctance to go, or is it more that this particular technique is just not working for me?"

(Sig)

I n this chapter, I have drawn together the threads which emerged from the patients' stories. I demonstrate how patients have constructed meaning from their experiences and, through doing so, have contributed to a fuller understanding of the analytic process.

---

*Paper based on this chapter presented to the RTP Fellows, IPA Congress, Chicago, July 2009.

A very interesting finding was that my aim in giving a voice to patients where they could be taken seriously had an interesting parallel in the process itself. Like the patients wanting to be heard, I found myself having to defend the authenticity of what I was exploring. This experience helped me to understand, at a personal level, the attempt to preserve the analyst as the one who would always know better than the patient. I will begin with describing this journey of mine in the process, and then discuss the key findings from the patients' analytic journeys.

A parallel process to the question explored

When I was thinking about this theme and playing around with ideas, I had some discussion with clinicians in the field. On one occasion, a senior analyst said to me that what I was doing would not be considered as research—rather, it was a "social study". Then, to my surprise, I received some vigorous denial that patients could actually know what they wanted, or know better than the analyst if their experience had been successful or not. It seemed that he was telling me that patients were not in the position to know whether they had benefited from their own analysis.

The argument as to which person in the analytic dyad has the authority to claim "who knows best" about the treatment outcome is quite a controversial one. Schafer (1996), for example, states that both analyst and patient are "variably reliable sources of evidence on their own subjective experiences and on those of the other" (p. 236) through the complex interplay between transference and countertransference processes. He argues that it is exceptionally difficult to tease out what is legitimate in such a contentious claim from "opposite sides" of the couch. However, as this book is about allowing the patients, generally not given a voice, to bring their own understanding and meaning to their analytic experiences, I believe it is important here to allow them to be taken seriously on what they think about, feel, and have desired from their analysis.

Tabin (2002) lends support to my thinking when he states,

> It is possible, of course, for a patient to feel an analysis was success-
> ful in dealing with what the patient came to deal with, and yet for

the analyst to feel uncomfortable about what was not dealt with. The fact still is that the patient's satisfaction with the analysis reflects an ongoing increased satisfaction in life. When a patient declares that an analysis was a failure, however, the analyst must be careful to avoid defensiveness in trying to understand why the patient retreated from further analysis, unsatisfied.

Another incident occurred, which again indicated to me that my exploration was perceived as rather threatening to practitioners in the field. I presented work in progress at a national Psychoanalytic Conference and, in discussing the impact of diverse personalities, I drew upon the published account of Hurwitz (1986), previously discussed (see Preface) as a training analyst's experience of two very different analyses. An analyst, whom I knew well, walked out of the presentation when I provided an example of Hurwitz's humour that drew laughter from the audience. I was amazed later to hear from a colleague that this analyst had seen me as mocking psychoanalysis.

Not long after these discouraging comments, I was accepted for the IPA Research Training Programme (1999) in London, with the opportunity to present my research question there. I received great encouragement from the Faculty of experienced analysts and my fellow participants, who gave me the confidence to continue. When I presented my work in progress, one of the Faculty members acknowledged the reality of Hurwitz's "unsatisfactory" experience, having personally worked with the particular training analyst referred to by Hurwitz. It was reassuring to hear an analytic experience recognized as authentic instead of being dismissed as though the analysand/patient was splitting the two analysts, in the transference, into "good" and "bad" objects. This analyst–researcher demonstrated how he had a mind for thinking about the actuality of Hurwitz's experiences, and did not perceive me as attacking analysis. I gained further reassurance about the importance of my work when I received two consecutive IPA funding grants to carry it out. My early experiences in my home country, however, highlighted for me the difficulty there has been for patients to be listened to and taken seriously.

This realization was helpful to me in understanding the group dynamic, which triggered a parallel response to my ongoing work when I presented a paper to my university peer group. It was a real challenge for fellow doctoral students to listen to what the patients were saying, and to enter into discussion without denying their voice by asserting that everything was transference. As I thought about the above experiences, and the group dynamics that aroused such strong responses, I recognized how the lived experience for me mirrored the material presented and was an even greater incentive for continuing the questioning of patients' experiences.

I would like to add, however, that there are many Australian analysts who have encouraged me in this exploration and have realized the importance of listening to the patient in order to provide greater mindfulness in their own clinical practices.

Key findings drawn from the major themes

The chapters throughout this book have loosely followed the format of an ongoing journey, paralleling, to some extent, the analysis itself. In order to provide some structure to this general discussion, I am following a similar format to present the key findings. Given the nature of the interview material and its link with free association by the patients, there has been some inevitable repetition in the various stages of their analytic journey. I have attempted here to avoid the repetition, and instead have focused on the major conceptual issues and themes which emerged, linking them to the current literature.

"Patient-partner", not "patient-victim"

One of the participants stated how, from the beginning of her analysis, she wanted to be a "patient-partner", not a "patient-victim". This was a significant statement, as it drew attention to the patient's need to be able to negotiate aspects of the analysis in a way that she found to be the most useful to her. Min was able to establish this from the beginning of her analysis, with an analyst who took her seriously. Other patients demonstrated a similar need for more negotiating power in the relationship, but did not have Min's capacity to articulate this. However, it seemed to permeate their experiences. Some were able to express how they felt helpless at times in the presence of an authority figure, as though experiencing feelings of being a "patient-victim". They became stuck in lengthy silences, or unable to "manoeuvre" around their analyst, when what they were requiring was someone able to understand their psychic pain and assist them out of an uncomfortable and seemingly impossible impasse. Min's capacity to think about what would be the most useful for the ongoing work of analysis, and her needs being met by an accommodating analyst, was a significant factor in the success of her analysis. This raises an important point about the role patients perceive that they play in the analytic dyad. The sense of powerlessness, and subsequent helplessness, is clearly evidenced by some of these patients, who felt imposed upon by an authoritarian or predominantly silent analyst. This left them expressing dissatisfaction, or leaving the analysis prematurely. It would be helpful for analysts to be more mindful of patients' expressed wishes and desires when initially interviewing for the analysis.

Lack of clarity about "what is psychoanalysis?"

One of the challenges I raised in Chapter One was the difficulty, if not impossibility, of finding a common definition for "psychoanalysis". This problem, or confusion around psychoanalysis, also arose when I sought participants to interview. In spite of stating specific criteria, I discovered a widespread ignorance in the "lay" public concerning the nature of psychoanalysis. Several volunteers who were keen to be interviewed failed to meet the criteria and were disappointed. Their experiences, on questioning, had been with a variety of counselling or other health practitioners, but not with professionally recognized psychoanalysts.

This confusion in a few of those wanting to discuss their experiences was partly due to their own naïveté about all forms of therapy "fitting" the same model; with others, the confusion occurred through a common misrepresentation by some health professionals who were not trained as analysts, yet were advertising that they were running psychoanalytic practices. When this occurred, the respondents automatically equated these practitioners with psychoanalysts; they did not know the difference from the actual experience. The branding or labelling of particular professional practices as psychoanalytic is clearly widespread and does no justice to psychoanalysis. If patients are unsatisfied they, in turn, can misrepresent their experiences of "psychoanalysis" when they have not been in treatment with people who are qualified to practise what is being offered.

As I became more involved in this exploration of patients' experiences, I discovered this confusion about the nature of psychoanalysis and its clinical practice was quite pervasive. It occurred even among the profession itself, as revealed by the literature. My experience at the IPA Nice Congress, 2001 was an endorsement of such diversity in both psychoanalytic understanding and clinical practice.

Patients' expectations

Patients undertake an analysis for multiple reasons. Some stated these clearly at the beginning; for example, wishing to work with personal, relationship, or work failures; other reasons are not so conscious, but emerge through the analytic process. There are, nevertheless, universal expectations, as evidenced by these findings; patients reported that they wanted to feel heard and facilitated in their exploration of painful internal conflict, by an analyst skilful enough to deal with all their communications in the transference. Their stories, however, have demonstrated that a satisfactory working through period did not always occur and such "universal" expectations were not invariably met.

Casement (2002) has drawn attention to psychoanalysts who sometimes arrogantly believe that they know best; thus, when anything goes wrong in the analysis, the patient is held accountable. Failures are attributed almost entirely to the patient's pathology, while the analyst fails to recognize that it could perhaps be the style of his/her clinical work that is problematic for the patient (Casement, 2002, p. xiii). As discussed previously in challenges to the research (Chapter One), some analysts have also argued that patients cannot know what they want because of the unconscious factors. If we accept the premise of the "dynamic unconscious", the analyst's position is necessarily privileged, as he/she has greater insight into the patient's unconscious. However, this is an exploration of the experiences and reflections of patients about their psychoanalyses, rather than the analysts' reflections—the usual position. In spite of the unconscious factors, I believe these patients have demonstrated some very sophisticated thinking and with evidence of knowing exactly what they wanted and how they hoped their needs would be met. It is a reminder of the importance of being able to listen to what patients are saying.

Some of the narratives confirmed Casement's statement of failures being attributed to patients' pathology, with a tendency for them to accept responsibility; other patients testified to liberating and productive work. These experiences have illustrated a very wide range of analytic styles and human qualities in the unique personality of the analyst. These characteristics contributed significantly to the patients' perceptions of their analysts' capacity to function in such a way that they felt understood and able to work constructively, or ended up in a premature departure from the analysis.

Tabin (2002) described one of the reasons why it has been difficult to listen to patients' expectations and understand more about the analytic process from their viewpoint. He stated that when analysts are discussing their work with peers, or attempting to learn from published clinical cases, the literature is usually provided by the analysts and not the patients; information from the latter has been difficult to acquire. Successful analyses are not easy to follow up, while failures are even less accessible, unless the patient seeks further analysis and then, as reported by Tabin (2002), "the previous analysis is seldom given importance in accounts of subsequent work" (p. 103). It is, thus, not surprising that the patients' expectations and hopes are not readily understood; or, as stated by Hinshelwood (1997), a paradox arises when the analyst believes he/she knows best what the patient should think and decide, and yet wants the patient to have found a mind of his/her own by the end of the analysis (see Chapter One).

The importance of adequate assessment procedures

The assessment period at the beginning of an analysis links with the previous section about patients' expectations. As discussed in Chapter Two, little has been published about preparing the patient for psychoanalysis. One of the key findings here was the significance of patient choice and the initial engagement with the analyst.

These two factors, which demonstrated patients' agency (or not) in the process, had a considerable impact upon the ongoing treatment and eventual outcome of the analysis.

Given this importance, I am surprised at the apparent lack of care and thoughtfulness in matching patients with suitable analysts. Many patients have drawn attention to the rather perfunctory way in which they ended up working with their particular analyst, and the general lack of preparation provided during the initial assessment period. Questions patients raised were disregarded by some analysts or met with silence, while others experienced a very different process of collaborative engagement from the start. The latter fostered a "patient-partner" rather than a "patient-victim" mentality. The considerable differences that were noticeable in assessment procedures have been discussed fully in Chapter Two.

It was, thus, not surprising to me that one of the patients in this study, Simon, could come to the end of his analysis and still express ignorance about the nature of his experience; or cite a book he had read by Skynner and Cleese, which provided him with information about the process he was undertaking. Other patients reported considerable knowledge of psychoanalysis, and even supervisory experience, yet articulated concerns that they did not fully understand its practice when they entered analysis, and then were not prepared adequately. Clarification of psychoanalytic goals would seem imperative for those seeking analysis, and especially in the early stage, when they find themselves entering such unknown territory.

There appears to be very different conceptual views about the value of assessments. These would seem to be based on the way analysts perceive the different roles and function between assessment and psychoanalysis proper. Stepping out of the classical position to adopt a more active role in learning about the patient is considered by some analysts to contaminate the ongoing process and, therefore, is undesirable. I would argue that the lack of clarity or reluctance around thoughtful assessment procedures denies a valuable opportunity for the analyst to get to know the patient, in a structured way, as a person and within a particular context. The assessment period also provides the space for the analyst to explore expectations and needs of the patients, thus enabling them to make a connection where they feel listened to and heard, and know that they are taken seriously. Another important aspect of the assessment phase is to offer an experience to the patient which provides some indication of what psychoanalysis is about, instead of primarily explaining about rules and boundary issues, as was described by many of these patients.

I think there is another crucial factor at this stage in terms of the analysts' own feelings and knowing whether they can work with a particular patient. The assumption is that once the analysis begins, everything will fall into place and "any analyst can analyse any patient". My experience in listening to these patients' stories demonstrates quite the opposite, with a number of premature terminations and "serial" analyses as a result of unsatisfactory or "failed" analyses. When a patient enters analysis with specific issues around relationships, if they cannot achieve some working through in a better relationship with the analyst they can remain "stuck" in a bad experience. They are repeating earlier patterns, as that is the only position they know. The experiences of Sig and Lucy are illustrations of this dilemma. In order to facilitate a good experience for the patient, the analyst needs to be mindful of the differences in personalities in both partners in the relationship, and also in other such variables as their religious values and culture. If there is enough incompatibility to raise questions about a good working relationship, it would seem imperative for the analyst to consider referring on to another analyst, unless these issues can be openly confronted and worked through.

What has emerged from these patients' accounts is the need for more clarity around the nature of assessments and preparation for the analysis, and ensuring that patients are matched with someone appropriate, rather than through expediency or current vacancy.

The significance of the analyst's personality in engaging with the patient

The powerful transference–countertransference relationship between patient and analyst has formed the larger part of patients' reflections on their experiences. They described the ways in which their analyst functioned in this relationship, which they linked with their perceptions of specific human qualities in the analyst.

In recent years, analyst/therapist qualities, which contribute to therapeutic change, have become among the most frequently studied variables (Beutler, Machado, & Neufeld, 1994). Research has increasingly demonstrated evidence of the analyst/therapist as a significant agent of change, independent of technique and theoretical orientation (Anastasopoulos & Papanicolaou, 2004; Bergin & Garfield, 1994; Crits-Christoph & Mintz, 1991; Kantrowitz, 1995; Luborsky & Crits-Christoph, 1986). I would like to argue further from these stories that it is the quality of the analyst's engagement in the relationship that is the most important factor, and this is based on their human qualities.

The majority of patients (13:18) were practising psychotherapists, and their sophisticated thinking was consistently reflected when they spoke about the ongoing process and analytic relationship. They also had expectations of what they hoped to achieve, and demonstrated their frustration when these were not met. Transference (defined in the Introduction and discussed in following chapters) was understood by most patients as the core element in the analytic process; they provided vivid examples to illustrate how they perceived whether their issues were worked through, or not, in the transference.

Issues to do with the engagement were paramount. Some patients described qualities such as "attunement", "receptivity", "nurturing", "holding and containing", being "in sync", "humour and playfulness", and "acceptance of reality", all of which facilitated a positive connection with their analyst in the transference. It could be assumed that these characteristics would be a given in any analytic experience, but, as revealed here, this was not the case. Other patients, and in particular the three who ended their analyses prematurely, perceived their analysts as "authoritative", "unwilling to engage", imposing extended periods of "punitive and critical silences", "disconnecting", "mediocre", and, at times, even "cruel".

All patients gave clear indications of how they were able to depict differences in their analyst's capacity to function in a helpful or unhelpful way. This was by virtue of their unique human qualities, rather than their specific training and acquisition of theoretical knowledge, which every analyst accomplishes. How analysts apply their training, using their own human qualities, would seem to be the major difference in whether the analytic treatment is successful or not. This is a key finding, and one that has important implications when thinking about training policies and practices for therapeutic treatment.

It is, of course, very difficult to accept these accounts as "the last word" when I have given a voice to patients only, excluding their analysts. However, as there was some consistency provided in these experiences, and particularly when three analysts each had two patients in treatment who described similar experiences (see Chapter Seven), I think it warrants some thoughtful consideration of the patients' perceptions. These cannot be dismissed lightly.

The analyst's "transference", or "unhelpful" countertransference

I noted earlier how peers in my seminar group, and some analysts I spoke with, were critical of any communications from the analyst as being able to be thought of outside the transference. This notion was also raised, in Chapter One, as one of the challenges to listening to the patients. This insistence by my peers was in spite of providing details of analytic work in which some patients clearly considered the analyst to be making extra-transferential interpretations; as, for example, Lucy's account of sending a postcard to the analyst while on holiday and his personal response. She was sophisticated enough in the analytic process to understand that this enactment by her called for exploration by her analyst, rather than a "thank you" and then closure. Another example, which I believe is relevant, was the analyst's response to Lucy when she remarked on the "leggy brunette" whom she saw leaving her analyst's rooms (discussed in Chapter Five). These illustrations would appear to support Lucy's beliefs that her analyst, at times, worked in the concrete rather than the symbolic, thus stepping outside his role as an analyst working with the transference. Most of these patients were sophisticated thinkers in psychoanalysis, and able to convey that they knew the difference between transferential issues and what was real.

The examples presented here, and others discussed in previous chapters, would seem to demonstrate countertransference reactions arising from within the analyst himself, rather than responses generated merely by the patient's material. This thinking is supported in the recent literature (Berman, 1949; Eagle, 2000; Gabbard, 1995; Sandler, 1987, 1993; Spillius, 1992), which acknowledges that not all countertransference difficulties can be blamed upon the patient, and that retraumatization can occur when the analyst's personal agenda is brought to the analytic situation (Kantrowitz, 1986; Racker, 1968; Sandler, 1987; Strupp & Binder, 1984). When a stance of neutrality is not maintained, certain cues emanate from the analyst to the patient, to which the patient in turn reacts (Eagle, 2000), and transference does not emerge independent of the analyst's social and interpersonal characteristics and reactions (Aaron, 1992). And, according to Kantrowitz (1986), "The analytic literature, while conceding both abstract and specific manifestations of counter-transference, rarely considers the impact that the particular qualities of an analyst may have on the treatment process" (p. 274).

The clinical illustrations presented by Lucy, and also clearly delineated throughout this book with other patients, draw attention to the mismatch which can occur in the analytic relationship. It seems that there are problems with analysts who become caught in an unsustainable transference–countertransference relationship, and are, therefore, not able to recognize the detrimental effect on their patient and think of referring on to another colleague. This reinforces my argument about the crucial nature of adequate assessment procedures, where the analyst provides an experience in which both partners can mutually assess their suitability for working with each other.

Writers such as Casement (2002) and Reppen and Schulman (2002) have emphasized the importance of analysts acknowledging failures in their experiences with their patients, or being able to hear when patients communicate to them that they are not receiving the kind of help they need. Recognition of such impasses would be helpful to both analyst and patient, who, with this acknowledgement, might then be able to continue in the same analytic relationship, or, if the impasse continues, the patient can then be directed to see another analyst. It is not a failure, or shameful, to acknowledge limitations in the analytic relationship and the possibility that other analytic "couples" might be able to function in a more constructive way when personalities, and other differences, are conceded as distorting or disrupting the analysis.

I have constantly used the term countertransference throughout this book, but this was not actually provided by the patients themselves. In reflecting upon their experiences, it seemed to me that this was implied when the patients were discussing personality issues of their analysts. The psychoanalytic usage of the term is discussed in the Introduction. Some patients give reports of responses by their analysts to verbal communications that indicate that these might actually link with ideas from McLaughlin (1981). He suggested that, at times, the analyst's attempt at interpretation can be prompted by his/her own transferences, rather than countertransference, and, thus, not restricted to a patient-centred focus. I considered that this distinction might relate to Lucy's examples, above. Her illustrations of how she sometimes perceived her experience do seem to demonstrate a "transference" reaction from her analyst, and not necessarily thoughts and feelings which reflect "what is going on in the patient's inner world" (Eagle, 2000, p. 36), and indicate countertransference.

Steve's comments about the analyst being "a victim of his own craft, of his own therapeutic approach" (see Chapter Five) bring to mind the third source of countertransference (Purcell, 2004; Stein, 1991). These writers suggested that the analyst's theory can interfere with his/her functioning, and, therefore, be considered as an unhelpful form of countertransference. Steve's point illustrates this when he ended his analysis stating that he believed his analyst was ". . . sensitive, skilled, ethical and professional", but still declared, "I don't think it really worked for me . . . I would really like to have closure but I don't know how to achieve it. It's like a lasting impression of a slightly bad taste."

Steve made a clear distinction between his perception of the analyst as a person, and the analyst's perceived "misuse" of theory, which he saw as detrimental to the analytic process. One example he gave was in reference to long periods of emotional destabilization; his analyst seemed to adopt the "classical" neutral position, and refused any response to questions that Steve asked about clarifications in boundary issues. Other illustrations that I believe could represent a "misuse" of theory as countertransference were the periods of prolonged silence, as endured by Rick, and Sig's description of the analyst telling him he was working from "his own agenda". In both these experiences, the analysts could have more usefully explored further how and why these patients remained "stuck".

The patients' experiences in relation to the quality of engagement with their analyst, and the diverse ways in which they perceived their analysts working in the transference–countertransference relationship, demonstrate sophisticated thinking about the analytic process. To me, they do clearly illustrate the "complexities of the clinical situation that develop between patient and analyst", which Roth and Fonagy (1996) emphasized was very important to understand. This was one of the challenges presented in Chapter One, and I believe it to be an important learning for analytic practitioners.

The significance of gender

The importance of gender has been discussed in previous chapters, and various arguments put forward as to its significance in analytic work. The emergence of a prominent theme around "fathering" issues I have linked with the predominance of male analysts in the study, in spite of more females participating as patients.

I addressed this theme, as a specific finding, in the chapter entitled "Paternal transference", and raised awareness of what I considered was of significance to gender issues in relation to this work. This is again highlighted in the next section, and indicates some complexity with the inclusion of a third party in the analysis. As the latter affected patient choice, I have argued that such a powerful theme around fathers emerged because the majority of analysts working with these patients were male.

The psychoanalytic literature (see Chapter Five) has indicated how psychoanalysis has developed from the historical stereotypes of fathering and mothering roles that promote the "traditionally" perceived masculine attributes of power, status, and money. In spite of this, for several decades gender was not considered important, the thinking being that any analyst could analyse any patient. The findings from these patients differed by demonstrating the importance placed on gender, particularly in relation to specific desires to explore past experiences with authoritarian or weak and passive fathers. However, these experiences revealed that not all male analysts were caught up in the universally based stereotypes of typical male functioning. Several patients described their male analyst as having human qualities which encompassed, among others, the traditional mothering attributes of "nurturing" and "receptivity", which led to very positive outcomes. I believe this can be explained by their unique personality characteristics, which made the difference, and the capacity for productive analytic functioning was more to do with the maturity of the analyst rather than because of his specific gender.

Third party influence

A critical issue to do with choice and gender was linked to the government funding policy, Medicare, which has been referred to in previous chapters. However, I wish to draw attention again to how the privileging of one group over another, because of a primary health qualification and not by their psychoanalytic training and expertise, has the tendency to "muddy the waters". As many of these patients were seeking a funded analysis because of financial restraints, this limited their choice to psychiatrically trained psychoanalysts, predominantly males on the Australian scene.

Medicare, by giving preference to one group of analysts over another in terms of monetary gain, can lead to a perception that the psychiatrically trained analysts have better qualifications and experience, which is not the case. It is noteworthy that Freud (1913c, 1927a) wrote about lay analysis being the preferred model, and even considered that a medical profession could be harmful to psychoanalysts. As stated by Kirsner (2000), "Freud saw psychoanalysis as based on psychology and not medicine and was implacably opposed to excluding lay analysts as the Americans did" (p. 6). Freud maintained this position until the end, as expressed in a letter dated July, 1938, and cited by Jones, saying: "The fact is, I have never repudiated these views and I insist on them even more intensely than before, in the face of the obvious American tendency to turn psychoanalysis into a mere housemaid of psychiatry" (Jones, 1953, cited in Kirsner, 2000, p. 253). It is interesting to note that the psychiatrically qualified analysts in Australia acted against Freud's express wishes and chose allegiance to the psychiatry profession, for political and, therefore, financial reasons, rather than remaining in the group with their non-medical psychoanalytic colleagues with whom they trained and had an analytic identity.

Another issue related to Medicare is its reporting requirements in order to maintain the funding. This can cause patients to be fearful of breaches of privacy and serve as an interference with the work of analysis. Patients may fear that their personal issues are not kept confidential and, therefore, be reluctant to open up in the "free association" method as espoused by their analysts. The above concerns have an impact upon both patient and analyst, and need to be brought openly into the analytic relationship for thoughtful working through. This lack of open discussion with the patient around what is required when funding is subsidized by a third party is an important finding, and one which needs to be addressed.

The points I have raised demonstrate a significant impact on the patients' choice of an analyst, and the subsequent influence on gender imbalance because of the predominance of psychiatrically trained analysts being male. This would appear to be an area where very little thought has been given to such consequences of an inequity in funding, and also to the perception of two "hierarchical" classes of trained analysts.

Significant issues around "termination"

I have previously made a link between the patients' eagerness to talk about their experiences and the termination phase. It is only recently that a follow-up on termination experiences has begun to be addressed in the psychoanalytic literature (Conway, 1999). The "unfinished business" which can remain with patients after their analysis was also addressed by one of the patients, Steve, in his statement fifteen years later: "I didn't ever achieve closure . . . the whole process has sat with me in a very odd way, in a very unfinished way. I find that disturbing."

As raised in Chapter Six, one cannot overestimate the importance of the termination phase, clearly articulated by Min, who stated, "I think it's important that a good analysis, when it terminates, it doesn't close the door. It's about having a good beginning, a good middle and a continuing end." What this highlighted for me was the artificiality of the psychoanalytic reference to "terminations", and also how this term itself might be thought about by patients because of its link with death, or an abrupt ending.

Diverse experiences of the ending of analysis were reported by patients and discussed in detail (Chapter Six). Unilateral decisions to finish, with consequences for the patient regardless of who makes the decision, have been reported as common experiences (Novick, 1997, Schacter, 1992). As raised earlier in this chapter, the difficulties inherent in the ending of an analysis did appear to have considerable impact on the eagerness of participants to talk about their experiences. I would like to suggest that an option be offered to all patients for a period of review at some stage after the termination, and particularly if it seems that the experience has been a difficult, incomplete, or unsatisfactory one. One patient, Jenny, was given this option by her analyst, with a very good result (see Chapter Six).

I am reminded of how attachment theory is now very prominent in psychoanalytic work in relation to separation and loss, and wonder how the endings in analysis could be thought about in similar terms. This important phase cannot be avoided, but, rather, needs more thoughtful space in the mind of the analyst, with an opening to consider a later follow-up period. According to Schachter (1992), "Many analysts believe that such contact risks damaging the patient" (p. 147). He states, however, that clinical assessments with such contacts (Schlessinger & Robbins, 1983; Wallerstein, 1986) have indicated "little or no damage to patients, and in some cases distinct benefits" (1990, p. 483). Analysts also use a very different standard for post-termination contact for themselves than for their patients. Schachter (1992) notes that "most analysts seek post-termination contact with their own training analyst beyond those contacts in professional situations that are virtually unavoidable" (Schachter, 1992, p. 147).

The opportunity for patients to reflect upon their experiences with me seemed to fulfil, to some extent, the purpose of closure. This was partially acknowledged by Kate, who implied the loss of the analytic hour in which she could speak freely. She stated, "I thought it would be a good opportunity to reflect on my analysis because you don't really get a chance to do that about lots of things, unless someone is interested to listen to you for an hour."

I draw attention, however, to Lucy, whose experience is detailed in previous chapters. I am focusing on Lucy as her interview and the distress it caused her left me feeling quite concerned. The possibility for talking prompted her response to the advertisement, but did not appear to offer relief from her anguish, not only about "a horrible experience", but also at feeling that she and her analyst had never reached closure. Her reasons for entering analysis and a phantasy of finding a "good daddy", unlike her real, abandoning father, were never resolved. As a result, it seemed that she felt she had done some irreparable damage to prevent the "good" father emerging, while she was left feeling like "a paraplegic who can't walk". Her interview appeared to be a cathartic experience where she was able to pour out memories she related to as both hateful and loving, but in the end said that the analysis left her feeling "that it was a hell of an experience". Our interview left her with similar powerful feelings of grief. Lucy did not seem to have the opportunity for a real mourning, and she reported how she was unwilling to try again as she was now really hard to please. "I think I want to get this impossible person, this all-knowing, all-wise being. And I don't think they exist."

The ending of analysis affects how a patient can process what has occurred over many years and look to the future; it also is linked with the whole journey. Those patients who had positive experiences talked of having some negotiation period for finishing their analysis and ultimately experiencing life changes; for others, the actual ending of analysis was coloured by the ongoing experience. For these patients with less than satisfactory or "bad" experiences, it could be argued that the ending of the analysis brought up images and feelings of again being left with "bad" or non-caring parents—some of the very reasons which brought them into analysis in the beginning. What is more concerning is that patients who have had a bad experience believe it is their fault and cannot allow themselves to think about the analyst as failing them. Instead, they take ownership of the failure as theirs.

The interminable nature of this pain, when it has been an unsatisfactory experience, would seem to indicate some urgency for the provision of more thoughtfulness in clinical practice around endings in analysis. This is compounded by what is implied by the actual psychoanalytic terminology used. The experience also of "having an analysis", a term commonly used, raises the notion of analysis as a "product", rather than a "process" which is ongoing and emotionally charged.

The eagerness of patients to participate in this research indicated a strong wish to tell someone their story, and suggested some closure was required when such a space was not provided elsewhere. Some patients informed me that they did, on their own initiatives, seek further and different forms of therapy following their unhelpful analytic experiences or unsatisfactory endings to their analysis.

Agency by patients as a prediction of better outcomes

An interesting question that emerged from the early beginnings of analysis and initial assessments was to do with personal choice and future outcomes. I thought it important to reflect upon any possible link between the beginning phase, ongoing process, and eventual termination. Therefore, I compared those who were proactive at the beginning in choosing their analyst with patients who passively accepted referrals, or felt some dissatisfaction with their initial analytic engagement. I am aware that every analysis has times when patients experience both helpful and unhelpful aspects; my assessment of a "good" analysis is based only on the patients' communications about their experiences ending in such a way that they felt progress had been made in life changes, relationship patterns, and feelings of being liberated.

In the experiences reported by all eighteen patients, I found that ten presented clear evidence of analytic work which they considered as liberating and generating personal transformations, both internally (for example "plumbing changed", or "considerable psychic changes") and externally in relationships, work, and other general life experiences; seven patients recorded experiences of leaving prematurely because of "feeling stuck", something not "completed" or "beneficial", or ending the analysis with detrimental effects, such as the development of adverse physical symptoms; one patient indicated some ambivalence as to the usefulness of his experience, wondering if he "would have changed anyway".

In thinking about the above experiences, I did conclude that the more assertive patients tended to have overall better analyses. Of the eleven patients who chose their analysts through some form of personal agency, which included previous contact, knowledge of the process, or shopping around, seven reported being very happy with the outcome of their analyses. A striking example was that of Kerry, who gave clear evidence of an immediate positive engagement with her analyst on assessment (see Chapter Two), and her subsequent insistence that he remains as her treating analyst. Her ongoing experience and thoughts at the end testified to her initial intuitive feelings about a "good fit".

In spite of choosing for themselves, four of this group were dissatisfied with their analyses, including Lucy, who declared it to be "a horrible experience". Her choice, however, was not based on confirmation of a previous, positive encounter, but was influenced by a phantasized wish about an analyst who physically resembled her abandoning father. Because of this identification, Lucy had hoped that he would provide the ultimate "good fathering" experience. As already discussed, the unconscious elements behind this phantasy did not seem possible to be worked with or attain any sense of resolution.

Three patients who accepted referrals with no preferences also had good experiences, while the remaining four of this group left prematurely or were very dissatisfied. I think, therefore, that an argument could be made for considering that a patient who has the capacity to be assertive and seek out what he/she wants has a greater likelihood of attaining a better outcome in analysis than those who show no preferences when starting the analysis. It is crucial that analysts are able to hold in mind the vulnerable states in which patients present for analysis, and, therefore, at that stage, are usually incapable of being able to think clearly or negotiate what is in their own best interests. This places the responsibility with the analysts, and indicates strongly how an adequate assessment procedure is of prime importance at this beginning stage of the analysis.

Ambivalence about recommending psychoanalysis

I have already registered my surprise at the general disinclination for patients to recommend analysis to colleagues or friends. I anticipated some reluctance by those who had talked of a "mediocre" or "horrible" experience, but had not considered such conservative responses from those patients who described very positive outcomes. There seemed a wish to protect people known to the patients from an ongoing experience that was difficult and painful, rather than endorsing a journey which was "liberating" and "life changing". This raised concerns for me about the future of psychoanalysis, when the majority of these patients, with satisfactory and enriching outcomes, were scarcely encouraging of its recommendation.

Most responses by patients were qualified, as described elsewhere. There were particular issues about ensuring that the analyst was chosen very carefully, was skilful enough to avoid offering the patient an experience that was "horrible" or "damaging", and that the patient seeking analysis was an adult "functioning reasonably well". Rosa, in spite of her very positive experience, remarked on how "harrowing it is", and said, "I wouldn't want to sell it." She also added that there was the necessity for the patient "to be well informed".

I think the comments around recommendations, or not, can be linked with aspects of the analysis concerning proper assessment procedures. They highlight the necessity for not only considering a "good fit" between the patient and referred analyst, and adequate preparation of the patient for analytic treatment, but also for evaluating the capacity of the patient to commit to such an intense and long-term form of therapy. These are all issues that these patients had reservations about.

A significant point was raised by Steve. He described how impressed he was with his analyst, but, nevertheless, felt that the analyst was hindered from working effectively by being "a victim of his own craft, of his own therapeutic approach". Steve further added that while this analyst was still on his list of preferred practitioners, which he recommended to others, he would not recommend the actual analysis. This is a very interesting contradiction, also noted by Steve. It seems to indicate quite clearly that he perceived his analyst as being hampered from functioning analytically through his adherence to theory rather than allowing his "impressive" human qualities to influence the way in which he worked. For me, this is a key finding for training institutes to take into consideration when supervising candidates in their clinical work. It would seem imperative that trainee analysts are encouraged to utilize their human qualities and not to hide behind theories, which are often perceived as the prime analytic force behind their practices.

Limitations to this book

One of the limitations I was mindful of in writing this book relates to the private and confidential nature of the analytic situation itself, as described in challenges I had to confront (Chapter One). As explained earlier, it is impossible to portray exactly what happens behind the "closed doors" of the analyst's consulting room. However, these interviews have produced very interesting and credible accounts of patients' experiences, in a way which has previously attracted little attention, and which provides a useful contribution for serious consideration in analytic training institutes and clinical settings. They have also enriched the current literature on psychoanalysis by providing a different perspective.

Other limitations are associated with the participant population and interviewing procedure. Exploring both analyst and patient perspectives of the same experience would provide interesting and, perhaps, quite different observations of the analytic relationship and ongoing process. However, I think that this exploration from only the patient's perspective is no less trustworthy than presenting just the analyst's experience, as has been customary to date. Gaining access to both patient and analyst in the same analytic experience is also a difficulty, presented by Australia having a relatively small psychoanalytic community and thus wishing to protect the privacy and confidentiality of the interconnected professional groups whose members comprise the majority of analytic patients.

With regard to the number of participating patients, eighteen could be considered relatively small. However, their stories have generated very rich information, and enabled an access to the analytic relationship that has seldom been revealed by patients in such a spontaneous and personal way.

I think further work focusing particularly on unsatisfactory or "failed" analyses of patients and their experiences after termination would make an interesting future exploration and considerably enrich the psychoanalytic literature.

Analytic qualities patients are seeking

I stated in the Preface and elsewhere that the aim of this work was to explore psychoanalysis from the patient's perspective. It was not my intention to discuss "good" and "bad" experiences *per se*, but rather to delineate the factors that patients perceived as helpful to their analyses or those which impeded the process to the extent that it became unworkable and the relationship could not be sustained. Not any one analysis was entirely "good" or "bad", but had elements that could be teased out as contributing to the overall experience.

One of the direct questions at the end of the interviews concerned what patients considered would make for a "good" analysis. Their responses included a list of human characteristics in the analyst that were actually experienced by many in their own analyses; other qualities they desired were added. I am including here only those characteristics that have not previously been explicitly stated, and examined in detail, through the findings: "kindness", a "greater presence", "humaneness, possibly the only thing that you actually need", and a "sense of love". The latter quality was added by Kerry, who said, "Can analysis work if love is not felt by either person at any time in the whole relationship?" Another patient said, quite determinedly, "You have to have results."

Some of the qualities offered were related more specifically to the analyst's technique: "being skilled enough to work with any confrontation without him/herself becoming embroiled in the conflict"; "more preparation and a sense of the broader plan ... the sense of a life sentence was a real killer"; "to have some feedback— that this person is letting you know he is hearing what you are saying"; "always thinking about things, thinking about the impact they have on the patient"; and, connected with this, "more thoughtfulness on the impact of interpretations". The comment about interpretative technique and congruence with the patients' communications was made by several patients. Carmel, for example, stated, "I think there are some people who just work from a space where they believe they know what is right and not from the patient being right. And that is very dangerous, if you think of transference and the fear and pain. And they are considered the experts."

Kate, having described how she was unable to work with her anger (see Chapter Five), said, "I would have liked more of his own personality ... It's hard to be angry at somebody so bloody neutral", while Marg, who left her analysis because she never felt heard, was quite specific in stating how she believed that "being listened to" was fundamental for a good analysis.

"If the patient comes to talk to you, and it can be for a whole lot of reasons but they are confused because they can't sort something out for themselves, they say, 'Can you help me sort this out?' So, that's what you do. In a nutshell, that's what you do. You help them sort something out so they can think for themselves about what is going on. And to have assistance with that with the analyst—that's pretty profound work."

This quality of being listened to seems such a fundamental aspect of the analyst's technique, but obviously was not always experienced here. Marg's other statements about "sorting out" the confusion that patients bring to the analysis for assistance in working through would also seem a major part of the analyst's function in his/her usual analytic practice.

In these key findings, expressed through the patients openly discussing their analytic experiences, it is very clear what they wanted and expected to receive from their analyses. Chapter Ten will now bring these narratives to a close with a brief discussion on clinical implications for psychoanalysis, its theory, and practice.

Clinical implications for psychoanalytic practice

"Do patients change because of psychoanalysis or in spite of what analysts do?"

(Guerrero, 2001, IPA Congress, Nice)

uerrero, a presenter at the Nice Congress (2001) raised an interesting question that is related to these findings. He asked, "Do patients change because of psychoanalysis or in spite of what analysts do?" If this question had been asked of the patients I interviewed, I believe the following comments, brought up spontaneously by two of the patients, would have been fitting responses to Guerrero. Tony, when reflecting on his experience, said, "I'm sure it [the analysis] did help me but I'm not sure how . . . I would have changed as a person anyway so it's difficult to say", while Rick remarked how his analyst provided the opportunity for him to make sense of his life but "nothing more helpful" than what he could possibly have done if he merely "sat in a corner and did my own thing". Other patients, however, were able to report that at the end of their analyses it had "completely changed" their lives.

This book contains rich and enlightening experiences of psycho-analysis "from the couch" by listening to patients talk, and has contributed many significant findings which are of importance to the developing body of psychoanalytic knowledge and clinical practice. Given the consistency in responses from the eighteen patients interviewed, it is important to take seriously the meaning of their strongly held views, which were maintained over consider-able periods of time. One patient, who reflected on his experience after fifteen years, admitted that he had never sat for so long with-out changing his mind or gaining any closure.

What does it mean for psychoanalysis and the techniques of its practitioners that these patients emerged with such varied experi-ences as presented here? The analysts' clinical training and theoret-ical knowledge cannot account for such different outcomes or how these patients perceived the ongoing process and relationship. What emerged as the most important aspect of the analytic journey was the relationship, a finding supported by recent literature. These patients have also drawn attention to the quality of engagement in the relationship, which was the critical factor leading to their res-pective outcomes. They identified the specific human qualities in their analysts that were helpful to the therapeutic relationship and those which were not. Where these qualities were not experienced, the patients were able to think clearly about the analytic process and, with some sophistication, suggested those characteristics that they believed were fundamental to good analytic work. The quali-ties they listed form a significant finding for analysts to thought-fully reflect upon in their clinical practice, particularly if the experience with some patients does not seem to be working successfully.

I have raised many questions about crucial analytic policies and practices, drawing attention specifically to the assessment and preparation of patients and the ending or termination phase. Both stages would seem to require a much greater focus in psychoana-lytic training programmes and subsequent clinical practices.

In the previous chapter, I identified key findings that could lead to further very interesting and worthwhile work in the future. The findings also raise important issues in thinking about how psycho-analysis can continue as a significant form of therapeutic treatment in a climate where other modalities are now producing promising results. These are being supported by funding bodies which seek evidence of economically efficient and effective clinical practice. This is a significant cultural shift, which has been occurring over the past twenty years. Patients seeking therapy are also more discerning now, more assertive and less willing to remain in a treatment that is not attending satisfactorily to their needs. Therefore, it is really important that psychoanalytic practitioners listen to those aspects of the analysis that these patients have described, with great clarity and sophistication, as either facilitating or impeding the process.

This raises another important point: when the relationship is of such significance, more so than interpretations, as revealed by these patients, and other modalities place emphasis on the relationship as well, what can psychoanalysis offer that is different? We are all aware, of course, that psychoanalysis provides a much more in-depth treatment for enduring pathological and debilitating symptoms. However, these can only really be addressed when there is a "good" working relationship to start with, which I have demonstrated here was not always possible. I also think psychoanalysts are not really good at marketing themselves. There is very little attention paid to publicizing good, qualitative, evidence-based research on the benefits of psychoanalytic treatment, compared with the more prolific studies on cognitive type therapies that are being produced.

The major confusion about the very nature of psychoanalysis itself, and who is qualified to practise or speak about it, is also a problem needing to be addressed. This lack of a clear consensus can have a considerable impact on the knowledge base and understanding of clinical practice. With such diversity in theoretical schools, particularly to do with the aims and essential elements of psychoanalysis, it is challenging to inform clearly defined and consistent institute policies. However, without these policies, it becomes very difficult for the layperson seeking psychoanalytic treatment to be sure that he/she is actually receiving what is being offered, by a practitioner qualified to practise.

What do patients want?

Significant aspects of the analytic experiences of eighteen patients have been presented and discussed throughout this book. Ten patients were highly satisfied with their analyses, which led to liberating and major life changes; for them it was a very good experience. Eight patients spoke of analyses that were mediocre or disappointing, two even experienced as damaging; three of these patients prematurely left the analysis. Factors that contributed to these experiences have been presented with clear illustrations by the patients; they have spelt out "what they want". Although they did not generally use psychoanalytic terminology, the patients demonstrated how they understood the role of transference and countertransference in the ongoing process; they demonstrated how they were able to work with it, or remained repeating experiences from the past, which could not be resolved. These patients have provided insight into how their expectations were realized or not, linking the human qualities of the analysts with what made the difference.

My entering the patient's world has, to some extent, paralleled the aims of a psychoanalytic treatment itself. Listening to the patient's voice has enabled the emergence of another side to the analytic "story". Through these narratives, I have argued the importance of including patients' experiences in literary accounts of psychoanalytic treatment, process, and outcome research. Through giving so much of themselves, with very personal stories and with such openness and honesty, I believe these patients have made a significant contribution to the knowledge base of psychoanalysis, analytic training procedures, and clinical practice.

REFERENCES

Aaron, L. (1992). Interpretation as expression of the analyst's subjectivity. *Psychoanalytic Dialogues, 2*: 475–507.

Aaron, R. (1974). The analyst's emotional life during work. *Journal of the American Psychoanalytic Association, 22*: 160–169.

Abel-Horowitz, J. (1998). Psychopharmacotherapy during an analysis. *Psychoanalytic Inquiry, 18*: 673–701.

Abend, S. M. (1989). Countertransference and psychoanalytic technique. *Psychoanalytic Quarterly, 58*: 374–395.

Abend, S. M. (1993). An inquiry into the fate of the transference in psychoanalysis. *Journal of the American Psychoanalytic Association, 41*: 627–651.

Abend, S. M. (2002). Prologue. *Psychoanalytic Inquiry, 22*: 299–306.

Abend, S. M., & Shaw, R. R. (1991). Concepts and controversies about the transference neurosis. *Journal of the American Psychoanalytic Association, 39*: 227–239.

Adler, E., & Bachant, J. L. (1996). Free association and analytic neutrality: the basic structure of the psychoanalytic situation. *Journal of the American Psychoanalytic Association, 44*: 1021–1046.

Adler, E., & Bachant, J. L. (1998). Intrapsychic and interactive dimensions of resistance. *Psychoanalytic Psychology, 15*: 451–479.

Akhtar, S. (1995). A third individuation: immigration, identity and the psychoanalytic process. *Journal of the American Psychoanalytic Association*, 43: 1051–1084.

Akhtar, S. (2000). From schisms through synthesis to informed oscillation. *Psychoanalytic Quarterly*, 69: 265–288.

Akhtar, S. (2009a). *Turning Points in Dynamic Psychotherapy: Initial Assessment, Boundaries, Money, Disruptions, and Suicidal Crises*. London: Karnac.

Akhtar, S. (2009b). *Comprehensive Dictionary of Psychoanalysis*. London: Karnac.

Allport, G. (1961). *Pattern and Growth in Personality*. New York: Holt.

Anastasopoulos, D., & Papanicolaou, E. (Eds.) (2004). *The Therapist at Work. Personal Factors Affecting the Analytic Process*. London: Karnac.

Appelbaum, A., & Diamond, D. (1993). Prologue. *Psychoanalytic Inquiry*, 13: 145–152.

Arlow, J. A. (1961). Silence and the theory of technique. *Journal of the American Psychoanalytic Association*, 9: 44–55.

Australian Psychoanalytical Society (APAS) website (2005). The Australian Psychoanalytical Society, Australia.

Bachant, J. L., & Adler, E. (1997). Transference: co-constructed or brought to the interaction? *Journal of the American Psychoanalytic Association*, 45: 1097–1120.

Bachrach, H. M., Galatzer, R., Skolnikoff, A., & Waldron, S. Jr. (1991). On the efficacy of psychoanalysis. *Journal of the American Psychoanalytic Association*, 39(4): 871–916.

Balint, M. (1942). Ego strength and education of the ego. *Psychoanalytic Quarterly*, 11: 87–95.

Balint, M. (1968). *The Basic Fault*. New York: Brunner/Mazel.

Baranger, M. (1993). The mind of the analyst: from listening to interpretation. *International Journal of Psychoanalysis*, 74: 15–24.

Baranger, M., Baranger, W., & Mom, J. (1983). Process and non-process in analytic work. *International Journal of Psychoanalysis*, 64: 1–15.

Baudrey, F. (1991). The relevance of the analyst's character and attitudes to his work. *Journal of the American Psychoanalytic Association*, 39: 917–938.

Beigler, J. S. (1977). A commentary on Freud's treatment of the Rat Man (unpublished paper, presented to the Chicago Psychoanalytic Society, February 1974).

Berenstein, I. (1987). Analysis terminable and interminable, fifty years on. *International Journal of Psychoanalysis*, 68: 21–35.

Bergin, A. E., & Garfield, S. L. (1994). *Handbook of Psychotherapy and Behaviour Change* (4th edn). New York: Wiley.

Bergmann, M. S. (1988). On the fate of the intrapsychic image of the psychoanalyst after termination of the analysis. *Psychoanalytic Study of the Child, 43*: 137–153.

Bergmann, M. S. (1997). Termination. *Psychoanalytic Psychology, 14*: 163–174.

Berman, E. (2001). Psychoanalysis and life. *Psychoanalytic Quarterly, 70*: 35–65.

Berman, L. (1949). Counter-transference and attitudes of the analyst in the therapeutic process. *Psychiatry, 12*: 159–166.

Berne, E. (1957). *A Layman's Guide to Psychiatry and Psychoanalysis*. New York: Grove Press.

Beutler, L. E., Machado, P. P., & Neufeld, S. A. (1994). Therapist variables. In: A. E. Bergin & S. L. Garfield (Eds.), *Handbook of Psychotherapy and Behavior Change* (4th edn) (pp. 229–269). New York: John Wiley & Sons, Inc.

Bick, E. (1968). The experience of the skin in early object-relations. *International Journal of Psychoanalysis, 49*: 484–486.

Bion, W. (1959). *Commentary*. In: *Second Thoughts. Selected Papers on Psychoanalysis* (pp. 120–166). London: Karnac.

Bird, B. (1972). Notes on transference: universal phenomenon and hardest part of analysis. *Journal of the American Psychoanalytic Association, 20*: 267–301.

Blackmon, W. D. (1993). Are psychoanalytic billing practices ethical? *American Journal of Psychotherapy, 47*: 613–620.

Blomfield, O. H. (1982). Interpretation: some general aspects. *International Review of Psychoanalysis, 9*: 287–301.

Boesky, D. (1991). *Counter-transference and Resistance: The Impossible Terms of the Impossible Profession*. San Francisco, CA: San Francisco Psychoanalytic Institute.

Bollas, C. (1989). *Forces of Destiny: Psychoanalysis and Human Idiom*. London: Free Association Books.

Bowlby, J. (1958). The nature of the child's tie to his mother. *International Journal of Psychoanalysis, 39*: 350–373.

Bowlby, J. (1960). Separation anxiety. *International Journal of Psychoanalysis, 41*: 89–113.

Breger, L. (1984). Discussion. *Contemporary Psychoanalysis, 20*: 583–588.

Brenner, H. (1992). On the importance of gender in the psychoanalytic relation. *International Forum of Psychoanalysis, 1*: 29–31.

Busch, F. N. (1997). Getting started: an introduction to dynamic psycho-therapy. *International Journal of Psychoanalysis, 78*: 1055–1057.

Cardinal, M. (1996). *The Words to Say It*. London: The Women's Press.

Casement, P. (2002). *Learning From Our Mistakes. Beyond Dogma in Psychoanalysis and Psychotherapy*. East Sussex: Brunner-Routledge.

Chaplin, J. (1975). *Dictionary of Psychology* (rev. edn). New York: Dell.

Chasseguet-Smirgel, J. (1984). The femininity of the analyst in professional practice. *International Journal of Psychoanalysis, 65*: 169–178.

Chodorow, N. J. (1989). *Feminism and Psychoanalytic Theory*. New Haven, CT: Yale University Press.

Chused, J. F. (1991). The evocative power of enactments. *Journal of the American Psychoanalytic Association, 39*: 615–639.

Chused, J. F. (1992). Interpretations and their consequences in adolescents. *Psychoanalytic Inquiry, 12*: 275–295.

Conway, P. C. (1999). When all is said . . . a phenomenological enquiry into post-termination experience. *International Journal of Psychoanalysis, 80*: 563–574.

Cooper, A. M. (1988). Our changing views of the therapeutic action of psychoanalysis. Comparing Strachey and Loewald. *Psychoanalytic Quarterly, 57*: 15–27.

Cooper, S. H. (1993). Interpretive fallibility and the psychoanalytic dialogue. *Journal of the American Psychoanalytic Association, 41*: 95–126.

Craige, H. (2002). Mourning analysis. The post-termination phase. *Journal of the American Psychoanalytic Association, 50*: 507–550.

Crits-Christoph, P., & Mintz, J. (1991). Implications of therapist effects for the design and analysis of comparative studies of psychotherapies. *Journal of Consulting and Clinical Psychology, 59*: 20–26.

Dewald, P. A. (1982). The clinical importance of the termination phase. *Psychoanalytic Inquiry, 2*: 441–461.

Dewald, P. A., & Neutzel, E. J. (1993). Learning from our unsuccessful cases. *Journal of the American Psychoanalytic Association, 3*: 743–754.

Dinnage, R. (1988). *One to One. The Experience of Psychotherapy*. London: Penguin.

Dinnage, R (1999). Personal communication. London.

Eagle, M. N. (2000). A critical evaluation of current conceptions of transference and countertransference. *Psychoanalytic Psychology, 17*: 24–37.

Edelson, M. (1975). *Language and Interpretation in Psychoanalysis*. Chicago: University Chicago Press.

Ehrenberg, D. B. (1996). On the analyst's emotional availability and vulnerability. *Contemporary Psychoanalysis, 32*: 275.

Erikson, E. H. (1962). Reality and actuality: an address. *Journal of the American Psychoanalytic Association, 10*: 451–474.

Etchegoyen, A. (2002). Psychoanalytic ideas about fathers. In: J. E. Trowell & A. Etchegoyen (Eds.), *The Importance of Fathers* (Vol. 42, pp. 20–41). East Sussex: Brunner-Routledge.

Ferenczi, S. (1949). Psychoanalysis and education. *International Journal of Psychoanalysis, 30*: 220–224.

Ferenczi, S., & Rank, O. (1924). *The Development of Psychoanalysis*. New York: Nervous and Mental Diseases Publishing.

Fonagy, P. (1999). Cited from his keynote address to the American Psychoanalytic Association, 16 April, 1999.

Fonagy, P. (Ed.) (2002). *An Open Door Review of Outcome Studies in Psychoanalysis* (2nd rev. edn). London: International Psychoanalytical Association.

France, A. (1988). *Consuming Psychotherapy*. London: Free Association Books.

Freedman, N., Hoffenberg, J. D., Vorus, N., & Frosch, A. (1999). The effectiveness of psychoanalytic psychotherapy: the role of treatment duration, frequency of sessions, and the therapeutic relationship. *Journal of the American Psychoanalytic Association, 4*(3): 741–772.

Freud, A. (1952). The mutual influences in the development of ego and id—Introduction to the discussion. *Psychoanalytic Study of the Child, 7*: 42–50.

Freud, S. (1895d). *Studies on Hysteria. S.E., 2*: 1–323. London: Hogarth Press.

Freud, S. (1900a). *The Interpretation of Dreams. S.E., 4–5*. London: Hogarth Press.

Freud, S. (1905e). *Fragment of an Analysis of a Case of Hysteria. S.E., 7*: 3–122. London: Hogarth Press.

Freud, S. (1912b). The dynamics of transference. *S.E., 12*: 97–108. London: Hogarth Press.

Freud, S. (1912e). Recommendations to physicians practicing psychoanalysis. *S.E., 12*: 109–120. London: Hogarth Press.

Freud, S. (1913c). On beginning the treatment. *S.E., 12*: 123–144. London: Hogarth Press.

Freud, S. (1915a). Observations on transference-love. *S.E., 12*: 158–171. London: Hogarth Press.

Freud, S. (1916x). *Introductory Lectures on Psycho-analysis. S.E., 16*: 431–447. London: Hogarth Press.

Freud, S. (1918b). *From the History of an Infantile Neurosis. S.E., 17*: 3–122. London: Hogarth.

Freud, S. (1923b). *The Ego and the Id. S.E.,* 17: 3–68. London: Hogarth Press.

Freud, S. (1927a). "Postscript" to The question of lay analysis. *S.E.,* 20: 251–258. London: Hogarth Press.

Freud, S. (1937c). Analysis terminable and interminable. *S.E.,* 23: 211–253. London: Hogarth Press.

Freud, S. (1960). *Letters of Sigmund Freud,* E. L. Freud (Ed.). New York: Basic Books.

Gabbard, G. O. (1995). Countertransference: the emerging common ground. *International Journal of Psychoanalysis,* 76: 475–485.

Gabbard, G. O. (1997). Borderline personality disorder and rational managed care policy. *Psychoanalytic Inquiry,* 17: 17–28.

Gans, J. S., & Counselman, E. F. (1996). The missed session: a neglected aspect of psychodynamic psychotherapy. *Psychotherapy,* 3: 43–50.

Gill, M. M. (1982). *Analysis of Transference, Volume I: Theory and Technique.* New York: International Universities Press.

Gill, M. M. (1984). Transference: a change in conception or only in emphasis? *Psychoanalytic Inquiry,* 4: 489–523.

Giovacchini, P. L. (1993). Schizophrenia, the pervasive psychosis. paradoxes and empathy *Journal of the American Academy of Psychoanalysis,* 2: 549–565.

Gitelson, M. (1952). The emotional position of the analyst in the psycho-analytic situation. *International Journal of Psychoanalysis,* 33: 1–10.

Gitelson, M. (1962). On the curative factors in the first phase of analysis. In: *Psychoanalysis: Science and Profession* (pp. 311–341). New York: International Universities Press, 1973.

Glover, E. (1955). *The Technique of Psychoanalysis.* New York: International Universities Press.

Goldberg, J. (1979). Aggression and the female therapist. *Modern Psychoanalysis,* 4: 209–222.

Goldberger, M., & Evans, D. (1985). On transference manifestations in male patients with female analysts. *International Journal of Psychoanalysis,* 66: 295–309.

Gonchar, J. (1995). Psychoanalysis and contemporary thought. *Psychoanalytic Quarterly,* 64: 203.

Gornick, L. K. (1986). Developing a new narrative. *Psychoanalytic Psychology,* 3: 299–325.

Gornick, L. K. (1994). Women treating men. Interview data from female psychotherapists. *Journal of the American Academy of Psychoanalysis,* 22: 231–257.

Gray, P. (1982). Developmental lag in the evolution of analytic technique. *Journal of the American Psychoanalytic Association, 30*: 621–639.

Greenberg, J. (1991). Countertransference and reality. *Psychoanalytic Dialogue, 1*: 52–73.

Greenberg, J. (2001). Thinking, talking, playing: the peculiar goals of psychoanalysis. *Psychoanalytic Quarterly, 70*: 131–147.

Greenson, R. R. (1961). On the silence and sounds of the analytic hour. *Journal of the American Psychoanalytic Association, 9*: 79–84.

Greenson, R. R. (1967). *The Technique and Practice of Psychoanalysis*. New York: International Universities Press.

Grunberger, B. (1966). Some reflections on the Rat Man. *International Journal of Psychoanalysis, 47*: 160–168.

Guerrero, C. G. (2001). Presentation. IPA Congress, Nice.

Guntrip, H. (1975). My experience of analysis with Fairburn and Winnicott. *International Review of Psychoanalysis, 2*: 145–156.

Hadda, J. (1991). The ontogeny of silence in an analytic case. *International Journal of Psychoanalysis, 72*: 117–130.

Hamburg, D. A. (1967). Report of ad hoc committee on central fact-gathering data of the American Psychoanalytic Association. *Journal of the American Psychoanalytic Association, 15*: 841–861.

Hartlaub, G. H., Martin, G. C., & Rhine, M. W. (1986). Recontact with the analyst following termination: a survey of seventy-one cases. *Journal of the American Psychoanalytic Association. 34*: 895–891.

Harty, M., & Horwitz, L. (1975). Therapeutic outcome as rated by patients, therapists and judges. *Archives of General Psychiatry, 33*(8): 957–961.

Heimann, P. (1950). On counter-transference. *International Journal of Psychoanalysis, 31*: 81–84.

Henry, W. P., Strupp, H. H., Schact, T. E., & Gaston, L. (1994). Psychodynamic approaches. In: A. E. Bergin & S. L. Garfield (Eds.), *Handbook of Psychotherapy and Behavior Change* (4th edn) (pp. 467–508). New York: John Wiley & Sons.

Herman, N. (1985). *My Kleinian Home*. London: Free Associations Books.

Herzog, J. M. (2001). *Father Hunger: Explorations with Adults and Children*. Hillsdale, NJ: Analytic Press.

Hill, C. A. (1996). Thinking in action: the relationship between theory and practice within a psychoanalytic framework. Unpublished Masters thesis, Monash University.

Hinshelwood, R. D. (1997). *Therapy or Coercion? Does Psychoanalysis Differ from Brainwashing?* London: Karnac.

Hinshelwood, R. D. (1999). Countertransference. *International Journal of Psychoanalysis, 80*: 797–818.

Holt, R. (1987). On reading Freud. In: C. L. Rothgeb (Ed.), *Abstracts of the Standard Edition of the Complete Psychological Works of Sigmund Freud* (pp. 3–71). New Jersey: Jason Aronson.

Hurwitz, M. R. (1986). The analyst, his theory, and the psychoanalytic process. *Psychoanalytic Study of the Child, 41*: 439–466.

Issacs, S. (1948). The nature and function of phantasy. *International Journal of Psychoanalysis, 29*: 73–97.

Jacobs, T. J. (2002). Secondary revision. on rethinking the analytic process and analytic technique. *Psychoanalytic Inquiry, 22*: 3–28.

Jiménez, J. (2001). Presentation. IPA Congress, Nice.

Jones, E. (1953). *The Life and Work of Sigmund Freud* (Vol. 1). New York: Basic Books.

Joseph, B. (1985). Transference: the total situation. *International Journal of Psychoanalysis, 66*: 447–454.

Kalb, M. B. (2002). Does sex matter? The confluence of gender and transference in analytic space. *Psychoanalytic Psychology, 19*: 118–143.

Kächele, H. (2001). Personal communication, Melbourne.

Kächele, H., & Thomä, H. (1999). The shared elements of all psychoanalytic therapies—twenty good reasons for a unifying perspective. Unpublished paper.

Kantrowitz, J. L. (1986). The role of the patient-analyst "match" in the outcome of psychoanalysis. *Annual of Psychoanalysis, 14*: 273–297.

Kantrowitz, J. L. (1995). The beneficial aspects of the patient–analyst match. *International Journal of Psychoanalysis, 76*: 299–313.

Karme, L. (1979). The analysis of a male patient by a female analyst: the problem of the negative oedipal transference. *International Journal of Psychoanalysis, 60*: 253–261.

Kassan, L. D. (1999). *Second Opinions. Sixty Psychotherapy Patients Evaluate Their Therapists*. New Jersey: Jason Aronson.

Kernberg, O. F. (1997). The nature of interpretation. Inter-subjectivity and the third position. *Annual of Psychoanalysis, 25*: 97–110.

Kirsner, D. (2000). *Unfree Associations. Inside Psychoanalytic Institutes*. London: Process Press.

Klein, M. (1943). Memorandum on her technique. In: P. King & R. Steiner (Eds.), *The Freud–Klein Controversies, 1941–1945* (pp. 635–638). London: Routledge, 1991.

Klein, M. (1952a). The origins of transference. *International Journal of Psychoanalysis, 33*: 433–438.

Klein, M. (1952b). The mutual influences in the development of ego and id—Discussants. *Psychoanalytic Study of the Child, 7*: 51–53.

Kulish, N. M. (1984). The effect of the sex of the analyst on transference: a review of the literature. *Bulletin of the Menninger Clinic, 48*: 95–110.

Kulish, N. M. (1989). Gender and transference. Conversations with female analysts. *Psychoanalytic Psychology, 6*: 59–71.

Kulosh, N., & Mayman, M. (1993). Gender-linked determinants of transference and countertransference in psychoanalytic psychotherapy. *Psychoanalytic Inquiry, 13*: 286–305.

Lacan, J. (1953). Funktion und feld des sprechens und der sprache in der psychoanalyse. *Ecrits* (pp. 237–322). Paris: editions du Seuil, 1966.

Lachmann, F. M. (1992). The importance of gender in the psychoanalytic relationship. *International Forum of Psychoanalysis, 1*: 32–36.

Langs, R. D. (1980). On the properties of an interpretation. *Contemporary Psychoanalysis, 16*: 460–478.

Laplanche, J. P., & Pontalis, J.-B. (1985). *The Language of Psychoanalysis.* London: Hogarth Press.

Lester, E. P. (1985). The female analyst and the erotized transference. *International Journal of Psychoanalysis, 66*: 283–293.

Levine, H. B. (1997). The capacity for countertransference. *Psychoanalytic Inquiry, 17*: 44–68.

Lichtenberg, J. (1985). *The Talking Cure: A Descriptive Guide to Psychoanalysis.* Hillsdale, NJ: Analytic Press.

Limentani, A. (1982). On the "unexpected" termination of psychoanalytic therapy. *Psychoanalytic Inquiry, 2*: 419–440.

Lipton, S. D. (1977). The advantages of Freud's technique as shown in his analysis of the Rat Man. *International Journal of Psychoanalysis, 58*: 255–273.

Little, M. (1951). Counter-transference and the patient's response to it. *International Journal of Psychoanalysis, 32*: 32–40.

Loewald, H. (1960). On the therapeutic action of psychoanalysis. *International Journal of Psychoanalysis, 41*: 16–33.

Loewenstein, R. (1951). The problem of interpretation. *Psychoanalytic Quarterly, 20*: 1–14.

Loomie, L. S. (1961). Some ego considerations in the silent patient. *Journal of the American Psychoanalytic Association, 9*: 56–78.

Luborsky, L., & Crits-Christoph, P. (1986). Measures of psychoanalytic concepts: the last decade of research from "the Penn studies", 35th International Psychoanalytic Congress. *International Journal of Psychoanalysis, 69*(1): 75–86.

Luborsky, L., Barber, J., & Crits-Christoph, P. (1990). Theory based research for understanding the process of dynamic psychotherapy. *Journal of Consulting and Clinical Psychology, 58*: 281–287.

Mahler, M. S. (1958). Autism and symbiosis, two extreme disturbances of identity. *International Journal of Psychoanalysis, 39*: 77–82.

Masson, J. (1991). *Final Analysis. The Making and Unmaking of a Psychoanalyst*. London: HarperCollins.

McGuire, W. (Ed.) (1974). *The Freud/Jung letters: The Correspondence between Sigmund Freud and C. G. Jung*, R. Manheim & R. F. C. Hull (Trans.), abridged by A. McGlishan. Princeton, NJ: Princeton University Press.

McLaughlin, J. T. (1981). Transference, psychic reality and countertransference. *Psychoanalytic Quarterly, 50*: 639–664.

Marks, M. (2000). Female sexuality: the early psychoanalytic controversies. *International Journal of Psychoanalysis, 81*: 835–837.

Matthis, I. (1998). Preface to the Swedish original edition. In: I. Matthis & I. Szecsödy (Eds.), *On Freud's Couch. Seven New Interpretations of Freud's Case Histories*. New Jersey: Jason Aronson.

Matthis, I., & Szecsödy, I. (1998). *On Freud's Couch. Seven New Interpretations of Freud's Case Histories*. New Jersey: Jason Aronson.

Mayer, E., & De Marneffe, D. (1992). When theory and practice diverge: gender-related patterns of referral to psychoanalysts. *Journal of the American Psychoanalytic Association, 40*: 551–585.

Meissner, W. (1998). Neutrality, abstinence, and the therapeutic alliance. *Journal of the American Psychoanalytic Association, 46*(4): 1089–1128.

Miller, L., & Twomey, J. E. (2000). Incoherence incognito. The collapse of the third in a fee-for-service structure. *Contemporary Psychoanalysis, 36*: 427–456.

Mitchell, J. (1974). *Psychoanalysis and Feminism*. New York: Pantheon Books.

Mitchell, S. A. (1993). *Hope and Dread in Psychoanalysis*. New York: Basic Books.

Modell, A. H. (1976). "The holding environment" and the therapeutic action of psychoanalysis. *Journal of the American Psychoanalytic Association, 24*: 285–307.

Morley, R. (2007). *The Analysand's Tale*. London: Karnac.

Novick, J. (1982). Termination: themes and issues. *Psychoanalytic Inquiry, 2*: 329–365.

Novick, J. (1988). The timing of termination. *International Review of Psychoanalysis, 15*: 307–318.

Novick, J. (1990). Comments on termination in child, adolescent, and adult analysis. *Psychoanalytic Study of the Child*, 4: 419–436.

Novick, J. (1997). Termination conceivable and inconceivable. *Psychoanalytic Psychology*, 14: 145–162.

Obholzer, K. (1980). *The Wolf-Man Sixty Years Later. Conversations with Freud's Patient*. London: Routledge & Kegan Paul.

Paniagua, C. (1985). A methodological approach to surface material. *International Review of Psychoanalysis*, 12: 311–325.

Pedder, J. R. (1988). Termination reconsidered. *International Journal of Psychoanalysis*, 69: 495–505.

Perelberg, R. (Ed.) (2005). *Freud. A Modern Reader*. London: Whurr Publishers Ltd.

Perron, R. (2001). The unconscious and primal phantasies. *International Journal of Psychoanalysis*, 82: 583–595.

Person, E. (1985). The erotic transference in women and in men: differences and consequences. *Journal of the American Academy of Psychoanalysis*, 13: 159–180.

Peterson, K. (1998). *de Simone, Gilda: Ending Analysis. Theory and Technique*. London: Karnac, 1997. *International Forum of Psychoanalysis*, 7: 54–55.

Piper, W. E., Debbane, E. G., Bienvenu, J. P., & Garant, J. (1987). A comparative study of four forms of psychotherapy. *Journal of Consulting and Clinical Psychology*, 52(2): 268–279.

Purcell, S. D. (2004). The analyst's theory: a third source of countertransference. *International Journal of Psychoanalysis*, 85: 635–652.

Racker, H. (1968). *Transference and Countertransference*. Madison, CT: International Universities Press.

Rangell, L. (1982). Transference to theory: the relationship of psychoanalytic education to the analyst's relationship to psychoanalysis. *The Annual of Psychoanalysis*, 10(1): 29–56.

Reich, A. (1951). On counter-transference. *International Journal of Psychoanalysis*, 32: 25–31.

Reich, A. (1960). Further research on counter-transference. *International Journal of Psychoanalysis*, 41: 385–395.

Reich, A. (1966). Empathy and counter-transference. In: *Anne Reich: Psychoanalytic Contributions* (pp. 344–360). New York: International Universities Press, 1973.

Renik, O. (1995). The role of an analyst's expectations in clinical technique: reflections on the concept of resistance. *Journal of the American Psychoanalytic Association*, 43: 83–94.

Reppen, J., & Schulman, M. A. (Eds.) (2002). *Failures in Psychoanalytic Treatment*. Madison, CT: International Universities Press.

Richards, A. D. (1984). Transference analysis: means or end? *Psychoanalytic Inquiry*, 4: 355–366.

Roazen, P. (1995). *How Freud Worked. First-Hand Accounts of Patients*. New Jersey: Jason Aronson.

Roth, A., & Fonagy, P. (1996). *What Works for Whom? A Critical Review of Psychotherapy Research*. New York: Guilford Press.

Rudominer, H. S. (1984). Peer review, third-party payment, and the analytic situation: a case report. *Journal of the American Psychoanalytic Association*, 32: 773–795.

Saks, E. (2007). *The Centre Cannot Hold*. Great Britain: Virago Press.

Samuel, W. (1981). *Personality Searching for the Sources of Human Behaviour*. New York: McGraw-Hill.

Samuels, L. (1985). Female psychotherapists as portrayed in film, fiction and nonfiction. *Journal of the American Academy of Psychoanalysis*, 13: 367–378.

Sandler, J. (1987). The concept of projective identification. *Bulletin of the Anna Freud Centre*, 10(1): 33–49.

Sandler, J. (1993). On communication from patient to analyst: not everything is projective identification. *International Journal of Psychoanalysis*, 74: 1097–1107.

Sandler, J., Holder, A., Kawenoka, M., Kennedy, H. E., & Neurath, L. (1969). Notes on some theoretical and clinical aspects of transference. *International Journal of Psychoanalysis*, 50: 633–645.

Satran, G. (1995). The patient's sense of therapeutic action: an introduction. *Contemporary Psychoanalysis*, 31(1): 124–132.

Schachter, J. (1990). Post-termination patient–analyst contact: 1. Analyst's attitudes and experience, II. Impact on patients. *International Journal of Psychoanalysis*, 71: 475–486.

Schachter, J. (1992). Concepts of termination and post-termination patient–analyst contact. *International Journal of Psychoanalysis*, 73: 137–154.

Schafer, R. (1992). *Retelling a Life*. New York: Basic Books.

Schafer, R. (1996). Authority, evidence and knowledge in the psychoanalytic relationship. *Psychoanalytic Quarterly*, 65: 236–253.

Schafer, R. (2003). *Bad Feelings*. London: Karnac.

Schlessinger, N., & Robbins, F. P. (1983). *A Developmental View of the Psychoanalytic Process: Follow-up Studies and Their Consequences*. Madison, CT: International Universities Press.

Segal, H. (1962). The curative factors in psychoanalysis. *International Journal of Psychoanalysis, 43*: 212–217.

Shapiro, D. (1976). The analyst's own analysis. *Journal of the American Psychoanalytic Association, 24*: 5–42.

Shapiro, E. R. (Ed.) (1997). The boundaries are shifting: renegotiating the therapeutic frame. In: *The Inner World and the Outer World* (pp. 7–25). New Haven, CT: Yale University Press.

Simon, B. (1993). In search of psychoanalytic technique: perspectives from on the couch and from behind the couch. *Journal of the American Psychoanalytic Association, 41*(4): 1051–1082.

Spillius, E. B. (1992). Clinical experiences of projective identification. In: R. Anderson (Ed.), *Clinical Lectures on Klein and Bion* (pp. 59–73). London: Tavistock/Routledge.

Spitz, R. (1956). Countertransference. *Journal of the American Psychoanalytic Association, 4*: 256–265.

Stein, S. (1991). The influence of theory on the psychoanalyst's countertransference. *International Journal of Psychoanalysis, 72*: 325–334.

Stone, L. (1981). Notes on the non-interpretive elements in the psychoanalytic situation and process. *Journal of the American Psychoanalytic Association, 29*: 89–118.

Strachey, J. (1934). The nature of the therapeutic action of psycho-analysis. *International Journal of Psychoanalysis, 15*: 127–159.

Strupp, H. H. (1969). Toward a specification of teaching and learning in psychotherapy. *Archives of General Psychiatry, 21*: 203–212.

Strupp, H. H. (1978). Suffering and psychotherapy. *Contemporary Psychoanalysis, 14*: 203–212.

Strupp, H. H., & Binder, J. L. (1984). *Psychotherapy in a New Key*. New York: Basic Books.

Symington, N. (1988). *The Analytic Experience. Lectures from the Tavistock.* London: Free Association Books.

Tabin, J. K. (2002). A sense of failure in analysis and the phenomenon of serial analyses. In: J. S. Reppen & M. A. Schulman (Eds.), *Failures in Psychoanalytic Treatment* (pp. 101–119). Madison: International Universities Press.

Target, M., & Fonagy, P. (2002). Fathers in modern psychoanalysis and in society: the role of the father and child development. In: J. E. Trowell & A. Etchegoyen (Eds.), *The Importance of Fathers* (Vol. 42, pp. 45–66). East Sussex: Brunner-Routledge.

Tessman, L. (2003). *The Analyst's Analyst Within*. New Jersey: The Analytic Press.

Tuckett, D. (2001). Congress presentation. IPA Congress, Nice.

Tulipan, A. B. (1983). Fees in psychotherapy. *Journal of the American Academy of Psychoanalysis, 11*: 445–463.

Vaughan, S. C., Spitzer, R., Davies, M., & Roose, S. (1997). The definition and assessment of analytic process: can analysts agree? *International Journal of Psychoanalysis, 78*: 959–973.

Waldron, S. J. (1997). How can we study the efficacy of psychoanalysis? *Psychoanalytic Quarterly, 65*: 283–354.

Wallerstein, R. S. (1986). *Forty Two Lives in Treatment: A Study of Psychoanalysis and Psychotherapy.* New York: Guilford Press.

Wallerstein, R. S. (1990). Psychoanalysis: the common ground. *International Journal of Psychoanalysis, 71*: 3–20.

Winnicott, D. W. (1949). Hate in the counter-transference. *International Journal of Psychoanalysis, 30*: 69–74.

Winnicott, D. W. (1956). Primary maternal preoccupation. In: *Through Pediatrics toPsychoanalysis. Collected Papers* (pp. 300–305). London: Karnac and the Institute of Psychoanalysis, 1992.

Winnicott, D. W. (1958). The capacity to be alone. In: The *Maturational Processes and the Facilitating Environment* (pp. 29–36). London: Karnac and the Institute of Psychoanalysis, 1990.

Winnicott, D. W. (1960). The theory of the parent infant relationship. In: *The Maturational Process and the Facilitating Environment* (pp. 37–55). London: Karnac and the Institute of Psychoanalysis, 1990.

Winnicott, D. W. (1963). Psychiatric disorder in terms of infantile maturational processes. In: *The Maturational Process and the Facilitating Environment* (pp. 230–241). London: Karnac and the Institute of Psychoanalysis, 1990.

Winnicott, D. W. (1965). *Maturational Processes and the Facilitating Environment.* London: Hogarth Press and the Institute of Psychoanalysis; Madison, CT: International Universities Press, 1965; London: Institute of Psychoanalysis and Karnac, 1990.

Winnicott, D. W. (1988). *Babies and Their Mothers.* London: Free Association Books.

Wolstein, B. (1997). The first direct analysis of transference and counter-transference. *Psychoanalytic Inquiry, 17*: 505–521.

Zetzel, E. R. (1966). Additional notes upon a case of obsession neurosis, Freud 1909. *International Journal of Psychoanalysis, 47*: 123–129.

INDEX